LOVE
IN THE
STARS

About the Author

Brad Kronen (Los Angeles, CA) has been using his talent as a professional astrologer and Tarot reader for the last 25 years. He first became interested in Astrology while earning his Bachelor's degree in Psychology at Fairfield University in Fairfield, CT.

His writing can be found at Scandalist.com and Examiner.com.

**Find Your Perfect Match
With Astrology**

LOVE
IN THE
STARS

Includes All 144 Sun Sign Combinations

BRAD KRONEN

Llewellyn Publications
Woodbury, Minnesota

FIRST EDITION
First Printing, 2015

Cover art: iStockphoto.com/9859463/©claudelle
iStockphoto.com/21085928/©alexokokok
iStockphoto.com/27234551/©artvea
Cover design: Kevin R. Brown
Editing: Amy Quale

Llewellyn Publications is a registered trademark of Llewellyn Worldwide Ltd.

Library of Congress Cataloging-in-Publication Data
Kronen, John, 1968–
  Love in the stars : find your perfect match with astrology / by Brad
Kronen. — First Edition.
     pages   cm
  ISBN 978-0-7387-4559-6
1. Astrology and marriage 2. Astrology. 3. Love—Miscellanea. 4.
Mate selection—Miscellanea. I. Title.
  BF1729.L6K76 2015
  133.5'864677—dc23

                                                    2015018837

Llewellyn Worldwide Ltd. does not participate in, endorse, or have any authority or responsibility concerning private business transactions between our authors and the public.
   All mail addressed to the author is forwarded but the publisher cannot, unless specifically instructed by the author, give out an address or phone number.
   Any Internet references contained in this work are current at publication time, but the publisher cannot guarantee that a specific location will continue to be maintained. Please refer to the publisher's website for links to authors' websites and other sources.

Llewellyn Publications
A Division of Llewellyn Worldwide Ltd.
2143 Wooddale Drive
Woodbury, MN 55125-2989
www.llewellyn.com

Printed in the United States of America

Contents

Introduction

Classic things withstand time. In this age when the latest model of laptop computer is obsolete faster than a carton of milk's range of freshness, one tried and true human need remains stronger than ever—to be loved.

Despite astrology having modernized itself with the twenty-first century, it's practically a guarantee the first thing a person will ask me when introduced is, "What sign should I date? I'm with a (fill in the sign). Is that bad?"

Before diving into this book, a few things must be emphasized. Oh, who am I kidding? First go ahead and tear through the book to see how compatible you are with the hottie/chick/dude who currently has your romantic attention. Feel better? Good. So as I was saying…

Every combination of sign can feasibly work together in a romantic setting. Some signs take more work to achieve a state of equilibrium than others. Some combinations of signs are inherently compatible together. Others clearly are not.

For those whose heart is set on someone born beneath a sign deemed to be incompatible with yours, consider the following options after reading this book: move romantically forward with a better sense of the inherent differences of personality between the two of you that will inevitably pop up, or reconsider your romantic pursuit after realizing your differences in personality are too great and not worth the investment of your overall time and energy. Either approach works after being enlightened by this book.

Regarding dating one's own sign, there are a few exceptions (actually, just one), but a good rule of thumb when considering whether to join romantic forces with another of the same astrological kind as yourself:

Look at it like dating your own gene pool. Would you date your cousin? (Keep your answer good and private, thanks.)

Love in the Stars is the best kind of manual to venture forward with into the world or battlefield of love, however you choose to see it. Understanding each sign's basic energy patterns or dynamics can make winning a prospective partner's heart a snap, and can also save you a fortune from going to divorce court.

For example, if you're going on a first date with a Gemini, be prepared to ask him at LEAST three questions about himself. Those who doubt their ability to pull off that labor of Hercules should either consider dating a different sign or at least write a few inquiries down in advance.

If you're married to a Scorpio and it's her 30th birthday, the LAST thing she'll want on her special day is a surprise party complete with every former friend from grammar and high school. What she'll really want after that fiasco is a mere five minutes with you—ALONE.

As we move forward into the future, the stress and frantic pace of life in the modern age seems to become more and more challenging for each of us as individuals. Despite the Internet exponentially expanding our ability to communicate and access information, technological innovation has caused many within today's world to become more detached and less likely to establish interpersonal relationships. Not only has dating become quite the daunting task in these current times, but twenty-first-century statistics show a sharp decline in marriages hand in hand with an increased spike in divorces.

This book was written with the hope of offsetting today's trend of personal detachment and societal isolation. For just as our need to be loved is both collectively ancient and more important than ever before, so too is astrology's role in assisting us with that core human need.

Godspeed with your labor of love, dear reader. May this book be the key in making those labors successfully complete.

Aries-Aries

Just so we're on the same page, Aries, you DO know you're romantically interested in one of your own, right?

I'll be honest with you two head butters. There are a few exceptions (actually just one, and you two sure ain't it), but overall it's not highly recommended for a person born beneath one sign to date another of the same astrological kind.

Each sign encounters their own unique set of challenges whenever romantically doubling up with itself. These challenges make themselves blaringly obvious whenever two Aries date each other. So obvious, they're akin to asking if one currently exists in the twenty-first century, or if your face possesses an actual nose.

But before ram-charging forward to discuss the overt pitfalls of problematic potential two Aries might face when romantically teaming up together, a quick overview of the first sign of the zodiac is required.

Aries is a fire sign. The essence of fire's foundation is action oriented and functions best whenever in motion or in the process of "doing." Hence, those born beneath any of the fire signs (Aries, Leo, Sagittarius) like being busy as often as possible.

The Aries need to be in action is so pure and strong, most rams get seriously fidgety even after just a few minutes of being seated or stationary. The typical Aries doesn't get too nitpicky as to exactly what kind of action they partake in as long as it's fast paced, and preferably spontaneous as often as possible. And doing ANYTHING is better for the firsts of the zodiac than doing nothing at all.

Dates for two rams, especially in the beginning stages of getting to know each other, will tend to be as physically active as romantically possible. The typical Aries prefers physical activities such as hiking, running, rock climbing, dancing (as long as their partner doesn't mind a guaranteed mid-move crash at least once per dance), attending a (insert any / all sport) game, and of course, "doing the bed creak," all with a sense of competitive drive throughout.

In discussing the romantic union between any two given fire signs, your Love Author must seriously stress the critical importance of the "F" word whenever these astrological hotties are getting to know each other more intimately.

Fun.

The fire signs function best when they sense there's some level of fun taking place at any given point in their action-oriented lives. Even an eyedropper's amount of fun can go a long way for the average fire sign. You rams want to impress / make up with / sexually lock horns with each other? Throw a little fun in the mix!

Now, even with the "F" word being tossed around like a (insert any / all sport) ball, as mentioned earlier, potential pitfalls exist within this ram-charged relationship that are more than overtly obvious.

Let's start with the most common pitfall of problematic potential that afflicts a vast portion of the fire-signed population, both individually, and even more so, while in romantic pursuit of each other.

Double Aries Potential Pitfall 1: Physical Exhaustion. Since the fire signs enjoy being as constantly active as often as possible, they tend not to hear their bodies' SOS call of alarm whenever approaching the brink of physical exhaustion.

For example, at the end of a day of relentless non-stop action, the fire person running on near empty will often stop in mid-motion while mumbling something along the following:

"Hey, you guys! I think I'm getting tire..." BOOM!

Your Love Author always furnishes his home with non-breakables, due to the booming sound signifying that the fire child has literally just hit the ground, and HARD!

When two Aries first meet, their excitement is usually quite hard to contain. So much so that they'll both exhaust themselves while doing things together as often as their physical bodies will allow.

It's best advised even the early phases of dating bliss, otherwise known as "the honeymoon period," be monitored if the romantic couple in question are two ram kids. Because if one fire sign should experience physical burnout, there should be enough energy left on reserve for the other fire sign to at least be able to hail a cab, or a stretcher.

Double Aries Potential Pitfall 2: Anger Issues. Aries is ruled by the heavenly body named after the Roman god of war, Mars. Astrologically, the red planet that oversees anger and aggression. It's no coincidence we use the Martian-colored term "seeing red" whenever describing a person who has lost themselves in a fit of rage.

The human emotion an Aries can readily tap into most is anger. One punchy Aries with anger issues is bad enough. Throw another enraged ram into the mix and the backdrop becomes the Ultimate Fighter octagon in the blink of a black eye if not monitored.

And just so everyone is on the same ram-charged page, the Aries female is NOT your shrinking violet or passive doormat of a girlfriend or wife. She does what she wants to do, and heaven help you if you stand in her way! These feminine flames think like dudes. They're strong willed, go after what they want, and can deliver a powerful right hook if they're told to be in any way submissive or subservient. You can't say your Love Author didn't warn you.

One other "physical" thing, rams. Quite often the body of many an Aries will move far too ahead of their thinking mind, causing any number of things to directly impair their way. Examples of these motion-impairing Aries incidents are as follows: the Aries male walking into any random wall, tree, or flag pole, or the Aries female wearing some sort of heeled shoe in public, resulting in her traversing any given flight of stairs while taking down all persons physically located within the trajectory path of her crash landing (prime example: the ram girl's prom or first formal dance while wearing heels).

The same suggestion supplied earlier regarding physical exhaustion still very much applies when two klutzes of the zodiac date each other —furnishing the home with non-breakables.

The last item on the list of clear and obvious pitfalls of double Aries romantic potential deals with your sign's strongest personality trait that's most frequently observed by others.

Double Aries Potential Pitfall 3: Self Concern. Being the first sign of the zodiac, Aries is also known as "the sign of self." The firsts of the zodiac like doing their own thing, whenever they choose to do so. Motivated by pure and unadulterated self-concern, the ram child is not used to considering the perspective of others within the framework of their spontaneously impulsive lives.

The key to relationship success for two people born beneath the sign of Me, Me, and a lot more Me is not about forcibly negating their natural sense of Aries self-concern, but rather taking the opposite approach.

Both rams should self-reference as often as possible whenever considering their same-signed love interest. Literally try to make it a habit (an Aries dirty word, I know) to ask your self-concerned selves, "Would I like it if ..." whenever considering your same-signed partner.

Have either of you hot heads ever heard the scientific theory that hypothesizes certain amounts of chaos exist within any given environment, and adding an equal amount of said chaos will inexplicably create order?

The same can be said of two Aries romantically joining forces. The more the child of Mars self-references whenever considering their partner, the more likely they'll incorporate such relationship surviving necessities as compromise, being considerate, and sharing to their double ram-charged romance.

Aries-Taurus

You two probably weren't even gestating yet as tiny calves and lambs, but way back when, people used an especially cornball phrase to sum up the different ways men and women approach relationships, Aries and Taurus: "If women are from Venus, then men are from Mars."

It's kind of silly with a smidge bit of boring sprinkled on top, but that kitsch catchphrase did hold a core truth when it was regularly used in its heyday.

And wouldn't you know? It's quite applicable to this astrological coupling, except replace the word "women" with Taurus and "men" with Aries.

In astrology, the terms "masculine" and "feminine" aren't gender specific. They describe the energy dynamic a person inherently possesses, regardless if one is male or female. The masculine signs function from a naturally aggressive dynamic that moves in an outwardly forward direction. The feminine signs function from the opposite spectrum, where they are naturally passive with things moving inward first before going out and about into the world. The fire and air signs are masculine. The earth and water signs are feminine. In regard to the Aries and the Taurus dating each other, Aries is the dude and Taurus is the chick.

To add extra emphasis to our astrologically modernized catch phrase, Taurus' actual planetary ruler is Venus, the heavenly body where women are from, and Aries' is, you guessed it, Mars, the dude planet.

Technically, the signs that border each other on the zodiac wheel are categorized beneath a most unexciting descriptor of astrological compatibility: neutral.

(A solitary cough can be heard in the very far off, remote distance.)

Every sign has the potential to work together, and some combinations take a lot more work than others to achieve a state of equilibrium. With the joining of the signs considered to be neutral of each other, the state of equilibrium is something very much like that solid borderline that naturally forms whenever oil and vinegar are put into the same container. In other words, mixing the two isn't a bad thing, but a whole lot of shaking is needed for there to be any kind of blend.

At their core, the signs of Aries and Taurus function from very different perspectives, making it seem many times as if these two signs lived on opposite points of the globe versus being astrological next-door neighbors. Aries is fast and furious. Taurus is slow and steady.

Being the action oriented fire sign, Aries likes things spontaneous, in the moment, and with a constant rush of fun, and often bordering on daredevil adventure. On the other horn, being the pragmatic earth sign, the Taurus likes things planned, with as much follow through and as few surprises as possible.

The Aries is all about action and adrenaline. The Taurus is all about luxury and leisure. The body of the Taurus can suffer due to not being physically active enough. The body of the Aries can suffer due to physical exhaustion brought about by being over active.

Being ruled by Mars, the planet of aggression and anger, the Aries has been known to explosively lose its temper in public from time to time. Being ruled by Venus, the planet of peace and quiet, the Taurus would rather lose a limb than its temper in any given public setting.

Many times, the Taurus can get so set in its way, it can become sedentary from too much sitting which can result in the bull experiencing ebbs of low energy. The natural energies of the Aries are usually revved so high, it barely has the ability to sit, let alone be sedentary.

Being the sign of "self," the Aries is always first on its priority list, with its needs being met first, followed by everyone else's. Being ruled by Venus, the planet of grace and manners, the Taurus always makes the needs and comfort of anyone who is its guest its first priority.

In order for this particular relationship to last, let alone have a pulse, a quality will need to be present from the first moments of this love union's inception—ACCEPTANCE.

Aries, accept the fact that your Taurean love interest is WAY more low key than your fast and furious self and won't necessarily be totally stoked at the random thought of going last minute bar hopping or partaking in the latest round of paintball war games. In fact, one of the Taurus' favorite pastimes is a word that doesn't even exist within the vocabulary of the typical Aries, which you rams will need to be semi-well versed in if you want to keep your bovine lover's affections: relaxing.

Taurus, accept the fact your Aries paramour has a much, MUCH higher metabolism and energy level than your peacefully calm self, and his or her constant state of self-concern mustn't be taken as a personal offense whenever displayed.

Both signs must be made aware of a trait that is particularly personal of the other if they would like to prevent their budding ram-bull romance from immediately crashing and burning.

Taurus, no matter how head over horns (or hooves) your Aries is in love with you and vice versa, know the following upfront: Every Aries needs some alone time on as regular a basis as possible.

Overlooking this straightforward Arien trait or constantly smothering your fire-signed love interest is tantamount to him or her severing romantic ties with no discussion allowed.

And speaking of non-discussion, we now come to the Taurean pitfall portion of the love program. Taurus' planetary ruler of Venus not only oversees such niceties as love and beauty, but peace and harmony, as well. This may sound all sugar and spice and Venusian nice at first, but in terms of a romantic relationship, these inherent niceties can turn out to be quite problematic. Allow your Love Author to explain.

A relationship is never 100 percent smoooooth sailing (sorry, couldn't resist a little bovine humor). There will be times within every human relationship where differences of opinion will occur and gripes and annoyances will arise. When these inevitable things take place, both partners will be called upon to either confront or debate each other over the contentious matters at hand in order to work things out. Except for the Taurus.

Should the person born beneath the sign of the bull have a gripe or difference of opinion with their partner, he or she more often than not won't say a word. Because of the planetary ruler's influence, many a Taurean will stifle the bother in order to maintain the peace/not rock the boat/keep things nice and quiet.

It's in the best interest of every child of Venus to be as upfront and vocal with gripes and differences as often as possible, and even more importantly, during the time of its occurrence.

Aries, your sign has a natural propensity for expressing anger and aggression. Your Love Author highly recommends the ram may want to gauge things besides monitoring its own temper to see that too much time doesn't pass without their Taurean love interest doing the same.

If the Aries can learn to relax enough so the Taurus can be cattle prodded by being actively present, the flames of romance between the ram and the bull could burn quite brightly instead of immediately fizzling out, due to it all astrologically being just a guy/gal thing.

Aries–Gemini

Did you lovebirds know the most damaging forest fires occur in areas that don't necessarily have the most flammable material but are susceptible to high winds?

Flame, unto its solitary self, doesn't make a fire burn fast and furiously. Take said flame and infuse it with the oxygen from the windy air and you have one serious scorcher, kind of like when Aries and Gemini join romantic forces.

In astrology, the four elements of earth, air, fire, and water are naturally paired off. Each grouping consists of two elements that are cohesive or naturally work well together, otherwise known as being complementary to each other. The elements of earth and water are grouped together, but more importantly for this particular pairing, the elements of fire and air are complementary to each other.

The element of fire is action oriented and functions best whenever in motion or in the process of "doing." Hence, those born beneath any of the fire signs (Aries, Leo, Sagittarius) like being busy as often as possible.

The Aries' need to be in action is so pure and strong, most rams get seriously fidgety even after a few minutes of being seated or stationary. The first sign of the zodiac doesn't get too nitpicky as to exactly what kind of action they partake in, as long as it's fast paced, and preferably spontaneous. And doing ANYTHING is better for the Aries than doing nothing at all.

Blowing right along to the Airy half of our complementary couple, the element of air has the mental functions of rational thought and communication at its foundational core. Being the first of the air signs (Gemini, Libra, Aquarius), one doesn't need to be Albert Einstein to observe the role communication plays with anyone born beneath the sign of the twins.

Behold! The jabberjaws/Chatty Chads and Cathys/motor mouths of the zodiac!

Ruled by Mercury, the fastest moving planet orbiting the sun, it can be quite the challenge to keep up with the speed-of-light pace of the Gemini mind and mouth.

The twins' astrological quality is "mutable," and the mutable signs occur when each of the four seasons draws to a close, right before another begins. Because they take place during a time of transition between changing seasons, the mutable signs function best in environments containing variety and change and are the multitaskers of the zodiac.

A mutable signed person can, in theory, attempt doing one thing at a time, but it's practically a guarantee things will be screwed up if it's a solitary dynamic of action. This is due to the traits shared amongst all the mutables of possessing not even the slightest shred of patience, as well as being susceptible to mind numbing boredom after sitting down for no longer than five minutes.

The mutables are known for doing as many simultaneous actions as physically possible, but are equally known for dropping said actions at choice times due to their susceptibility of being easily distracted.

Both Aries and Gemini crave variety, get bored almost instantaneously, and have less than an eyedropper's full of patience amongst the two of them put together. Thus, those born beneath the ram and the twins like to change the backdrop of their scenery as often as possible.

Matching the inherent energies of the Aries personality with that of the Gemini's usually makes for quite the well-fitting union, since the two signs are already compatible from a core, foundational level thanks to the complementary nature between the elements of fire and air.

You can guarantee when the Aries and Gemini's budding romance initially begins, these two signs will never partake in the same date activity twice. Things should never get too stale and will usually have a fast paced level of romantic interest for this astrological coupling.

The Gemini's voracious mental curiosity is a great partner for the Aries' spontaneously impulsive actions. The mind and mouth of the twins-born person should find it both a breeze and a blast shifting gears with whatever the ram child feels like doing in the moment, at any given time.

With all the super great aspects behind romantically combining the elements of fire with air, potential problems arise should either sign become bored or distracted. Geminis, no matter how good the lovin' is with your ram-charged lover, the Aries will always need some alone time. This is a natural component for the first sign of the zodiac, which is otherwise known as the "sign of self."

Being the sign of self, the ram child likes doing its own thing, whenever he or she wants to do it. Motivated by pure and unadulterated self-concern, the Aries isn't used to considering the perspective of others within the framework of its impulsive life.

Should the Aries need some alone time, it is imperative for the Gemini not to take personal offense or misinterpret the ram's solitary needs as a form of romantic rejection!

When a twins person is feeling either self-conscious or nervous, their mental energies will often go into overdrive, resulting in its naturally talkative self revving into Gemini power babble (another way of saying talking up a blue streak in triple time about a whole lot of nothin').

Should this nervous fast-forwarding of the Gemini mouth and mind take place, the Aries' need to retreat into solitary isolation will become even more motivated than initially intended. The best way the ram can assuage the twins fear? Clear and regular communication.

Gemini isn't necessarily a clingy or needy sign (leave that issue with their astrological next-door neighbor, Cancer), but it's more like those born beneath the sign of the twins are highly sociable creatures and like knowing there's a human source nearby at any given time to talk to/joke with/mimic.

Wish to avoid Gemini power babble AND still have your alone time, Aries? Keep this Mercurial rule in mind: A little communication goes a long way for the Gemini, and no communication whatsoever is cause enough to be a romantic deal breaker for the typically twinish person.

If the Aries can romantically reassure the Gemini by keeping the channels of communication open while the ram is allotted their much-needed solitary time, then let the good times roll and burst into spontaneous, air stoked flame!

But it must be noted, neither sign has a spotless rep for being faithful, especially during the beginning phases of their romantic relationship. For those adulterous rams and twins, may your Love Author provide the REAL reason for your extra-curricular bed creaking?

In a word: BOREDOM.

It's a problem that can just as easily be remedied. Should the ram and the twins allow their worst shortcomings to take over (which both signs happen to naturally share), namely boredom and distraction, the spark of stimulation that excitedly began when they first met will be immediately doused like a lightning-caused flickering flame being squelched by the overwhelming din of a raging thunderstorm.

Conversely, if the ram and the twins concentrate their romantic focus strictly on each other, the initial spark of stimulated attraction between these two complementary signs stands to become a steadily burning flame of a loving bond with the passage of time.

Aries-Cancer

Hold up, Aries and Cancer. I need to step out for a bit and find me a Red Bull and hopefully any cheap excuse of an energy bar, 'cause you two are WORK.

Alrighty, then! Now that I've done what's humanly best to crank my energies up to as maximum a non-illegal level as I can, allow me to start by being brutally blunt: The two of you are SURE you're dating each other, right?

I should preface things by stating that every sign has the potential to work together in a romantically involved way, it's just that some signs take a lot more work to achieve a state of equilibrium than others. And to repeat what was stated earlier, you two are WORK!

Of the twelve signs, Aries and Cancer are each other's biggest challenge to relate with naturally, due to each sign's placement on the zodiac wheel being positioned from each other at the harshest astrological angle possible of 90 degrees, better known as the square.

When two signs square each other, a consistently high probability exists for either sign to easily rub the other the wrong way. This happens quite often because either or both signs are simply being their natural selves.

Besides squaring each other, the ram and the crab often find they have very little common ground for a foundation that's needed to build a solid relationship. This is due to the first representatives of the elements of fire and water being fundamentally different from each other on multiple levels.

Aries is the first representative of fire. Cancer is water's first representative. The ram expresses being in action in its most pure and concentrated form, and the crab does the same with expressing emotion.

Being fire's first sign and of all the zodiac at large, the need to be in action is so pure and strong for those born beneath the sign of the ram, most Aries get seriously fidgety even after a few minutes of being stationary. The Aries doesn't get too nitpicky as to exactly what kind of action it partakes in, as long as the energies of the ram are in some kind of motion and preferably as spontaneous as often as possible.

The most pure and unadulterated way which a Cancer expresses its emotions is by nurturing others. If a Cancer feels emotionally connected to someone, he or she will literally "mommy" that person in order to best express their emotional state, regardless if they are related by blood or not. And just like the most overprotective of mothers, the typical Cancerian is keenly sensitive as to how nurturing energies are received.

Wanna make your Cancerian "mom" proud and pincer-pleased? Give full attention and thanks for nurturing actions and energies.

Wanna have your Cancerian "mom" turn into one big giant crab of hyper-sensitivity? Ignore their attempts to nurture.

But what to do when the Cancer chooses to mommy the sign least likely to want, or even appreciate, those intensely focused maternal energies? (Psssssst! Aries, that means you.)

When the crab realizes the object of his or her nurturing affections is the independent, self-concerned Aries, the natural defense reaction is to mommy the ram even more.

And by "mommying more," your Love Author really means smothering, followed by life endangering asphyxiation.

This watery defense mechanism of a reaction will, in turn, result in the Aries defensively reacting with behavior even MORE standoffish than before, but instead of actions carrying a whiff of self-concern, everything now reeks of outright selfishness!

On the other side of the crab horn/ram claw, what's the most effective way to put out a fire? Throw a nice, big pail of passive water on it.

If the Aries senses something is amiss in the relationship with the Cancerian, or worse, if the ram wants to make amends, the fire sign will attempt to actively "do" something with the crab. The Cancer will then proceed to thwart every bit of Arien activity through the passive, yet very undermining tactic of non-reactive non-action (otherwise known as being passive-aggressive to the hilt).

Your Love Author shall clarify his enlightening point in the form of a little ram-crustacean reenactment of romantic role reversal.

It's the day AFTER your birthday, Cancer, which coincidentally, your Aries partner failed to remember ... AGAIN.

Upon the clock striking 12:01 a.m. on the day following the anniversary of your Cancerian birth, you proceed to remind the Aries of his or her short term memory loss. And by "remind," I mean engage in an all out confrontational war.

Things get argumentatively messy, resulting in a deadlock of the crab and the ram not speaking to each other.

To make up for the lack of consideration, and by "lack of consideration," your Love Author really means the inability to register anything which doesn't directly deal with itself, the Aries comes up with a plan to make up for things by strategizing an entire weekend of Cancer-kiss-and -make-up activities!

In Aries time, we now return to about a week or so having passed after the Cancer's birthday.

The Aries enters the room where the Cancer is seething, I mean, sitting.

"Hey Babe!" the Aries says while approaching the seething, I mean, seated Cancer, whose locked gaze is fixed staring out the window at a most visually fascinating bush nearby.

"Hey," the Cancer replies without shifting a molecule of energy away from the vital task of staring at the all-important bush outside.

The Aries notices that the Cancer doesn't even look up to visually recognize its presence entering the room. The ram person then comes right out and asks, "Babe, are you still upset?"

Never straying its eagle eyed focus from that most crucial of neighboring bushes, the Cancer replies in as flat a tone as humanly possible, "No. I'm fine."

The Aries absentmindedly responds with "Okay" and leaves, forgetting why he or she walked into the room in the first place.

THE END. TA-DAH!

Sorry to sound like a broken romantic record, Aries and Cancer, but as I've said before, which I now feel compelled to say again, you two are WORK!

If the ram needs to be made aware of the crab's need to nurture, just as importantly, the Cancer needs to greatly adjust to the Aries' need to be periodically alone.

Cancerians, no matter how good the lovin' is with your ram-charged lover, the Aries will always need some alone time. This is a natural component for the first sign of the zodiac, who otherwise is known as the "sign of self."

Because it's the sign of self, the Aries likes doing its own thing. Motivated by pure and unadulterated self-concern, the ram child is not used to considering the perspective of others within the framework of its spontaneously impulsive life.

Should the Aries need some alone time, it's imperative for the Cancer to not take personal offense or misinterpret the ram's solitary needs as a form of romantic rejection!

Overreacting to the Aries' need to be alone or worse, smothering them and getting even MORE within their personal space, is tantamount to leading your ram relationship right to the boiling pot of breakup soon there afterwards, Cancer.

If the ram non-selfishly displays some crustacean consideration by allowing the Cancer to mommy him or her at various non-solitary times, with the crab remembering its Aries love child is first and foremost born free, this pairing of squaring signs may just end up worth the work after all.

Aries-Leo

Astrologically, the best romantic unions are those made up of two people born beneath the same element. And guess what, Aries and Leo? Given the fact both the ram and the lion are fire signs, YOU WIN!

Things really don't get much romantically better when the first and middle representatives of the family of flame join romantic forces.

The fire signs are action oriented and function best whenever in motion or in the process of "doing." Hence, those born beneath the element of flame like being busy as often as possible.

Now, despite hitting the romantic jackpot astrologically as a couple, it's best advised for the Aries and the Leo to give their budding love union a longer than usual period of adjustment if they hope to achieve any kind of lasting romantic success. Why? The difference lies with each fire sign's astrological "quality."

Aries' astrological quality is "cardinal," Leo's is "fixed." When comparing the ram's and the lion's astrological qualities, many times it'll seem as if the two fire signs came from opposite reaches of the solar system. Their overall approaches to things can differ that greatly from each other.

The cardinal signs (Aries, Cancer, Libra, Capricorn) take place at the starting point of each of the four seasons. Aries begins on the first day of spring, otherwise known as the spring equinox. The cardinal signs function best when their actions are starting or initiating things that are fresh, new, and never before experienced.

The fixed member of the fire sign family functions and operates quite differently than its cardinal signed counterpart.

The sign of Leo occurs smack dab in the middle of summer, during its dog days. Just as it sounds, the word used to describe the astrological quality of the mid-seasoned signs (Leo, Taurus, Scorpio, Aquarius) fits neatly into describing their overall temperament as well—FIXED.

As a whole, the fixed signs do not have the easiest time (more like next to never) seeing other people's perspectives that aren't their own. Other fixed characteristics that are anything but non-challenging are as follows: a natural tendency to resist change; a mental proclivity to see things in a one-dimensional, black or white way; an inherent inclination to not want to compromise; and a consistent knack for being obstinate, which is a polite way of saying, "pig-headed stubborn."

Even with what is mentioned above, the fixed signs tend to be the most tenacious of the entire zodiacal bunch. Whereas the Aries is able to start things with ease, its cardinal nature tends to inherently lack the necessary follow through to make sure those well begun things reach full completion.

The fixed nature of the Leo, on the other hand, contains an inherent strength of purpose that's truly impressive. Getting their energies jolted into action is the biggest challenge for those who are fixed, but once up and running, they are unstoppable and never lose their intense focus until the tasks are fully completed.

After all the astrological quality talk, let's take the overall essence behind the qualities of fixed and cardinal and compare and contrast them specifically to the members of the fire-signed family.

Of the twelve signs, Aries is the most impulsive and spontaneous. The words "impulsive" and "spontaneous" don't exist within the vocabulary of the all-controlling Leo.

Leo has a slow and steady approach to Life. Aries is fast and furious.

Leo likes a sense of regimented routine in its day to day life. Aries would rather jump, horns first, off the highest precipice than have any kind of regimented routine imposed upon its day to day life.

The Leo LIVES for romance! The Aries lives for itself.

The Aries' lack of concern about what others might think gives it the ability to throw on a backwards baseball cap and sweatpants without a care and go out in public either unwashed or ungroomed. The Leo's abundance of ego makes them so concerned about what others think, the Lion would rather have its head mounted in a trophy room than be seen in public with hair that's either unwashed or ungroomed.

The Aries LOVES surprises! The Leo fantasizes about devouring those that love surprises.

The Leo has the patience of a saint. The Aries can become a saint's worst nightmare if it has to wait more than half a microsecond longer than expected for anything.

The two biggest points of contention that could easily douse the romantic bonfire between these two fire signs deal with spontaneity versus planning, and alone time versus couple time.

The cardinal-signed Aries loves being "in the moment" during as many moments of its ram-charged day as possible. Doing things off the cuff, or from a randomly spontaneous angle is totally radical for the Aries and radically insane for the fixed sign of royalty, Leo, who likes to control every aspect of the monarchy that is its world.

Problems emerge when the monarchy turns into an absolutist dictatorship of Leonine control, where all romantic activities are pre-scheduled agendas and any kind of Arien last minute changes or in the moment impulses are strictly forbidden.

On the fiery flip side, for the love of Mars, Aries, do NOT do the "surprise!" thing with your Leo love interest, especially showing up to its place unannounced!

Despite the shock of dropping by on your Leonine lover and finding them with, (I almost can't say it), UNPRIMPED HAIR, you impetuous rams probably won't remember much afterwards, due to the taken by surprise Leo roaring you right out of its lair.

Another thing, Aries, a key personality difference between the Leo and your sign is that beneath the killer exterior of the deadly lion lies the sensitively gooey heart of a hopeless romantic. And beneath the exterior of the ram are ram guts.

In order for the Aries to capture its Leonine love interest and cage its heart, some amount of romance is required.

But here lies the problem, rams. Being romantic is a way of making your Leo lover feel truly special and adored, but in order to do that (your Love Author hasn't even said it yet, and his eyes are watering from the stinging pain of it all), the Aries has to think of someone else besides its self-concerned self.

It's asking a TON, but you horn heads can do it! I just know ... you ... can?

Quickly changing astrological flame throwers ...

Leo, no matter how good the lovin' is with your ram-charged lover, the Aries will always need some alone time. This is a natural component for the first sign of the zodiac, which otherwise is known as the "sign of self."

Aries folks like doing their own thing, whenever they want to do it. Motivated by pure and unadulterated self-concern, the ram child is not used to considering the perspective of others within the framework of its spontaneously impulsive life.

Should the Aries need some alone time, it is imperative for the Leo to not be personally offended or misinterpret the ram's solitary needs as a form of romantic snubbing.

Dramatically overreacting to the Aries' need to be alone or worse, getting even MORE in their personal space is tantamount to leading your ram relationship right to the slaughter soon there afterwards, lions.

So after all that, if both fire signs take the time to adjust, as well as remain aware of their key differences of personality, your Love Author sees no reason why the Aries and Leo shouldn't be playing with each other's fire as often as they romantically can.

Aries–Virgo

Seriously, Aries and Virgo. I need to throw this one out there, first and foremost. Are you two SURE you're dating each other?

Maybe you both have other romantic partners who either got lost or separated while all parties foraged their way to this particular chapter of the book?

Close, but no Cupid doll, huh?

So both of you are unshakably sure in your convictions that one half of this newly budding romance is an Aries, and the other, a Virgo, correct? Okay, then. Boldly forward we go.

Sorry for all the obnoxious obviousness just then, Aries and Virgo, but the two of you romantically joining forces is definitely NOT a common occurrence one hears about every day, nor is your astrological union considered to be in any way obvious.

When looking at the prototypical wheel of the zodiac, the sign of Virgo lies at a 150 degree angle away from the sign of Aries. The proper astrological term for this very particular angle is the "quincunx." Everyone repeat along with me. Ready? Ku-win-kwunx. Very good!

Now, the quincunx is also known by the much easier pronounced, astrological reference word "inconjunct." When two signs are placed at an inconjunct angle of each other, nothing remotely matches, and every inherent aspect of one sign is square pegged against the natural energies of the other.

Some keywords associated with the inconjunct are: re-direction, challenge, diversion, and that which requires adjustment.

I won't kid either of you, Aries and Virgo. Most of the outside world has a hard time picturing the two of you together due to your union's high factor of "unobviousness." When viewed individually, one would think you both were hardcore polar opposites. Each sign's inherent energies seem THAT different from each other.

Aries is an action-based fire sign. Doing things that are new and never before tried works best for them. Virgo is an earth sign that relies on the tangible. Doing things they have repeatedly worked on before with the intention of perfecting over time is its optimal set up.

Being ruled by the planet named after the Roman god of war, Mars, the typical Aries tends to be rambunctious and straightforwardly aggressive more often than not. Being one of the karmic signs with a pre-awareness to be of service to others, the typical Virgo tends to be quiet and unobtrusively humble more often than not.

Virgos are neat and tidy. Aries are anything but.

Aries are impulsive and love to push the envelope by being the daredevil at times. Virgos are pragmatic and identify themselves with the work they do. Any envelopes being pushed on their end tend to be strictly desk bound with the intention of being post marked on the same business day.

Aries is the sign of the self and often isn't aware of other people's needs until its needs are met first. Virgo's karmic duties can make him or her far too aware of meeting other people's needs first before their own and is often called the selfless sign.

The Aries has a "devil may care" attitude overall and hardly ever worries. Look up the word "worry" in the dictionary and the term "See also, Virgo" follows its definition.

Virgo has a tendency to repress. Aries has a tendency to explode.

Aries is the sign of the leader. Virgo is the sign of that leader's administrative assistant.

You can never tell an Aries what to do. A Virgo prefers being told what to do.

The Virgo is proactively healthy and hardly ever sick, due to making regular checkups with the doctor. The phrase "checkup" doesn't exist in the vocabulary of the Aries, who far too often will make an appointment to see a doctor only when they are seriously sick.

Every sign has a key phrase, and looking at the mottos of these two signs individually might assist with making all this unobvious talk a bit more defined.

Aries' key phrase is "I AM." Virgo's is "I ANALYZE."

Said another way, the sign of me, me, and more me paired together with the sign that could make internalized worry an Olympic event isn't necessarily the easiest astrological union, but it's not impossible either.

Why these two signs don't even mingle, let alone join forces is due to each not bothering with the other after a blanket evaluation is made: The Aries will tend to initially sum up the Virgo to be a wet blanketed prude who critically finds fault with not just itself, but the world at large.

The Virgo may at first judge the Aries to be a self-obsessed, never-ending risk liability who throws caution to the wind with every impulsively untidy move they make.

Along with adjusting to the Aries' constant state of self-concern, the Virgo must always keep in mind the following astrological key difference between their signs, as well. The Aries is never too concerned about what others think, whereas the Virgo pretty much always is.

The biggest pitfalls of problematic potential within this particular love union are the core differences of approach either sign takes regarding issues of maturity, spontaneity, and fun.

An Aries will often leap off the romantic precipice due to the ram feeling pinned into a corner of Virgoan non-spontaneous activity that never lets up on what the neighbors think, or worse, never allows sweat gear of any kind to be thrown on and worn in public EVER!

Conversely, many a Virgo will take their ram virgin union to the slaughter after no longer finding amusement in those specifically Arien things that lack maturity, like random dirty laundry being left in any given spot of the house (including the refrigerator), beer funnels, beer pong (or a mixture of both), as well as joke punching.

The Virgo will need to consistently work on lightening things up for its Aries love interest. Plus, it would substantially help things romantically if the virginal one made a concentrated effort to add a factor to its fire-signed partnership that isn't usually associated with their sign: Fun.

A little fun goes a LONG way for an Aries. The Virgo's hard-working nature can make many born beneath the middle of the earth signs appear to always be intensely driven and constantly need to appear perfectly put together, which over time can be rather un-fun.

Things extend past the realm of uninterested neutrality when the Aries stops being so self-conscious and allows the Virgo to bring some much needed organization and streamlined efficiency into the ram's worry-free but messily haphazard life.

Similarly, the virgin olive oil can blend quite nicely with that ram-kicking pungent vinegar if the Virgo loosens up a little (who am I kidding, a whole lot) and gets seriously wild by spending an entire ram-charged weekend without a single "to do" list anywhere on or near its self-efficient person!

Trust me, Aries. For the Virgo that IS seriously wild, bordering on the unthinkable.

If the Aries can allow the Virgo to clear out some of its chaos (along with blow-torching the living quarters clean), then the Virgo may let his or her hair down just enough in order to have more surface space to butt heads with its playful ram of romance as they wrestle, rock climb, play beer pong, etc. POST blow torching, of course.

I know, Virgo. There's nothing worse than contracting beer pong pinkeye due to non-sterile glass wear.

Aries-Libra

(Entering Room) Oh, hey! Aries. Libra.

(Casually strolling past, then stopping to give each of you a prolonged glancing over.)

If I didn't know any better, my view upon entering the room of the two of you sitting all relaxed and casually hanging out usually wouldn't give me cause to wonder if anything out of the ordinary was going on.

But I do know better. Much, much better.

I just happen to know the astrological fact that The Ram and The Scales are polar opposites of each other, and not to be trite in a nasal Paula Abdul way, but opposites attract.

And when two opposites are within close physical proximity of each other, the attraction factor turns into an all-out starved shark feeding frenzy of kissing touchy-feely!

Hey, lighten up you two! There's nothing wrong with the romantic fact your Love Author is astrologically savvy enough to deduce that just before entering the room, you two were groping for each other like wild primates.

Some would say you oppositely attracted lovebirds were merely obeying an inalterable law of both astrology and science.

Remember those magnet experiments used back in junior high to demonstrate the law of attraction? Take those same oppositely charged pieces of metal that slammed into each other whenever one was within remote proximity of the other, except now one of the magnets is called "Aries" and the other "Libra."

(uncomfortable silence)

Okay then! How about we skip the science talk to give an overview of the ram and the scales' astrological backgrounds to see how different and similar you opposite signs are together.

Aries, your sign is ruled by Mars, the planet named after the ancient god of war and aggression. Libra, your sign is ruled by Venus, the planet named after the ancient goddess of peace and harmony.

Aries, you're the sign of self-concern as evidenced by your spontaneous and often sloppy impulses. Libra, you're the sign of tact and grace as evidenced by your neat and tidy social skills and impeccable manners.

Phrases like "decision-making time" don't exist in the vocabulary of the ram. When an Aries wants something, it goes after it. Done deal. Whereas imagine a camera panning away from a Libra trying to decide whether he or she wants Chinese or Italian for dinner. Observe how the seasons change through the outside window as the camera motions further away from this time-stopping ordeal of indecisiveness.

Aries, now and then you lose your cool and volcanically erupt in public. Libra, you would rather lose a limb than your cool in public.

Even with all of the above mentioned the rule with polar opposites is they share just as many similarities as differences.

Both signs have no problem finding the initial motivation to go after their basic needs. Since Aries rules over the house of the physical body, the ram's needs are straightforward and simple, similar to the core things the human body requires in order to function: food, shelter, warmth, exercise, and even sex.

The basic needs for the Libra, however, aren't so basic. The scales person functions best when it is in a relationship. Because its core need is to be united with another, many a Libran will be motivated to not be single and be driven in a very determined way to change its relationship status to that of "taken." The Libra's need to be in a relationship is just as strong as the Aries' need to eat when hungry.

Because the ram child is motivated by its core needs, the first of the zodiac is always first on its list of priorities, with everyone else second. For example, if an Aries is hungry, it will eat. You can join him or her to dine if you want, but if an Aries is hungry, it is going to eat. Or if an Aries is tired it will go to bed. There may be a party with a house still full of guests, but no matter, the Aries is still going to bed. Everyone else can let themselves out whenever they want to leave.

You can't say your Love Author didn't warn you.

Keeping in mind the first sign of the zodiac is also known as the sign of self, it doesn't matter how horns over heels your Aries is in love with you or vice versa. Every Aries needs some alone time on as regular a basis as possible.

Overlooking this straightforward Arien trait, or constantly smothering your Aries love interest is tantamount to severing romantic ties with no discussion allowed.

And speaking of non-discussion, we now come to the Libran problematic portion of the love program.

Libra's planetary ruler of Venus not only rules over such niceties as love and beauty, but peace and harmony as well. This may sound all sugar and spice and Venusian nice at first, but in terms of a romantic relationship, these inherent niceties can turn out to be quite problematic. Allow your Love Author to explain.

A relationship is never 100 percent smooth sailing, or in scale terms, perfectly balanced. There will be times within every human relationship where differences of opinion or gripes will occur. When these inevitable things take place, both partners will be called upon to either debate or argue over the contentious matters at hand in order to work things out. Except for the Libra.

Should the scales person have a bone to pick with its partner, he or she more than likely won't say a word. Because of its non-confrontational nature, many a Libran will stifle whatever problem in order to maintain the peace/not rock the boat/keep things nice and quiet.

It's in the best interest of every child of Venus to be as upfront and vocal with gripes and differences, and just as importantly, during the time of the occurrence.

The converging of polar opposite signs has an all or nothing effect. There is never a middle of the road/not really sure (even Libran unsure) end result when opposites cross paths, especially after initially mauling each other like crazed wild animals.

Even with that blushingly said, if there is nothing more other than a few fast and furious bed creaks, or in other words, nothing of binding common interest beyond the initial attraction, the polarized spark will be snuffed out just as quickly as it began. Why?

Many times the flames of opposing desire are quickly doused due to both signs driving each other naturally crazy after the passing of five post-bed creaking minutes, give or take.

But conversely, if the polar opposites can stand each other's presence for more than five minutes post you know, and have a thing or two they like about the other, or even better, share a few things in common, then here is where we find those fairy tale relationships that stay together.

In fact, when there are binding factors beyond the initial opposite attraction, many of these dualistic duos literally last until "death do they polar-opposite part."

Aries–Scorpio

Seriously, Aries and Scorpio. I need to throw this one out there, first and foremost. Are you two SURE you're dating each other?

Sorry for all the obnoxious obviousness, but your two signs romantically joining forces is definitely NOT a common occurrence one hears about every day, nor is the ram and the scorpion dating each other considered to be in any way obvious.

When looking at the prototypical wheel of the zodiac, the sign of Scorpio lies at a 150 degree angle away from the sign of Aries. The proper astrological term for this very particular angle is the quincunx. Everyone repeat along with me. Ready? Ku-win-kwunx. Very Good!

Now, the quincunx is also known by the much easier pronounced, astrological reference word, "inconjunct." When two signs are placed at an inconjunct angle of each other, nothing remotely matches, and every inherent aspect of one sign is square pegged against the natural energies of the other. Some keywords associated with the inconjunct are: redirection, challenge, diversion, and that which requires adjustment

I won't kid either of you, Aries and Scorpio. Most of the outside world has a hard time picturing the two of you together, due to your union's high factor of unobviousness. When viewed individually, one would think the ram and the scorpion were polar opposites. Their inherent energies seem THAT different from each other.

Being the first sign of the zodiac, the Aries lives in the moment and is the most impulsively spontaneous of signs. The words impulsive and spontaneous don't exist within the vocabulary of the Scorpio, a sign that tries to wield absolute control over its life by having everything pre-planned.

Aries' astrological quality of cardinal makes them quite good at starting things. However, the ram's biggest challenge is taking the things it naturally starts so well and following them through to completion. Finding the motivational energy to begin things is the Scorpio's biggest challenge, but once begun, this fixed sign has the tenacity and focus to make sure things are followed all the way through to completion.

The Aries is an open book. What you see is what you get with this most straightforward of signs. The Scorpio feels most secure having an air of mystery attached to him or her. Their book is closed shut and perish the thought what'll happen if one tries seeing anything the Scorpion is unwilling to show.

The Aries loves surprises! The Scorpio loves to fantasize about disposing of those who love surprises.

The Scorpio has the patience of a saint. The Aries is a saint's worst nightmare if it has to wait 5 milliseconds longer than expected.

If an Aries is mad at you, it will explode and yell, then ask if you're hungry and whether you want to join them to eat. If a Scorpio is mad at you, it will explode and yell, then eat and digest every detail of how you hurt them for the purpose of future emotional weaponry.

Combining the romantic energies of the Aries with the Scorpio isn't only about their glaring differences of personality. Romantic potential actually exists between the first of the fire signs and the middle of the watery ones, but it's as unobvious as their inconjunct compatibility.

Much like a treasure chest of gems being furtively hidden in the ocean's sands due to its unobvious placement lying slightly outside one's field of vision, these two signs usually don't even mingle, let alone join forces.

Romantic success for the Aries Scorpio relationship lies deep below the external surface of both of these strong-willed signs. The more these two hot heads of the zodiac make the investment of getting to know each other, the greater the chances that out of view treasure chest will be discovered and eventually unlocked.

A most unique bond exists between the ram and the scorpion that despite being hidden and far from sight, was forged by an ancient astrological union between both signs that reaches back to mankind's archetypal beginnings.

Before racing back through time, here's a little astrology 101 reminder. Every sign is ruled by one of the planets of the solar system, otherwise known as the planetary ruler of a sign. Aries, your planetary ruler is Mars, the ultimate fighter of outer space. Scorpio, yours is Pluto, the planetary grand daddy of goth.

But as recently as a century ago, this Aries Scorpio planetary rulership simply was not the case.

Hey, Aries, did you know a time existed when computers didn't? Swear to Scorpio!

Believe it or not, the digital age has lasted for a fraction of a millisecond when realizing 99.9 percent of human history involves vast stretches of time that had not a single computer, electrical gadget, working toilet, nor any form of ice cube whatsoever!

Add a few telescopes over the centuries, throw in some electricity into the passage of decades, toss in an extra planet per century after 1600, and let's fast-forward much closer to the abundantly ice-cubed present, shall we?

Uranus was stumbled upon by humankind in the 1700s. Neptune's presence was added to man's awareness in the 1800s. It was only as recently as 1931 when the existence of Scorpio's planetary ruler, Pluto, was made known to the residents of planet earth.

Before the twentieth century, Scorpio was ruled by the red planet, Mars. By sharing what's properly called an ancient planetary ruler, the ram and the scorpion are archetypally connected by the following positive Martian personality traits that both inherently possess bravery of heart, strong instinct, straightforward directness, and a vibrant life force tied to an unabashed will to survive.

Should the ram and the scorpion decide to commit to each other, the Aries should be well aware in advance there is nothing casual about this union! When the Scorpio commits its serious self romantically to another, it does so for the long haul. The Aries needs to know from the get-go that romance with the scorpion has nothing to do with seeing each other now and then, nor simultaneously playing the field. The ram should not become the object of the Scorpio's very intense affections unless the Aries is ready to fully commit.

As previously mentioned, if an Aries loses its temper and proceeds to chew you out, it does so, immediately followed by announcing its state of hunger and asking if you're ready to eat. The Scorpio has a proclivity to hold on to past hurts, and tends to carry grudges of the longest standing kind, which in the larger scheme of things, hurts no one but the seething scorpion the most. It would behoove many a Scorpio to model its behavior more towards the Arien trait of being emotionally in the moment, followed by being in the next moment, and then the next, with no emotional residue.

If both strong-willed signs manage to avoid any/all displays of astrological domination over the other, the inner gems of their anciently shared strengths will fiercely shine forth, leaving the ram and the scorpion agog with mutual wonder and admiration.

Aries–Sagittarius

Welcome to the carnival, Aries and Sagittarius!

When both your spitfire signs become romantically involved together, the world can be likened to a festive carnival where both the action and fun seem non-stop!

Astrologically, the best romantic unions are made up of two people born under the same element. Since Aries and Sagittarius are both fire signs, it really doesn't get much better than when these two members of the family of flame join romantic forces.

The elemental foundation of fire is action, and fire signs in general (Aries, Sagittarius, and Leo) function best whenever they are in motion or in the process of "doing." Said another way, the members of the fiery family like staying active and busy as often as they can.

Since Aries is the first representative of the element of fire, the need to be in action is so pure and strong for those born beneath the sign of the ram that most Aries get seriously fidgety even after a few minutes of being seated or stationary. The first sign of the zodiac doesn't get too nitpicky as to exactly what kind of action they partake in, as long as it's fast paced and preferably spontaneous. And doing ANYTHING is better for the typical ram than doing nothing at all.

The mutable signs (Sagittarius, Gemini, Virgo, Pisces) occur as each of the four seasons draws to a close. Sagittarius takes place at the tail end of autumn, just before the winter solstice. The mutables function best in environments containing some level of variety and change and are the multitaskers of the zodiac.

A mutable-signed person can, in theory, attempt doing one thing at a time, but it's practically a guarantee things will be screwed up if it actively chooses that intensely focused dynamic. This is due to the traits shared amongst all the mutables of possessing not even the slightest shred of patience, as well as being susceptible to mind-numbing boredom after sitting down for no longer than five minutes.

The mutable signs are known for doing as many simultaneous actions as physically possible, but they're equally known for dropping said actions at choice times due to their susceptibility of being easily distracted.

Dates for two fire signs, especially in the beginning stages of getting to know each other, will tend to be as physically active as romantically possible.

The ram enjoys partaking in such physical activities as hiking, running, rock climbing, dancing (as long as its partner doesn't mind a guaranteed mid-move crash at least once per dance), and of course "doing the bed creak," all with a touch of competitive drive throughout.

The centaur takes its action-oriented core and enjoys doing things against a big-picture-sized backdrop, such as attending a (insert any/all sport) game in an arena setting, gambling the night away at a casino, or traveling to the most exotic locales on the globe.

Romantically joining the Aries with the Sagittarius is a great match because neither will have a single qualm about doing the other's activity. Plus, if one's suggested action just happens to be spontaneously switched at the last minute by the other, the fun factor gets stoked up even more for either fire child!

Whenever discussing the ram-centaur union, your Love Author must seriously stress how critically important it is for the "F" word to be present as often as possible whenever these two naturally hot ones come together: Fun.

The fire signs always need to feel there is some level of fun taking place somewhere in their lives at any given time. As little as an eyedropper's amount of fun goes a long way for them.

But even with the F-word being tossed around like a (insert any/all sport) ball, specific pitfalls of problematic potential need to be discussed between these two fiery folk.

We'll start with the problem that afflicts a vast portion of the fire-signed population, both individually and even more so while in romantic pursuit of each other.

Aries-Sag Potential Pitfall 1: Physical Exhaustion. Cardinal-signed Aries loves being "in the moment" during as many moments as possible of its ram-charged day. Doing things off the cuff or from a randomly spontaneous angle is most radical for them. Mutable-signed Sagittarius is the multitasker of the zodiac with its energy best being burned up doing as many simultaneous things as physically possible.

Since the fire signs enjoy being constantly active, they tend not to hear their bodies' SOS call of alarm whenever approaching the brink of physical exhaustion.

When the ram and the centaur first meet, their excitement is usually quite hard to contain. So much so that a high probability exists for the two fire signs to run themselves ragged while attempting to do things together as often as their physical bodies will allow.

Injuries can also be a common occurrence whenever two fire signs go out and play and throw caution completely to the wind.

Speaking of injuries…

Aries-Sag Potential Pitfall 2: Anger Issues. Aries is ruled by Mars, the heavenly body named after the Roman god of war. Along with action and energy, Mars oversees anger and aggression.

It's no coincidence we use the Martian-colored term "seeing red" whenever describing a person in a fit of rage. Many children of Mars tend to naturally have bad tempers due to anger being the one human emotion an Aries can easily tap into most.

As stated earlier, Sagittarius' quality of being mutable instills within the centaur an inherent need for variety and change as well as the ability to multi-task. But the Sag's mutability also instills a level of patience that is minimal to non-existent.

Test the patience of a sign inherently known for having a clear absence of it and risk the likelihood of some out-of-the-blue (Sag's color) pony punches being hand-delivered right at you.

And every fire child should know the following upfront: the fire-signed female is NOT your shrinking violet or passive doormat of a partner. She does what she wants to do, and heaven help you if you stand in her way! These feminine flames think like dudes. They're strong-willed, go after what they want, and can deliver a powerful right hook at will if they're told to be in any way submissive or subservient. You can't say your Love Author didn't warn you.

Aries-Sag Potential Pitfall 3: Cheating. With Aries' heavenly body of Mars ruling over all of the body's physical drives, including those burning ones emanating from the loins, and with Sag's mutability factor craving variety, what's it spell?

Philandering. Being unfaithful. Adultery. You get my bed-creaking drift.

Both Aries and Sagittarius are signs naturally endowed with stronger than average sex drives. Should the burning need for adulterous activity arise, both signs are more than capable of switching up the sexual fun exclusively with each other.

Besides those potential pitfalls, your Love Author sees no reason why you two hotties shouldn't be allowed to enter the carnival fairgrounds and run rampant!

HEY, ARIES AND SAG! OVER HERE!

Jump on! Your heated love seat for two on the ferris wheel of fiery fun has arrived! Wait until you catch the view of what a carnival life can be when this thing reaches the top!

Given both of you are astrological daredevils, do not, under any circumstance, dare each other to play ferris wheel chicken upon reaching said top.

Aries-Capricorn

"And He shall separate them one from another, as a shepherd divideth his sheep from the goats. And He shall set the sheep on His right hand, but the goats on the left." Matthew 25: 33

See, Aries and Capricorn? It's not just me. Even the big G thinks you two should be separated.

Just kidding! (Kind of.)

Of the twelve signs, Aries and Capricorn are each other's biggest challenge to naturally relate with due to each sign's placement on the zodiac wheel. The ram and goat are positioned from each other at the harshest astrological angle possible of 90 degrees, which is better known as "the square."

When two signs square each other, a consistently high probability exists for either sign to easily rub the other the wrong way. This happens quite often because either or both signs are simply being their natural selves.

Not only do both signs' inherent traits sound almost like polar opposites when compared to each other, the core foundations behind what makes an Aries and a Capricorn tick practically appear to negate themselves when placed side by side.

Being the first representative of the element of fire, Aries is the sign of impulsive spontaneity that goes into action at will. Being the last representative of the element of earth, Capricorn is the sign of formal restraint whose vocabulary doesn't even contain the words "spontaneous" or "impulsive."

The Aries' upfront and straightforward nature gives it the ability to chat with anybody. The Capricorn's detached manner of being business formal means he or she won't just chat with anybody, especially strangers!

When excited, the Aries tends to talk as fast and furious as a teenager. The Capricorn tends to talk as distant and formal as a bank teller and never gets excited. Ever.

The Aries likes to spend time with/hang out with/date those that are close to its age. The Capricorn likes to spend time/hang out with/date those that are much older or much younger.

The Aries can have a serious temper. The Capricorn is serious yet tempered.

Now Aries and Capricorn, after all that, did you think your Love Author would give the impression that astrology gives only an across the board "thumbs down" regarding your signs romantically pairing up together? Good ram goats, no! Biology seconds that notion.

Ironically, sheep and goats look quite similar and are often hard to differentiate by their physicality alone. Only by observing their behavior patterns and core genetics can one see just how much these two creatures do not biologically m-a-a-a-a-a-tch.

Astrology plays a key role with both cloven-hooved beasts, right down to their biological genus categorization. A sheep is biologically housed within the species, *Ovas aries*, a goat within *Capra hircus*. Although both are members of the antelope family, the ties that bind these two animals are muted compared to their core deviations.

A ram is a male sheep. A goat refers to a male or female version of such. All goats have horns, and only some types of rams do. When rams fight, they butt heads. When goats attack, they charge at their opponent's backside or hind legs. Goats have beards, rams do not. Mountainous rams live in rocky terrain that borders grass and clover-rich meadows. Mountainous goats live in the highest rocky terrains known to any mammal and will eat whatever they are able to forage at those stratospheric heights.

Now here's a real horn curler. The biggest difference between a ram and a goat is the number of chromosomes each has at its genetic core. The ram's *Ovas aries* species has 54 chromosomes, whereas the goat's *Capra hircus* species has 60. In biological summation, the ram is a simple creature by nature, whereas the goat is far more complex.

Of the two, the Capricorn will need to do more of the initial adjusting than the Aries when first dating due to a quality that is a constant state of being for the ram and not nearly as much for the goat: self-concern.

Being in a relationship with an Aries is about as straightforward a situation as one can find, but the romantic partner of a ram child must always take into consideration the following rule of Arien self: The Aries is going to do whatever it wants to do, whenever it wants to do it.

This is the sign of self that follows its most basic core needs. In other words, the Aries is always first on its list of priorities with everyone else second. For example, if an Aries is hungry, it's going to eat. You can join him or her to dine if you want, but it will eat when it's hungry no matter what. Or if an Aries is tired, it's time for bed. There may be a party with a house still full of guests, but no matter, it's time for bed and everyone else can let themselves out whenever they want to leave.

Along with the Capricorn adjusting to the Aries' constant state of self-concern, the earth sign must take the following into consideration. The Aries is never too concerned about what others think, whereas the Capricorn pretty much always is.

The biggest pitfalls of problematic potential within the Aries Capricorn union are the core differences of approach either sign takes regarding issues of maturity, responsibility, spontaneity, and fun.

An Aries will often leap off the romantic precipice due to the ram feeling pinned into a corner of Capricorn non-spontaneous activity that never lets up on what the neighbors think or worse, never allows athletic gear of any kind to be worn in public. EVER!

Conversely, many a Capricorn will take its ram goat union to the slaughter after no longer finding amusement in those specifically Arien things that lack maturity, like random dirty laundry being left in any given spot of the house (including the refrigerator), beer funnels, beer pong (or a mixture of both), as well as joke punching.

The Capricorn will also need to consistently work on lightening things up for its Aries love interest. It would greatly behoove (get it?) the goat to put a concentrated effort into adding a factor to its sheep goat love union that isn't usually associated with its sign: Fun.

A little fun goes a LONG way for an Aries. The Capricorn's hard-working nature and high status goals can cause many a goat guy and girl to be intensely driven and always needing to appear perfectly put together, which over time, can be rather unfun.

If the Aries can set a goal of some (not all) time spent with the Capricorn having some sort of structured purpose, (as well as plans on never getting caught in public wearing sweats with a backwards baseball cap on in front of its goat guy or girl), there just may be romantic comingling in the pasture.

And if the Capricorn can add some fun into the romantic mix while figuring out a way to come up with as genuine a human-sounding laugh whenever it doesn't get the Aries (or anyone else's) jokes, then this particular pairing may end up being lovingly lined in the highest quality of woolen fleece and silky mohair after all.

Aries–Aquarius

Did you lovebirds know the most damaging forest fires occur in areas that don't necessarily have the most flammable material but are susceptible to high winds?

Flame, unto its solitary self, doesn't make a fire burn fast and furiously. Take said flame and infuse it with the oxygen from the windy air and you have one serious scorcher. Kind of like when the Aries and the Aquarius join romantic forces.

In astrology, the four elements of earth, air, fire, and water are naturally paired off. Each grouping consists of two elements that naturally work well together, otherwise known as being complementary to each other. Hence, the elements of earth and water, but more importantly for this particular pairing, the elements of fire and air are complementary to each other.

When fiery Aries is romantically paired with airy Aquarius, the erratic nature of the furiously fast burning wildfire is made more constant and tempered down to that of a slow and steadily burning flame.

In order to fully comprehend that romantically hot concept, individual overviews of the first of the fire signs and the last of the air signs must be presented.

The elemental foundation of fire is action, and the signs that make up the family of flame, namely Aries, Leo, and Sagittarius, enjoy being in as constant a state of action as often as possible. Hence, the fire signs function best when they are in motion or in the process of "doing." Said another way, the members of the fiery family like being busy.

Being the first representative of the element of fire, the need to be in action is so pure and strong that most Aries get seriously fidgety even after a few minutes of being seated or stationary. The first sign of the zodiac doesn't get too nitpicky as to exactly what kind of action it partakes in as long as the energies of the Aries are in some kind of motion that's preferably spontaneous. And doing ANYTHING is better for the typical Aries than doing nothing at all.

Blowing right along to the airy half of our complementary couple, human intellect is the foundational core of the element of air, and the air signs function best through the mental processes of thought and communication. The range of intellectual complexity and communicative output of the signs that comprise this element (Gemini, Libra, and Aquarius) can be likened to something along the lines of a *Goldilocks and the Three Bears* astrological scenario.

Much like the three different variations of bear sizes in the children's fairy tale, the first representative of the air signs, Gemini, can be likened to the baby bear of the air-signed bunch due to that sign's constant state of mental curiosity. The middle representative of the airy ones, Libra, is comparable to the mama bear due to that sign's mental capabilities being so graciously well-mannered. Last but certainly not intellectually least, the Aquarius can be no one else but the papa bear of the air-signed family by virtue of the water bearer's innovative intellect towering way above every other resident of the breezy bunch and the rest of the zodiac.

What steadies the fiery nature of the Aries Aquarius union into a steadily burning flame of high romantic potential is the astrological quality of the stoking wind supplied by the last of the air signs. In other words, it's the "fixed" quality of the water bearer.

The fixed signs (Taurus, Leo, Scorpio, Aquarius) are each positioned at the mid-point of each of the four seasons, with the sign of Aquarius taking place during the dead of the winter season. Unlike Aries' quality of cardinal, whose specialty is the ability to start things or begin from scratch, the fixed signs usually have a hard time finding the motivation to getting things started or begun. But where the cardinal sign's biggest challenge is following the things he or she starts so well all the way through to completion, the fixed person almost always methodically keeps its energies moving until whatever task that has been slowly started is fully done. Among the fixed, nothing is ever rushed or approached with a fast and furious pace. Slow and steady wins the race with these heavy hitting signs.

Combining the daredevil of fire signs (Aries) with the fixed sign of airy genius (Aquarius) may at first sound like a union of polar opposites due to the ram and the water bearer working from such differing dynamics. However, returning once more to our original "wind + fire = serious scorcher" formula of complementary elements, joining the romantic energies of the Aries with the Aquarius usually results in a serious romance of long-lasting potential versus a burning ball of passion that extinguishes itself as quickly as when it first combusted.

In fact, both sign's core differences of dynamic tend to be seen as refreshingly fun by the other versus any kind of romantic obstacle that could get in the way of the Aries and Aquarius' budding intimacy upon first dating each other.

The Aries' highly energetic and straightforward approach to things has a special way of keeping the brilliant mind of the Aquarian thoroughly entertained. While the water bearer's unique intellect can captivate the attentions of even the most fidgety of rams, leaving it agog with wonder and stunned to silence.

With all the super great aspects behind the complementary nature of fire and air, potential problems arise should either element become too isolated.

In their own strong ways, both Aries and Aquarius are signs of solitary independence. No matter how good the lovin' is for either sign, both the ram and the water bearer will always need some alone time. This is a natural component for the Aries, who otherwise is known as the sign of self. For the Aquarian, this is an imposed state despite the water bearer being known as the sign of groups.

Upon entrance onto this plane of existence, the Aquarius longs to be part of a social group. However, this almost always never materializes to the water bearer's liking, especially during the teen years and twenties, due to its inherently fierce sense of individuality.

Without trying, the Aquarian's natural quirkiness and ahead of its time flair makes it stick out like a sore thumb within any group, be it friends, classmates, co-workers, or social clubs. Over time, the typical water bearer becomes accustomed to being a lone wolf due to years of longing to belong but admiring those together from a distance.

The ram child, on the other hand, likes doing its own thing, whenever it wants to do it. Motivated by pure self-concern, the Aries isn't used to considering the perspective of others within the framework of its spontaneous, impulsive life.

But that's exactly what needs to be done when Cupid's arrow slams the ram with amorous intentions for an Aquarian love interest!

If the Aries steps outside of its own self-concerned perspective and coaxes the Aquarian out of its self-imposed solitary confinement by reassuring the water bearer its inherent uniqueness isn't incomprehensible but oh so lovable, then let the good times roll and burst into air-stoked flame!

Aries-Pisces

Tonga and Samoa.

That's how I see the two of you romantically together, Aries and Pisces. Aries, you're Tonga, Samoa is Pisces. Perfect, right?!

(Crickets.)

Guess a smidge more explaining is needed, huh?

Well Aries and Pisces, even though you both technically are next to each other on the big wheel of the zodiac, your Love Author would rather equate your romantic compatibility to something more along the lines of the bordering islands of Tonga and Samoa in the South Pacific Ocean.

Aries, let's say I forward pass you via your astrological body part, head first, right onto the island of Tonga. Pisces, your sign will be sent through space and time via your body part, feet first, onto the neighboring island of Samoa.

Both islands share the same time of day, but at the precise moment of it being noon for Aries, it would be 12 noon for Pisces as well, but on the previous day.

Despite being geographically next to each other, these two islands in the South Pacific were recently separated by the International Date Line.

Tonga is located in the eastern hemisphere of the globe and is a day ahead of the majority of the world's population. The island of Samoa is in the western hemisphere and is set furthest back in time.

From a circular perspective, Aries and Pisces lay right next to each other on the wheel of the zodiac. However, when comparing the two signs with a linear approach, things become practically inversed a full 180 degrees. Linearly, Alpha Aries is positioned first at the very start of things and Omega Pisces is placed last at the end of the zodiacal road.

Where the zodiac begins with the sign of self, Aries, things are seen through a simple, straightforward lens of instinctual self-concern. We close astrological shop with the sign of universality and intuitive awareness symbolized by the cosmic fish of Pisces.

The last sign of the zodiac's interconnected intuition propels the Piscean soul far beyond anything individualized. What began as an individualized perspective of pure self-concern (Aries) both dissolves and extends itself to include an awareness of the furthest reaches of the universe (Pisces).

This sense of universality endows those born beneath the sign of the cosmic fish with an inherent awareness of various planes of existence that lie beyond our perceived notions of the here and now.

So after all that intense "karmic apple versus cosmic orange" comparison stuff, this next oddball tidbit should throw you both off and right back on track. Did either of you know when looking at people's birth order (one's placement in its family amongst siblings), there is an unusually high propensity of married couples comprised of an oldest child paired with a youngest child?

The sociological theory behind this matrimonial phenomenon hypothesizes that one member of the couple can effectively learn from, as well as teach the other, areas of experience its partner would most likely not be as readily familiar with and vice versa.

In order for the love union of the ram with the fish to not just thrive, but materialize at all, it's imperative for this astrological duo to approach things from a cosmic birth order perspective. And guess what, Aries? This time around you're not first, as is ALWAYS the case.

If we take this unique astrological pairing and apply the theory of cosmic birth order, then Pisces is the eldest of your cosmic family and Aries is the youngest of your karmic clan.

In this romantic setup, the Aries must adjust to the mammoth task of putting all its natural impulses on the back burner. Nor should the ram child immediately act or react without stopping to think, or at least pause, while joining romantic forces with its water-signed love interest.

In other words, if the Aries Pisces relationship is to even have a pulse, all impulses of the Aries doing what it wants, whenever it wants, must be kept under wraps, especially in the beginning stages of getting to know its Piscean partner.

Why should the ram be so non-ram-like? We all know when an Aries is hungry/sleepy/cold due to the firsts of the zodiac tending to its basic needs, right then and there, regardless of who else is present.

With that sentiment in mind, let's do a little science experiment of the psychic kind. Aries, picture your spitfire self at your hungriest. A black hole of gnawing hunger has just formed at the base of your guts and you simply have GOT TO EAT NOW! Feeling it? Good.

So does your Piscean partner, even though it just came from a lavish three- course meal.

Your Love Author likes to personally call those born beneath the sign of the cosmic fish the psychic anemones of the zodiac due to the last of the water signs existing in a near constant state of feeling. Even with that said, the state of Piscean feeling goes way beyond our imaginary hunger experiment.

If emotionally connected to another, a fish person has an inherent ability to feel what another feels. Taking that sentiment to an even more intensely private place, if someone born beneath the last of the twelve signs feels emotions for another very deeply, then quite often it will experience its partner's joy, sorrow, disappointment, and even hunger if it's extreme enough.

Piscean sensitivity is powerful. So much so the fish person will tend to be cautious with the outside world, holding back on taking any kind of initiative or doing anything it considers too forward.

If the Aries does what the Aries is used to doing, whenever the mood strikes them, the Piscean will more than likely misinterpret that to mean the ram has no interest or doesn't care, often resulting in each of the Pisces' cosmic fish darting off in opposite directions for good.

Both signs need to behave atypically from their inherent proclivities and from there ALLOW things to unfold.

In this astrological coupling, the Aries can, for once, take a back seat and allow the Pisces to take the driver's seat.

Stay calm, fish folk! Taking any kind of initiative, let alone the driver's seat, is a terrifying prospect for the most sensitively psychic of the twelve since it doesn't come from an inherently natural place within its Piscean person. But if your Love Author may immediately interrupt all Pisces protestation by insisting that a little self-empowerment, just like cod liver oil, is seriously tough to swallow at first but is so good for you.

By displaying behavior that isn't typical for each of its respective signs, the Aries and the Pisces will in all likelihood reveal their inherent core strengths quite powerfully to each other. Should that occur, the romantic possibilities associated with joining the Alpha and the Omega of the zodiac will present themselves as vast as the furthest reaches of the universe itself.

Taurus-Taurus

It's no secret, bull boys and girls. Earth signs like their stuff.

The element of earth, which is the sign of Taurus' astrological foundation, derives security from that which is tangible: money, homes, cars, diamonds that are at least five carats (never lower) in variations of white, pink, brown, with the occasional yellow thrown in.

Ya know. Stuff.

With Taurus being the first representative of the element of earth, the sign of the bovine enjoys taking the concept of the tangible to the extreme!

But honestly, bulls. Does the Bentley REALLY need a juice bar installed? And I think you cow kids will survive if the vacation villa doesn't have its own coat of arms AND flag.

Now don't misunderstand me, Taureans. There's nothing wrong with owning nice things and having wads of cash. It's when the tangible becomes master over those who are based in the tangible that things become a smidge problematic.

But more on that in just a bovine bit.

I'll be honest with you two. There are a few exceptions (actually just one, and you two sure ain't it), but overall it's not highly recommended for a person born beneath one sign to date another of its own astrological kind.

Each sign encounters its own unique set of issues whenever romantically doubling up with itself, and more than the other residents of the zodiac, the sign of Taurus has some of the toughest pitfalls of problematic potential when dating its own.

Taurus is a fixed sign by astrological quality, and joining two fixed signs together is one of the most challenging combinations to maintain, due to the following fixed traits: a natural tendency to resist change; a mental proclivity to see things in a one-dimensional, black or white way; an inherent inclination to not want to compromise; or a consistent knack for being obstinate, which is a polite way of saying "pig- (or in this case bull)headed stubborn."

When two Taureans first meet and decide to date, things couldn't be more bovine beautiful! Given their sign's need for all that is pretty and peaceful, along with their natural disposition of being romantic to a fault, when the dating process commences, both bulls put every effort into looking their best and being on their best behavior.

A date who is just as mild-mannered and inherently romantic as myself? What could possibly go wrong? Plenty.

Picture this pair going mad cow for each other amidst the puffy clouds of that particular slice of romantic heaven, and then a disagreement or difference of opinion occurs.

Instantaneously, both bulls will dig their hooves into the ground, determined never to budge a millimeter for the duration of their bovine lives!

Upon seeing their fixed sign partner doing the aforementioned hoof digging, the other fixed sign will become even MORE unrelenting, stupefied at how obviously wrong its fixed sign love interest is about everything.

Ironically, with the sign of the bovine being inherently well versed in romance and courtship, the first official difference of opinion between two Tauruses can be quite unexpectedly shocking for all obstinate parties involved.

When this occurs, only one thing exists within the tangible world that has the power to offset this clash of the fixed signed titans: COMPROMISE.

Not just one, but both fixed signs need to regularly compromise with its fixed signed partner in order for this relationship to NOT have an ending of romantic armageddon. Taurus is one of the most stubborn signs in the known universe, and many seasons shall change and pass over this scene of bullish opposition before either earth sign realizes its bovine lover is just as stubborn as him or herself.

Along with the problematic potential of two bulls locking horns in stubborn opposition, should one Taurus have a bovine bone to pick with the other or feel the need to debate or argue its point, it tends to never moo a word, keeping every gripe or problematic issue held in. Why? Blame the Goddess of Gorgeous.

Taurus is ruled by the heavenly body named after the ancient goddess of love and beauty. The downside to having Venus as one's astrological ruler is that she can be a total priss.

Besides love, the planet of pretty also rules over such niceties as peace and harmony People who are Venus-ruled abhor any kind of overt displays of aggression. Even a lively debate can make a Venusian personality run and take cover. Confrontations of any kind are so distasteful to the Venus ruled that some will often do anything just to keep the peace and not rock the boat.

Many times the partner of the Taurean may not even be aware its bovine lover has an issue due to the Taurus keeping every cow-tentious issue to itself the entire time.

Imagine if both holders of the cow-tention are both cows themselves.

Taureans, there comes a time, in any given relationship occurring on this planet, where differences and held in hurts must be voiced. Communication is vital for a relationship to not only be healthy but survive no matter how uncomfortable the issues needing to be discussed should seem.

Lastly, as this chapter exaggeratedly joked about in its opening, the sign of the bull derives the most security from owning tangible things. Not only that, but with its planetary ruler also overseeing such money driven concepts as luxury and commerce, those born beneath the sign of the bovine tend to have exceptional tastes that often are just as exceptionally expensive.

Take the sense of security Taureans derive from the tangible, mix it with their Venusian taste for the expensive, and place the combination of the two entirely within the negative spectrum. What do you get? The Taurus' natural need for things morphing into the unevolved bull being enslaved by greed and materialism.

Every Taurean should be aware of the negative effect the tangible can have over him or her as individuals, but when the bull romantically doubles up with itself, the allure for bigger, better, and nicer things can become an overpowering force greater than both bovines if left unmonitored.

Relationships comprised of two born under the same sign aren't the easiest. Some are for obvious reasons. Others, as in the case of two bulls, are for what lies beneath the relationship radar.

If both bulls fight their natural tendencies of forcing every aspect of their relationship to be all sugar and spice and everything non-confrontational, as well as battle against the forces of greed and materialism together as a Taurean team, then life truly shall become bovine beautiful for this double-signed pairing.

Taurus–Gemini

You both must have heard that ancient adage that applies as much today as it did in times of old, right, Taurus and Gemini? It goes something along the lines of people can choose their friends, but not their neighbors.

This neighborly concept applies astrologically as well, yet at the same time is completely irrelevant when it comes to playing the zodiac dating game. Take you two for example.

Nothing can change the astrological fact the signs of Taurus and Gemini are next door neighbors with each other on that big wheel of life, otherwise known as the zodiac. Yet that inalterable information is neither karmic apples nor cosmic oranges during those not so common times when the bull and the twins decide to join romantic forces.

Moving from old astrological adages to contemporary rules of cosmic thumb, it's generally understood the signs that border each other are categorized beneath a most unexciting descriptor of astrological compatibility: neutral.

(A solitary cough can be heard in the far off, remote distance.)

Every sign has the potential to work together. Some combinations take a lot more work than others to achieve a state of equilibrium. With the joining of the signs considered to be neutral of each other, the state of equilibrium is something like the solid borderline that naturally forms whenever oil and vinegar are put into the same container. In other words, mixing the two isn't a bad thing, but a whole lot of shaking is needed for there to be any kind of blend.

At their core, the Taurus and Gemini function from very different perspectives, making their inherent energies seem as if these two signs lived on the opposite ends of the globe versus being astrological next-door neighbors.

Do either of you remember the children's fable, *The Tortoise and The Hare*? A tale for tots, I know, but applicable none the less as a suitable representation displaying the inherent differences of dynamic between the bull and the twins.

Taurus, can you guess which fabled animal you are? (Hint, it even sounds a lot like you, and I don't mean mooing.)

Yes, Gemini! I'm well aware you had the answer well before I even asked the question, but we're asking if the Taurus knows!

While the bull is taking its sweet and oh so slow time deliberating the correct response, could the over-excited air sign PLEASE move its franticly waving hand away from my face and proceed to exhale before passing out? Thanks so very much, Gemini!

The verbal wrist-slapping alone should give things away that the Taurus is the tortoise and Gemini the hare. Slow and steady wins the race versus fast and furiously going off in all directions while barely breathing.

Here's an idea! Let's take the dynamic differences between the Taurus and the Gemini and make things really fun by suggesting random activities and applying them to both signs!

Your Love Author will let the astrological games begin by suggesting the first activity: EATING.

In the time it takes for the Taurus to slowly chew and savor its first forkful of a meal, the Gemini has already vacuumed its entire plate down and is wondering why the server is taking so long to bring the check.

Wasn't that fun? (The same solitary cough can once again be clearly heard in the far off distance.)

Taurus, while you're still adjusting to the very nature of how this game works, and Gemini while you're still in the process of deciding upon the myriad of subjects you've already chosen to play the game with, your Love Author would like to continue the festivities by suggesting yet another activity: TALKING.

The Gemini should be well versed with this particular activity, given it does so much of it and at a lightning-fast rate. Being the first representative of air, the element that is communication based, the Gemini doesn't just like to talk. It NEEDS to. This airy foundation of communication provides those born beneath the sign of the twins the inherent ability to talk to anyone, even with its solitary self.

On the flip side of the cow coin, if the Taurus had things its way, talking would be reserved for emergencies only. The bull's manner of speech is short, deliberately slow, and to the bulls eye point. And the less chattering there is for the Taurus, all the more bullish better.

If the Taurus has something to say, it will talk in a most straightforwardly direct manner using the plainest of language with basic, simple words.

Stepping away from specific activities or functions, but still keeping the fable of *The Tortoise and The Hare* in mind, these two astrological next-door neighbors operate from an overall dynamic that is worlds apart from each other.

Where the Taurus gets security from a familiarized sense of repetitive routine, the Gemini thrives from the mental stimulation brought about by variety and change.

It's usually the case that when one of you is leaving, the other is just about to come in. Like the fabled hare, the Gemini zooms about at typical Mercurial speed, and usually zips right past the tortoise-like Taurus, never allowing any romantic sparks to form or relationship seeds to take root.

Both signs need to go against their natural grain in order for the union of the bull with the twins to last beyond the very temporary or extremely short-lived.

Why these two signs don't even mingle, let alone join forces, is due to each not bothering with the other after a blanket evaluation is made.

The Taurus will tend to initially (and lest we not forget, stubbornly) sum up the Gemini to be a vapid airbag whose shallowness is clearly apparent by how often and much the chatterbox babbles about a whole lotta nuthin'.

On the other hoof, the Gemini will often pre-determine in a matter of nanoseconds the Taurus to be a creature of habit SO set in its stodgy ways, it has to shake off layers of sedentary sediment whenever lumbering from one room to the next. In turn, the end result is many a twin summing up the bull to be a beast of the worst kind of burden imaginable: boring.

If these two zodiacal next-door neighbors are willing to erase the initial blanket evaluations about each other, as well as consciously adjust their natural pace as to be more in sync with its partner's overall lifestyle, then this seemingly incompatible pairing stands to be transformed into an astrologically updated fable for the modern day.

A fairy tale, which despite its oil and vinegary start, has a revised ending where the tortoise crosses the romantic race's finish line hand in hand with the hare. A tale of potential romance that when formed by the consistent efforts of coupled compromise, actually entitles the bull and the twins to live, and more importantly, love happily ever after.

Taurus-Cancer

Behold, Taurus and Cancer! Your Love Author places before your coupled selves one of the best examples representing the union of your elemental foundations of earth and water: the bath salt.

Much like adding a generous heaping of fragrant bath salts to a warm, inviting bath, teaming up the first of the earth signs (Taurus) with the first of the water signs (Cancer) creates a romantic union known for its swimmingly natural compatibility. It's an affinity of coupled cohesion that quite often bears the potential, much like the chunkiest of sodium citrates (aka organic salt), of becoming a romantically rock-solid bond that stands the test of time.

In astrology, the four elements of earth, air, fire, and water are naturally paired off. Each grouping consists of two elements that naturally work well together, otherwise known as being complementary to each other. The elements of fire and air are grouped together, but more importantly for this particular pairing, the elements of earth and water are complementary to each other.

Along with being complementary, Taurus and Cancer share another common tie by virtue of both signs being the first representatives of each of their respective elements. The first representatives express the inherent energies of their element in the purest and most uncomplicated of ways. So much so the elemental firsts are sometimes known as their respective element's true sign.

The bull expresses its connection to the tangible in its most pure and concentrated form, and the crab does the same with expressing emotion.

The earth signs derive the most security from what can be seen, touched, tasted, and felt. Said in more tangible Taurean terms, those born beneath the sign of the bull derive the most security from their possessions, how much money is in the bank, and the work output it produces.

Being the first representative of earth, the senses of the Taurean are at their purest and most uncomplicated. The bull will take its bovine sweet time fully employing its senses while partaking in such sensual activities as stopping to smell the roses (its flower), slowly savoring every bite of a scrumptious meal, or feeling the stratospherically high thread count of its sheets while resting or relaxing in bed.

A water sign's first reaction to the outside world is through emotions. The water- based person will gauge everything initially by how it literally "feels" at first.

Being the first of the watery ones, the Cancerian feels every emotion from its core, but much like the tides that are pulled by its ruling planet, the moon, the crab person innately knows that human feelings are not controllable. Similar to how its core element of water can't be contained, those born beneath the sign of the crab inherently know the palette of human emotions functions within a constant state of flow and change.

Picture a crab as it sidles along the beach near the lapping waves of the ocean. The sea creature never runs freely forward. A crab's motion is always tentative. What gives this caution-filled animal the allowance for movement of any kind is the security and shelter the crab's hardened shell provides.

Now picture a person born beneath the sign of the crab. The crab person functions best when it has the security of a home base. This is NOT a sign that can live out of a suitcase or on a friend's couch for an indefinite period of time.

The Cancer is motivated through its watery essence to seek security with its emotions. Thus, those born beneath the sign of the crab derive the most security from the two core foundational aspects of life that human beings have held closest to them since the dawn of civilization: home and family.

Despite Taurus and Cancer being two of the most security driven signs of the zodiac, it doesn't take much to make either the bull or the crab happy or fulfilled. Neither is impressed by anything too grandiose or layered with complexity, and both signs are deeply moved by gestures and actions that come from a genuinely heartfelt place.

When the Taurus and the Cancer first begin seeing each other, they'll often fall off their friends' and family's radar due to much of their initial dating time being spent at each other's places of residence.

Both signs are known to have living spaces that are warm and inviting, decorated with simple richness, and where comfort both for themselves and their guests is emphasized the most.

Besides having a roof over one's head, what's that one other basic thing in life that gives every person on this planet a sense of core security, and just as much, if not more, insecurity when he or she doesn't have it? Food.

Along with enjoying the time spent at each other's homes, another main reason why no one sees the Taurus or the Cancer when they commence the dating process is due to both signs trying to outdo and impress each other with their cooking skills. Truly, Taurus and Cancer are the gourmands of the zodiac. Both signs are inherently GREAT cooks and can whip up the most satisfying, nourishing, and lest we not forget delicious home-cooked meals.

Even if they don't necessarily enjoy nor have the time to play master chef in their home kitchens, the bull and the crab will still be hard to find when first joining romantic forces because they'll always be out to lunch! Or dinner, or brunch, or late breakfast, or high tea. You get the gustatory picture.

Every astrological combination within a given relationship has its potential downsides. Since this particular combo is so home based, many times even a cattle prod connected to an electric fishing net won't get the Taurus and the Cancer to leave their snug and comfy love shacks.

The other cautionary note for the two master chefs of the zodiac cooking for each other deals with an issue nearly every person born beneath the bull and the crab grapples with individually: weight gain.

The bull tends to be physically thicker than most, and being Venus ruled, tends to have quite the hankering for the sweeter side of things, especially CHOCOLATE.

Fluctuations of weight for the crab, interestingly enough, are almost always directly related to its emotional state. The Cancer's emotions are so strong and pure that many times the crab's inner feelings will trigger weight gain. So much so the physical body of many a crustacean will often retain both water and fat as a protective way of "padding" the physical self from the self that is wholly emotional.

Weight gain is a factor to be expected when the complementary couple of the bull and the crab initially get to know each other more intimately. However, both signs will need to regularly monitor exactly how much thicker their shells and hides become over time with all the constant good eats throughout the course of their romantic relationship.

Should things become significantly "heavier," you lovebirds merely need to incorporate a few calorie burning activities both in and out of the house. This should be followed up with both signs partaking in a particular activity that, as mentioned at this chapter's beginning, best represents the complementary nature of your earth and water love union.

After any kind of strenuous activity or exercise, it's highly recommended the bull and the crab draw a soothing bath made even more inviting by the addition of the most fragrant of bath salts. Together, of course.

Taurus-Leo

Your Love Author is a total sucker for early Japanese sci-fi flicks, Taurus and Leo.

My personal favorite is the 1964 classic from the Showa period, *Godzilla Versus Ghidorah*, where Godzilla, the king of the dinosaurs is pitted against the three-headed 1,000 year old king of the dragons, Ghidorah.

These cult status pseudo horror films were able to effectively relay a constant and ever growing sense of tension that emerged whenever two monsters of titan-like strength and willpower, such as Godzilla and Ghidorah, crossed paths.

It's very much like when the Taurus and the Leo date each other.

Don't get me wrong you two. The horror show action doesn't commence after the curtain goes up, immediately when the bull and the lion first meet. Just as in any proper sci-fi horror flick, the atmosphere needs to be picture postcard perfect to juxtapose the truly horrific nature of what lies above or below, which soon shall volcanically descend upon the film's idyllic surroundings and peaceful townsfolk.

Both powerhouse signs are very aware of their public presence. Being ruled by Venus, the planet of beauty, looking good in front of others is a strong and valid need for the Taurus. Similarly, having the sun as its ruler, the Leo would rather be a carpet skin than look unpresentable or unable to shine in the public's eye.

Along with looking their very best, when the Taurus and the Leo first meet and date, both are on their best behavior. In fact, things really ARE romantically pristine and picture postcard-esque when the bull and the lion initially begin dating since both signs are inherently programmed to be romantic through the culturally dying art of courting.

Courting (noun): A way of getting to know a person through gradual stages of increased intimacy by incorporating romance with social activities.

Romance isn't just important for both the bull and the lion. It's vital.

Taurus' planetary ruler is named after Venus, the goddess of romance; and Leo's natural house of rulership, the fifth, is also known as the house of romance. Both signs respond and interact best through the romantic process of courting, as defined above.

The best way to a Taurus' heart is through its senses. Courting a bovine love interest will be a matter of the Leo tantalizing the fine-tuned senses of the bull with sensual pleasantries such as roses (Taurus' flower), champagne, Swiss chocolate (no American), deliciously inviting room sprays, etc.

The best way to a Leo's heart? Straight in and all the way through—literally! Once the process of courtship has begun, the Taurus should understand that romance for the Leo is most especially felt when the lion is made to feel as special and wonderfully unique as possible. The tools of romance won't matter nearly as much to the Leo as long as the bull delivers them with an approach that is romantically dramatic and genuinely heartfelt.

Returning once more to our romance film of ultimate horror...

The film's lead lovers walk hand in hand down the promenade, past the school as the closing bell rings, while the teacher stands in the entrance way waving in slow motion, mouthing "Goodbye, children!" to her happily exiting students. The camera pans up and away, allowing the viewing audience to see far off in the distance, the churning volcano, darkening sky, or bubbling ocean's surface.

Terror is about to descend upon Romanceville!

In other words (dramatic orchestral chords while a woman hysterically screams), the Taurus and the Leo are about to have their first difference of opinion!

Did I forget to mention to either of you that your love interest is a fixed sign? Oh my. Did it also slip my mind to inform both of you two fixed signs that dating each other is one of the most challenging relationship combos out there? Oopsie.

Both Taurus and Leo are fixed signs. The fixed signs are in the middle of each of the four seasons, and the word used to categorize this sign quality also fits neatly into describing their temperament as well: FIXED.

Overall, the fixed signs do not have the easiest time (more like next to never) seeing other people's perspectives that aren't their own. Other "colorfully challenging" personality traits the fixed signs inherently share are a natural tendency to resist change; a mental proclivity to see things in a one dimensional, black or white way; an inherent inclination to not want to compromise; or a consistent knack for being obstinate, which is a polite way of saying, "pig (or in this case bull)-headed stubborn."

Picture the Taurus and the Leo jumping through romantic hoops and completely mad cow for each other, experiencing that particular slice of romantic heaven known as the honeymoon period, and then a disagreement or difference of opinion occurs between them.

Instantly, both fixed signs will dig their heels into the ground, determined never to budge a millimeter for the duration of their bovine and leonine lives!

Upon seeing their fixed sign partner doing the aforementioned heel digging, the other fixed sign will become even MORE inflexibly unrelenting, stupefied at how obviously wrong their Fixed sign partner is about everything.

Godzilla has officially crossed paths with Ghidora, ladies and gentlemen!

Ironically, the bull and the lion's inherent awareness of romance and the proper processes of courting makes their first official difference of opinion (aka clash of the fixed signed titans) even more shockingly unexpected.

Like the townspeople from the celluloid Japanese seaside town of placid perfection, everyone is taken completely off guard. No one sees it coming when Godzilla emerges from the ocean's depths, while simultaneously, the three-headed dragon Ghidora swoops down from the sky to have a screaming showdown of monster-sized proportions with the gargantuan lizard.

But just like the dapper and well-suited male lead whose mouth moves well before the audience hears his dubbed-in-English voice, your

Love Author would like to inform you feuding fixed ones, "There may just be a way."

Hold on to your boyfriends and plug your ears because this one's gonna be a real screamer. COMPROMISE. It's the only way to save Romanceville, Taurus-uku and Leo-san!

Not just one, but both fixed signs need to regularly compromise with its fixed sign partner in order for this relationship to NOT have a horror flick ending of romantic armageddon. Taurus and Leo are two of the most stubborn signs in the known universe, and many seasons shall pass over this monster scene of ultimate obstinance before either side realizes its partner is just as stubborn as itself.

Does anybody recall Godzilla ever relaxing or even exhaling a flaming sigh of relief? If Ghidorah was strong-armed out of the picture, Rhodan or Mothra soon took its screaming place and the monster wars raged on and on.

The film's lead lovers may have been separated while Ghidorah was deflecting that flying school bus hand-flung by Godzilla, but they always figure out a way to find each other in a tearful hug towards the film's end. Just as the camera pans up and away, displaying the smoking carnage as peace once more returns to the town of Romanceville. Or does it?

So what'll it be, Taurus and Leo? A showdown of stubbornness with a horror flick ending worse than any Godzilla, Jason, or Chuckie movie combined, OR a partnership of mutual respect and compromise that can't have anything else BUT a romantically happy ending?

The choice is of your own making.

Taurus-Virgo

Taurus and Virgo! Come on down! You're the grand prize winners on *Bind or Grind*, the show where couples dive head first into the whirlpool of love and either sink or swim together!

Welcome to the VIP Room of *Bind or Grind* romance winners, bulls and virginal ones. Only the most compatible couples make it past this particular velvet rope, and you two get the big ol' green light.

In astrology, the best romantic partnerships are comprised of two people born beneath the same element. With Taurus and Virgo both being earth signs, we not only have a match, we have a romantic winner because this is one of the best astrological pairings out there!

Now, on to showing our earthy couple what they've won by way of what they haven't lost!

Janice, if you may be so kind as to show our love winners what's behind curtain number one.

(Janice enters from stage left, smiling far too hard with the most vacant of outward stares as she flicks huge placards with the following non-earth–signed qualities plastered in bold lettering): extreme mood changes, jobless (by choice), penniless, hallucinogenic drugs, slovenly or sloppy (whichever is more horrifying), bad hygiene, or blatantly needing dental work.)

Since both signs are members of an element known for the security it derives from the material plane and all things tangible, neither the Taurean nor the Virgoan will have the following traits inherently associated with its individual sign or persons!

On to Curtain number two!

A romantic date neither earth sign will be going on with each other, since it'll most likely hearken back to a sense of nightmarish déjà-EW-WW with your last few romantic train wrecks!

(Audience applause track interspersed with occasional hyena laugh.)

For our custom-made "Date from Earth-signed Hell," the lovely Holly has just been invited by her new beau to a fun-filled, last-minute weekend getaway vacation to Viva Las Vegas!

What Holly didn't plan on was being ignored the entire weekend, due to her big spending paramour, Gary Gambler, who doesn't know when to call it quits in the casino as he loses his shirt... and Holly's!

For someone who wouldn't budge from that blackjack table all night, empty pockets Gary sure does burn rubber out of town mighty quick! Because after losing everything and the kitchen sink if he could bet on it, Gary gives the sweetest adieu by doing a fast disappearing act and footing the bill to no one else but Holly!

Good thing you earthy ones are reliably responsible with decent paying jobs to cover all the gambling addicted mess that was irresponsibly left behind.

Am I right, audience? Of course I am!

(Audience applause track interspersed with occasional hyena laugh.)

At this point, you two must be thinking, "If this is what winning is like, I'd escape at all costs if I lost." And we actually will reveal exactly why the Taurus and the Virgo had to go down romantic memory lane via the highway to hell in just a game show minute!

But first I'd like to remind every non-Virgoan pet owner to have its dog or cat spayed or neutered. We know that task was checked off every Virgo's "to do" list a long time back given the middle representative of the earth signs oversees the maintenance and upkeep of the domesticated animal realm, most especially dogs and cats.

Back to our earth-signed game show of romance!

Taurus and Virgo, you already know the elemental foundation for both your signs is earthy to the core. And it's already been mentioned how the earth signs concentrate most of its hard-working energies on the material plane and that which is tangible (what one can see, touch, taste, and feel).

Taurus, being earth's first representative, you react to the tangible world in the most pure and concentrated of ways: through your senses. Food that tastes utterly delicious, flowers that smell heavenly, bed linen with thread counts so high they feel out of this world, etc. You get the sensual picture.

Virgo, you focus on the tangible through your various work piles of efficiency and organization; your "to do" lists; and your immaculately clean clothes, body, and home. The home of the typical Virgo is so spotless a person could actually eat off the floor, which, in all actuality, you'd rather internally implode than commit such unhygienic insanity.

For you non-earthy types, a particular word exists that's directly interchangeable with the phrase "that which is tangible." It's called "reality."

The earth signs are most adept at dealing with what we call reality by being naturally practical and pragmatic. However, there's another P-word, which if left unmonitored, holds the potential to be the downfall of every earth-signed couple and individual. Intriguingly, both the Taurus and the Virgo are especially prone to this particular P-word if they are not careful.

When observed individually, the Taurus is susceptible to only partial maiming by this dreaded word since many born beneath the sign of the bovine will abuse it mostly from an idealistic perspective and for strictly romantic purposes.

For the Virgo, however, addiction to the P-word has the potential to be all encompassing.

Should that dreaded word be applied or introduced to the Taurus Virgo relationship in any way, defeat is soon to follow, no matter how well suited these two signs are for each other.

Despite all the tangible reality talk, this P-word is seriously out there, in an almost hallucinogenic, la-la land kind of way. Ready? Brace yourselves! Perfection.

The Taurus is guilty in applying the P-word to the concept of love. The Virgo is guilty in applying it to the concept of life at large.

This brings us to curtain number three, ladies and gentlemen, where behind lies the grand prize for our romance winners!

(Stage darkens. Drumroll starts. Curtain number three dramatically lifts, to reveal ...)

A mirror.

Stand in front of the mirror, Taurus and Virgo. The third and most grand of romantic prizes is yourselves!

(Audience wildly cheers while applauding in triple speed.)

We reenacted a few romantic trainwrecks from the past in order to emphasize how much potential there is when the bull and the virgin partner up! The romantic possibilities the two of you have together will be mountains better than what we saw behind curtains one or two.

(As would a root canal or colonoscopy for that matter).

Even with that said, you earthy ones need to keep in mind no relationship is perfect, including yours. But your astrological compatibility will make it feel like it is most of the time.

The key to making this astrological blend of earthy lovin' an actual grand prize and not some cheaply made Ginsu knife parting gift is for neither the Taurus or the Virgo to ever let the P-word cross their minds or lips, especially while together.

Now let's give our studio audience a big *Bind and Grind* kiss so the bull and the virgin can roll up their sleeves and begin working on their very own non-perfect partnership together!

MWAH!

Taurus-Libra

Mirror, mirror on the wall, which sign's taste and style is the greatest of them all?

Mirror? Hello? Mirror, we're waiting. MIRROR!!!

(CRACK)

Wow, Taurus and Libra! You two broke my magic mirror! It literally couldn't decide what sign is superior in aesthetic appreciation, which is a fancy way of saying taste.

Just to inform you two wickedly attractive signs, the bull and the scales are both ruled by Venus, the goddess of love, harmony, and all things pretty.

When the goddess of gorgeous is your planetary queen, it's no contest. Throughout the zodiac kingdom, Taurus and Libra lay claim to being the signs that possess the best taste, aesthetics, and sense of style over all others.

Even with all the high praises of prettiness and despite both signs sharing the same planetary ruler of high style and fashion sense, it must be said Taurus and Libra are two very different astrological creatures.

Taurus' astrological quality is fixed. The bull has quite the hard time finding the energy to initially start things, but once begun, has the tenacity and focus to make sure everything is carried out to full completion. Libra's astrological quality is cardinal. The scales are quite good at starting things, but following what has been started all the way through to completion is one of its biggest challenges.

When it comes to being decisive, the mental process of the Taurus can be so resolute and finalized that the decisions made by many a bull tend to be inflexibly set in stone and defined by the most black and white of terms.

The best way to describe the decision-making process of the Libra can be very much likened to the changing of the seasons or listening to one's hair grow. Its indecisive weighing back and forth and hemming and hawing can be that time consuming.

Being the first representative of the element of earth, the sign of the bovine is fundamentally basic, right down to its speech. Short and sweet is the best form of Taurean talk, with not a single moo ever being too flowery or overly complex.

Being the middle representative of air, the element that utilizes communication the most, the Libra is a master at the art of conversation and delights in language that has intellectual flair and sprinkled with flowery ornamentation. The more basic the talk, the quicker the Libra succumbs to the affliction most commonly found amongst air signs: boredom.

Now on to some compare/contrasts of both the prettier (and deadlier) kind.

Along with being fashionably fabulous, both the bull and the scales are motivated most by a force that also happens to be quite the addictive influence Venus holds over her children: romance.

When playing the game of love with the Venus-ruled, romance must be actively involved nearly every step of the way, beginning with the process of courtship.

Courting (noun): A way of getting to know a person through gradual stages of increased intimacy by incorporating romance with social activities.

I'm sure all Venus-ruled parties are already well aware how painfully unromantic the world is these days.

Mention the word "courting" in the present time and most people will think you're referring to the latest basketball stats or your plans to actively sue someone. This has led many a Venusian person to become almost convinced that chivalry is dead and romance went out of style long ago.

Because the bull and the scales inherently know the rules of proper courtship, the initial phase of getting to know each other, otherwise known as the honeymoon period, can be so intoxicating for both Venus-ruled parties one would think either sign was residing in a fairy tale world due to their romantic sensibilities being fully utilized and stimulated.

What could possibly go wrong with a proper suitor who is just as pretty as my beautiful self and meets the romantic requirements of the Venusian courting process? Plenty.

The planetary queen of love and beauty can transform into the evil queen of fairy tale legend by tempting either sign with a poisoned apple custom made for the Venus ruled: romantic idealism.

After being denied anything remotely romantic for so long, when a Taurus and a Libra first begin dating, either Venus-ruled sign could easily go into ROMANCE OVERLOAD, which could lead to ROMANCE OVERDOSE, which if not treated by heaping spoonfuls of hard-cold reality could be followed more alarmingly by HALLUCINOGENIC ROMANTIC IDEALISM!

In other words, Taurus and Libra can become completely addicted to a false world of romantic idealism and never want to return to icky reality.

Since the sign of the scales is based in the mentally driven element of air, Librans are especially prone to becoming addicted to the romantic fantasy that unfolds within their minds. The addicted Libran longs to overdose on the poisoned apple of romantic idealism, never to return to the crass and coarse world of unromantic reality.

The partner of the OD'ing victim will be put on a pedestal and romantically worshipped as if a deity. The more this happens, the less the romantic OD'ing victim will want to deal with its partner in reality, desperately loving a fabricated idea and not the actual flesh and bones person.

You Venusians may be wondering about the remedy for this romantic fairy tale gone way too far. Incredibly the answer is as hyper realistic as possible and far more fantastical sounding than any given fairy tale. Did either of you love fools know that in the original versions of both *Sleeping Beauty* and *Snow White*, when the Prince comes upon his passed out damsel in unconscious distress, the plan of attack he uses to bring her back to reality wasn't a kiss?

Actually, it was, but it wasn't just one wet one. It was a sexy slew of them. And it wasn't just kissing that snapped Snow White back into reality, it was a good, ol' fashioned bed-spring creaking.

Hey, someone had to break the spell by not being able to fully spell things out.

Don't be so shocked! Come on, how do you think Snow White got those rosy cheeks? Dust mopping? Yeah, right!

Now that we've discussed the most problematic of pitfalls the Taurus and Libra could face when dating each other with romantic idealism covered, a challenge that places a very close second is Venusian non-confrontation.

Should the Taurus or the Libra have a bone to pick with the other or feel the need to debate or argue a point of contention, he or she tends to never say a word, keeping every gripe or problematic issue held in. Why? Once again, blame the goddess of gorgeous.

Besides love and the rest of all the pretty crap, Venus also rules over such niceties as peace and harmony. People who are Venus-ruled greatly dislike confrontations of any kind. Even lively debate is considered SO distasteful to the Venusian personality that some will often do whatever it takes just to keep the peace or not rock the boat.

Taureans and Librans, there comes a time in any given relationship on this planet where differences and held in hurts must be voiced. Communication is vital for a relationship to not only be healthy but survive no matter how uncomfortable the subject matter.

If both Venus-ruled parties fight its natural tendency to make the relationship all sugar and spice and everything non-confrontational, as well as learn to openly communicate with each other anytime a problem or gripe should arise, then life truly will take the form of a fairy tale romance, but within reason! We'll be keeping a close eye on you Libran romance junkies all the same.

Taurus-Scorpio

(Entering room.) Oh! Hey, Taurus. Scorpio.

(Casually strolling past, then stopping to give each of you a prolonged glancing over.)

If I didn't know any better, my view upon entering the room of the two of you sitting all relaxed and casually hanging out usually wouldn't give me cause to wonder if anything out of the ordinary was going on.

But I do know better. Much, much better.

I just happen to know the astrological fact the signs of the bull and the scorpion are polar opposites of each other, and not to be trite in a nasal Paula Abdul way, but opposites attract.

When two astrological opposites are within close physical proximity of each other, the attraction factor turns into an all-out starved shark feeding frenzy of kissing touchy feely!

Hey, lighten up you two! There's nothing wrong with the romantic fact your Love Author is astrologically savvy enough to deduce that just a few moments ago, you were groping each other like wild primates. Some would say you oppositely attracted lovebirds were merely obeying an inalterable law of both astrology and science.

Remember those magnet experiments used back in junior high to demonstrate the law of attraction? Take those same oppositely charged pieces of metal that slammed into each other whenever one was within remote proximity of the other, except now one of the magnets is called "Taurus" and the other "Scorpio."

(Uncomfortable silence.)

Okay then! How about we skip all the scientific talk and provide both romantic parties an overview of each other's individual astrological backgrounds to see just how different, as well as similar, the bull and the scorpion are together.

Taurus, you're the sign of sensuality. Scorpio, you're the sign of sexuality.

Taurus, your sign rules the house of money. Scorpio, your sign rules over the house of other people's money.

Taurus, the time of year when your sign takes place is associated with growth and material abundance due to the earth being in full bloom at the height of springtime.

Autumn's harvest has already come and gone when your time of year arrives, Scorpio. Hence, your sign is associated with the survival instinct where one makes the most of the barest of necessities.

Taurus, your planetary ruler of Venus is named after the goddess of gorgeous, and you'll do your utmost to maintain an environment that all is sugar and spice and everything non-intense on the surface. Scorpio, with your planetary ruler of Pluto named after the god of the underworld, pretty much everything you do is intense and never surface level.

Along with being polar opposites, the bull and the scorpion share the same fixed astrological quality.

Far more than any of the other astrological qualities, the fixed signs experience the most challenge whenever joining romantic forces.

As a whole, the fixed signs don't have the easiest time seeing other people's perspectives that aren't its own. Other fixed characteristics that are anything but easy are a natural tendency to resist change; a mental proclivity to see things in a one dimensional, black or white way; an inherent inclination to not want to compromise; or a consistent knack for being obstinate, which is a polite way of saying "pig-headed stubborn."

Picture this pair going mad cow for each other during that particular slice of romantic heaven otherwise known as the honeymoon period when the bull and the scorpion initially begin dating each other. And then a disagreement or difference of opinion occurs.

Instantly both fixed signs will dig their heels into the ground, determined never to budge a millimeter for the duration of their bovine and scorpionic lives.

Upon seeing its fixed sign partner doing the aforementioned heel digging, the other fixed sign will become even MORE inflexibly unrelenting, stupefied at how obviously wrong its fixed sign love interest is about everything.

When this occurs, only one solution exists within the tangible world that can offset this clash of the fixed signed titans: COMPROMISE.

Not just one, but both fixed signs need to regularly compromise with its fixed sign partner in order for this relationship to NOT have a horror flick ending of romantic armageddon. Both Taurus AND Scorpio are two of the most stubborn signs in the known universe, and many seasons shall pass over this non-budging scene of opposing opinion before either fixed sign realizes its pig-headed partner is just as stubborn as itself.

If no form of compromise is put into effect, the inherent obstinance of both the bull's and scorpio's personality will propel this most stubborn of stalemates through the unfolding future with neither fixed sign showing the slightest inclination of ever caving in.

As stated earlier, the polar opposites have diametric differences that are noticeably obvious, but many forget these special pairings share just as many similarities as well. Usually the similarities between polar opposites aren't nearly as obvious as their differences, but there is an exception with the coupling of the bull and scorpion.

Taurus and Scorpio, you're the polar opposite team that wins the prize for consistently liking each other once the immediate factor of opposite attraction wears off.

Neither of you over-reacts. Both of you embrace a "slow and steady wins the race" approach to things. The bull and the scorpion take their sweet time committing to anything or anyone, but once done, both signs are loyal to a fault.

And each of you are damn good in the sac ... carhine amounts regularly used as sweetener. You know, as an alternative to pure sugar. (clearing throat)

Attraction is what almost always brings the polar opposites together, which in turn yields some initial and immediate physical "sweetness."

Even with that blushingly said, if there is nothing more than a few fast and furious bed creaks, or nothing of binding common interest beyond the initial attraction, the polarized spark between polar opposites will be snuffed out just as quickly as it blowtorched began. Why?

Many times the flames of opposing desire are quickly doused due to both signs driving each other naturally crazy after the passing of five post-bed creaking minutes, give or take.

Ah, but conversely, if the polar opposites can stand each other's presence for more than five minutes post you know, and have a thing or two they actually like about the other, or share a few things in common, then here is where we find those fairy tale relationships that tend to stay together.

In fact, when there are binding factors beyond initial animal attraction, many of these dualistic duos literally last until death do they polar opposite part.

Taurus-Sagittarius

Seriously, Taurus and Sagittarius. I need to throw this one out there, first and foremost. Are you two SURE you're dating each other?

Sorry for all the obnoxious obviousness just then, but the two of you romantically joining forces is definitely NOT a common occurrence one hears about every day, nor is your particular partnership considered to be in any way obvious.

When looking at the prototypical wheel of the zodiac, the sign of Taurus lies at a 150 degree angle away from the sign of Sagittarius. The proper astrological term for this very particular angle is the quincunx.

Everyone repeat along with me. Ready? "Ku-win-kwunx." Very good!

The quincunx is also known by the much more easily pronounced astrological reference word "inconjunct." When two signs are placed at an inconjunct angle of each other, nothing remotely matches, and every inherent aspect of one sign is square pegged against the natural energies of the other. Some keywords associated with the inconjunct are: redirection, challenge, diversion, and requires adjustment.

I won't kid either of you, Taurus and Sagittarius. Most of the outside world has a hard time picturing the two of you together due to your union's high factor of unobviousness. When viewed individually, one would think the bull and the centaur were hardcore polar opposites. Each sign's inherent energies seem THAT different from those of the other.

Taurus is one of the slowest moving and heaviest of signs. Sagittarius is one of the fastest moving and lightest of signs.

A zodiacal sign's speed is directly influenced by its astrological element and, more importantly, its quality. Only by analyzing the bull's fixed quality alongside the centaur's quality of mutable does it become more than abundantly clear how vastly different these two signs are from each other.

Just as it sounds, the word used to categorize Taurus' astrological quality also fits neatly into describing its overall temperament as well: FIXED.

As a whole, the fixed signs do not have the easiest time seeing other people's perspectives that aren't their own. Other fixed characteristics that are anything but easy are as follows: a natural tendency to resist change; a mental proclivity to see things in a one-dimensional, black or white way; an inherent inclination to not want to compromise; or a consistent knack for being obstinate, a polite way of saying "pig-headed stubborn."

With fixed signed energy, nothing is ever rushed, spontaneously unplanned, or approached with a fast and furious pace. Slow and steady wins the race with these heavy-hitting signs.

Busting out of slow and steadytown and speedracing into fast and furiousville, the mutable signs occur as each of the four seasons draw to a close. The sign of Sagittarius takes place at the tail end of autumn, just before the winter solstice. The mutables function best in environments containing variety and change and are the multitaskers of the zodiac.

A mutable signed person CAN, in theory, attempt doing one thing at a time, but it's practically a guarantee he or she will screw things up if it actively chooses that intensely focused dynamic. This is due to the traits shared amongst all the mutables of possessing not even the slightest shred of patience, as well as being susceptible to mind numbing boredom after sitting down for no longer than five minutes.

The mutables are known for doing as many simultaneous actions as physically possible, but they're equally known for dropping said actions at choice times due to their susceptibility of being easily distracted.

Just so everyone is on the same astrological page, there are four elements in astrology: earth, air, fire, and water. The earth signs are based in the tangible: what they can see, touch, taste, and feel. The fire signs are action-based and -oriented. Water complements earth and air complements fire.

Combining elements that are non-complementary such as Taurus' earth with Sagittarius' fire adds even more strangeness to an already unobvious astrological mix, especially in the following areas: physical activity, energy levels, motivation/impetus, body constitution, recreation, and eating habits.

Let's bring all this unobviousness onto the tangible plane by providing some Taurus/Sagittarius practical application! Taurus has a slow and steady approach to life. Sagittarius' is fast and furious.

Taurus likes to have a sense of regimented routine in its day to day life. The only kind of regimented routine a Sagittarian will accept is regular doses of variety and change in its day to day life and as often as possible.

In the time it takes for the Taurus to slowly chew and savor its first forkful of a meal, the Sagittarius has already vacuumed its entire plate down and is wondering why the server is taking so long to deliver the check.

Taurus likes peace and quiet and abhors any kind of arguing or heated debate. Sagittarius loves to debate or loudly argue, many times getting in one's face and finger pointing while doing so.

The body of the bull can suffer due to not being physically active enough. The body of the centaur can suffer due to physical exhaustion brought about by being over active.

Fixed-sign Taurus prefers being in total control by planning things in advance. Hence, it's practically a guarantee the bull will arrive at any scheduled activity on time, every time. Sagittarius prefers being spontaneous and tends to procrastinate to the last possible minute. Hence, it's practically a guarantee that most of the time the centaur is never on time.

Taurus has the patience of a saint. Sagittarius becomes a saint's worst nightmare if it has to wait more than half a microsecond for anything.

Why these two signs don't even mingle, let alone join forces, is each sign not bothering with the other after a blanket evaluation is made.

Upon first meeting, many a Sagittarian will often tend to sum up the Taurus to be a boring stick in the mud who will move only in the case of dire emergency, such as an earthquake, tsunami, armageddon, etc., while the Taurean may at first judge the Sagittarius to be an irresponsible, empty promiser who will keep its word only in the case of dire emergency, such as an earthquake, tsunami, armageddon, etc.

Things extend past the realm of uninterested neutrality when both signs adjust their natural sense of speed to incorporate their partner's very different pace. If the Sagittarius can refrain from being its usual Tazmanian Devil self of frantically paced activity, it may just let the Taurus teach it a thing or two about the art of relaxing.

Similarly, the bull's sense of regimented routine may get a breath of much-needed fresh air after following the centaur around on one of its typical days, which are usually anything but typical. The Sag's varied and numerous activities can transport the Taurus far from its daily cow path to unexplored, never-before-experienced adventures.

So how about it, Taurus and Sagittarius? Do you two remain sticks in the mud that allow a blanket evaluation of each other destroy any romantic potential, or do you ditch all the book-by-the-astrological-cover stuff in order to make something that's not so obvious astrological relationship-wise into something romantically substantial?

The choice is up to both of you.

Taurus–Capricorn

It's no secret, Taurus and Capricorn. Earth signs like their stuff.

The element of earth, which is the astrological foundation for both your signs, derives security from that which is tangible: money, homes, cars, and diamonds that are at least five carats (never lower) in variations of white, pink, brown, with the occasional yellow thrown in. Ya know. Stuff.

However, when the first representative of earth (Taurus) joins romantic forces with the last representative of that same element (Capricorn), their astrological pairing takes the concept of the tangible to the extreme!

But Taurus, does the Bentley REALLY need a juice bar installed? And Capricorn, does the vacation villa HAVE to have its own coat of arms AND flag?

Now, don't misconstrue what I'm trying to relay, you two. There's nothing wrong with owning nice things and having wads of cash. It's when the tangible becomes master over those based in the tangible that things become a smidge problematic.

Speaking of the tangible, I picked up a little something to celebrate your earthy love union. It's a couple of dual-purposed souvenirs picked up for quite a pretty penny (you can pay me back later) that serve as both gifts and realistic reminders for the earth-signed couple to keep their love of the tangible in check during their romantic time together.

But I jump far too ahead of myself.

Astrologically, the most romantically compatible couples are made up of two people born beneath the same element. With the bull and the mystic mountain goat both being earth signs, we not only have a match, we have a romantic winner!

When two signs are of the same element, a strong likelihood exists that both parties will get along harmoniously well together and see things eye to eye as partners.

Since they are ruled by Venus, the planet of beauty and aesthetics, those born beneath the sign of the bull have exceptionally good taste. The typical Taurean loves to be aesthetically pleased by surrounding itself with pleasantries as well as things that are visually beautiful.

As the first representative of the earthy element, the bull derives the most security from the tangible things it possesses and its senses are at their purest and most uncomplicated. The Taurus will take its bovine sweet time to fully employ its physical senses whenever partaking in such sensual activities as stopping to smell the roses (its flower), savoring every bite of a scrumptious meal, or feeling the stratospherically high thread count sheets while resting or relaxing in bed.

Optimal comfort for the typical Taurean is when his or her "things" are highly stylish, visually pleasing, and luxuriously comfortable.

As the last representative of the element of earth, the perspective of the tangible and one's "things" for the Capricorn shifts away from the purely personal and moves up—waaaaaaaaaaaay up—for everyone and their mother to see.

Status (noun): The position of an individual believed to confer elevated rank or stature.

Capricorn is known as "the sign of status." Naturally ruling over the zodiac wheel's highest point, the tenth house of career and the public, the goat has a work ethic like no other. What the rest of the zodiac thinks is a hard day's work, is what the typical goat guy or girl takes care of on its day off.

The Capricorn's work is most productively effective when a particular concept is present: THE GOAL. No matter how high up or far off, the work ethic of the mystic mountain goat is used to its full potential should the Cappie have an aspired goal in mind.

Because a goodly portion of the work they do is predominantly goal oriented, the majority of goats have an inherent need to drive the latest model of Mercedes or BMW and/or wear the most frightfully expensive eye gear as an expression of their hard earned labors.

In other words, the Capricorn has a natural need to display its level of status as if openly declaring to the world, "I EARNED THESE FRIGHTFULLY EXPENSIVE THINGS BY WORKING MY GOAT HOOVES TO THE BONE!"

Needless to say, for both the Taurus and the Capricorn appearance is of the utmost importance. Here are two signs that would rather lose a limb versus being spotted in public donning sweatpants or have an exposed body part that's either unmanicured or unshaved. This rule of appearance for the bull and the goat applies to every degree of public exposure for them, be it attending a gala charity event in the early evening or stopping at the local convenience store for milk in the early morning.

Individually, both the bull and the goat tend to have rather expensive tastes and are usually allergic to anything remotely resembling low quality or secondhand.

As stated earlier, there's nothing wrong with having nice things and earning wads of cash, Taurus and Capricorn. However, your Love Author would like to remind both earth-signed lovers that too much abundance isn't always an automatically defaulted good thing.

A landslide of problematic potential exists when two earth signs become an asset-amassing entity of one couple. Should either the Taurus or the Capricorn allow the material plane to take absolute control, chances are quite strong its partner will also fall prey to that most dangerous kind of earth-signed greed, otherwise known as blatant materialism.

Tangibly speaking of which, your Love Author's love tokens! Okay you two. Shuck the expensive eye gear and shut your peepers tight! Ready?

POP THE CAGES OPEN AND LET 'EM OUT, BOYS!

My gift for the earthy couple? Giant peacocks on the verge of molting! The male form of this species is the version we associate with the peacock. Its massively grand tail is the tool of attraction the peacock uses to impress the aviary opposite sex of its kind, otherwise known as the peahen.

But there's a price to pay with being the mate of choice amongst the choicest chicks of peahen persuasion. If the peacock's tail becomes too expansively large without actively molting or having any excess feathers removed, it will restrict the cocky bird to the material plane by making him too weighed down to fly or even strut in a brisk manner.

If not quickly addressed, the plight of the portly peacock becomes a most welcome dilemma for the lions or tigers located anywhere within the near vicinity of this overtly oblivious bird.

Let the peacock's pared-down tail of floating emerald green and ultramarine serve as a reminder for both earth signs to keep their mutual need to amass things on as grounded a level as possible.

The more this is mutually done, the greater the chances you earthy ones will be catapulted from this tangible plane of existence into a realm of romantic bliss that's out of this material world!

Taurus–Aquarius

The chapter has barely begun, and already you two have put me in quite a pickle, Taurus and Aquarius!

I planned on generalizing the overall positive and negative dynamics when the bull and the water bearer join romantic forces by presenting things via the traditional but trite "I have good news and bad news" format, but even THERE we have issues.

Taurus likes things cushy and comfortable. The bull's love of luxury and leisure makes it openly receptive to the good news in any of its variations but ready to stampede in resistance should the slightest bit of bad news be broadcasted.

Aquarius likes things, well, different. Why should it conform to such a pigeon-holed range of limitation such as "good" or "bad" when there is an entire universe's worth of choices that lay in between? It's almost as bourgeois as asking the politically savvy whether they are merely Republican or Democrat.

(Smiling hard while walking slowly backwards away.)

So what to do, you two?

How about we change the initial formatting altogether by starting over from satirical scratch?

And rather than present the usual compare/contrast discussion between two signs where the more generalized traits are discussed first, followed by the details of distinction, how about we seriously shake things up by doing the inverse (if only to please the sign that "dares to be different," AKA Aquarius)?

Being the first representative of the earth signs, Taurus is most concerned with what is tangible, namely its things and possessions, along with the security and pleasure it derives from them. Being the last member of the air-signed clan, affairs of the mind are of the utmost importance to the Aquarius, who tends to frown upon any overt over-attachments to the material world.

The Taurean is truly uncomplicated and straightforward in nature. The Aquarian is by far one of the most complex of the zodiac, whom even its own kind has a hard time understanding.

Taurus is ruled by Venus, the planet of harmony and prettiness, and will many times suppress or stay silent regarding any gripes or misgivings it has with others just to keep things quiet and peaceful.

Aquarius is ruled by Uranus, the planet of rebellion. It enjoys questioning the powers that be, hypothesizing a never before thought of conspiracy theory, or championing for those whom it considers to be victims of circumstance, none of whom the Aquarian knows personally. Keeping the peace for this sign is about loudly protesting for the rights of all and defending those who can't voice their grievances.

Being Venus-ruled, Taureans have congenial dispositions, pleasant sounding voices, and tend to get along swimmingly well with others. Being Uranian in nature, Aquarians are naturally quirky and unique, tend to speak with odd sounding voices, and overall are known for being cold and standoffish with those it doesn't know well. Taurus is Muzak. Aquarius is thrash metal punk.

Moving inversely from the detailed to the general...

Both Taurus and Aquarius are of the same astrological quality: fixed.

Far more than any of the other astrological qualities, the fixed signs experience the most challenge in getting along with one another and merely achieving a state of relationship equilibrium.

As a whole, the fixed signs do not have the easiest time seeing other people's perspectives that aren't their own. Other fixed characteristics that are anything but easy are: a natural tendency to resist change; a mental proclivity to see things in a one dimensional, black or white way; an inherent inclination to not want to compromise; or a consistent knack for being obstinate, a polite way of saying "pig-headed stubborn.

In fact, the dating process between the fixed signs of Taurus and Aquarius can be likened to a particular genre of Japanese sci-fi horror film, *Godzilla*.

Much like the unfolding plot that is the formulaic standard for any of the *Godzilla* movies, the atmosphere needs to be picture postcard perfect when the Taurus and the Aquarius first begin dating.

When these two fixed signs first meet and decide to date, things couldn't go any romantically smoother! Both the bull and the water bearer put every effort into looking their best, and just as importantly, being on their best behavior.

The initial dating phase between the Taurus and the Aquarius may be so intoxicatingly good at first that assumptions may be erroneously made that this highly romantic love vibe will be a permanent fixture for the two fixed signs going forward.

But it's exactly that same type of sentiment in the *Godzilla* film when the lovers are walking hand in hand down the promenade, past the school as the closing bell rings, where the teacher stands waving in slow motion, mouthing "Good-bye, Children!" to her happily exiting students. The camera pans up and away allowing the viewing audience to see far off in the distance the churning volcano, darkening sky, or bubbling ocean's surface.

Terror is about to descend upon Romanceville!

In other words (dramatic orchestral chords while a woman hysterically screams), the Taurus and the Aquarius are about to have their first difference of opinion!

Picture the bull and the water bearer walking hand and hoof together, strutting amidst the puffy clouds of honeymoon phase bliss, and then a disagreement or difference of opinion occurs.

Instantly, both fixed signs will dig their heels and hooves into the ground, determined never to budge a millimeter for the duration of their bovine and Aquarian lives!

Upon seeing its fixed sign partner doing the aforementioned heel digging, the other fixed sign will become even MORE inflexibly unrelenting, stupefied at how obviously wrong its fixed sign partner is about everything.

Godzilla has officially crossed paths with Mothra/Ghidora/Rhodan/ or Hidorah the smog monster, ladies and gentlemen!

Mirroring the same reaction as the townspeople who reside in the celluloid hamlet of placid perfection, everyone is taken completely off guard.

But, much like the dapper and well-suited male lead whose mouth moves well before the audience hears his dubbed-in-English voice, your Love Author would like to inform both feuding fixed signs, "There may just be a way."

Hold on to your boyfriends and plug your ears because this one's gonna be a real screamer: COMPROMISE.

It's Romanceville's only hope, Taurus-uku and Aquarius-san!

Not just one, but BOTH fixed signs need to regularly compromise with its fixed sign partner in order for this relationship to NOT have a horror flick ending of romantic armageddon.

Both Taurus and Aquarius are two of the most stubborn signs in the known universe, and many seasons shall pass before either fixed sign realizes that its pig-headed partner is just as stubborn as him- or herself.

The two *Godzilla* film lovers may have been separated while Ghidorah was deflecting that flying school bus hand flung by Godzilla, but they always figure out a way to find each other in a tearful hug towards the film's end just as the camera pans up and away, displaying the smoking carnage as peace returns to the town of Romanceville once more. Or does it?

Best of luck dating each other, Taurus and Aquarius. But both signs should be warned: If compromise isn't part of your loving landscape together, both of you should enter at your own romantic risk.

Taurus–Pisces

Behold, Taurus and Pisces! Your Love Author places before your coupled selves one of the best examples representing the union of each of your elemental foundations, earth and water, and one of the oldest as well: the bath salt.

Much like adding a generous heaping of fragrant bath salts to a warm inviting bath, teaming up the bull with the cosmic fish creates a romantic union known for its swimmingly natural compatibility.

In astrology, the four elements of earth, air, fire, and water are naturally paired off. Each grouping consists of two elements that are cohesive and naturally work well together, otherwise known as being complementary to each other. Hence, the elements of fire and air are grouped together, but more importantly for this particular pairing, the elements of earth and water are complementary to each other.

The earth signs are based in the tangible. When reacting to any given stimuli from the outside world, the earth signs utilize their senses first and foremost. Since Taurus is the first representative of the element of earth, its physical senses are at its purest and most uncomplicated.

The bull will take its bovine sweet time to fully employ its senses whenever partaking in such sensual things as stopping to smell the roses (its flower), slowly savoring every bite of a scrumptious meal, or feeling the luxuriously high thread count sheets while resting or relaxing in bed.

A water sign's first reaction to the outside world is through its emotions. The water-based person gauges everything initially by how it literally makes him or her "feel" at first. By far, the sign of Pisces is the most sensitive of all the signs. So sensitive in fact, your Love Author personally calls those born beneath the sign of the cosmic fish, "the psychic anemones of the zodiac," due to its near constant state of emotional reception.

The Taurus derives security by having a stable foundation of things that are anchored to the material plane. The Pisces gains security by feeling bonded to those whom it is strongly connected to emotionally.

The grounded stability of the Taurus matched with the otherworldly intuition of the Pisces at first sounds like a relationship dynamic of polar opposites, but in actuality, the energies of the bull and the fish romantically joined together usually results in a partnership of balanced contentment. These two signs complement each other by virtue of their mutual energies merging the weighted with the weightless, and joining the material with what is immaterial.

Plus, both the bull and the fish share the same source of motivation: Romantic inspiration.

With Taurus' planetary ruler named after Venus, the goddess of love, and Pisces' ruling heavenly body of Neptune overseeing romantic poetry, as well as the romance movement at large, the bull and the fish don't just have a natural propensity to be romantic. These two signs take romance and make it seriously hardcore!

Unfortunately the world is quite the unromantic place these days. Mention the word "courting" in the present time and most people will think you're either talking about the latest basketball stats or your plans to actively sue someone. Even with such a romantically restrictive backdrop painted, both Taurus and Pisces still respond to and interact best through the process of courting.

Courting (noun): A way of getting to know a person through gradual stages of increased intimacy by incorporating romance with social activities.

Upon first meeting, the Taurean and the Piscean will more than likely make each other's better romantic acquaintance by engaging in the proper rules of courtship.

The biggest pitfall of romantic potential for the Taurus Pisces union is the tendency for either sign to REPRESS or SUPPRESS any problems, gripes, or differences the couple needs to work on together.

Taurus' planetary ruler of Venus not only oversees such niceties as love and beauty, but peace and harmony as well. This may sound all sugar and spice and Venusian nice at first, but in terms of a romantic relationship, these inherent niceties can turn out to be quite problematic.

Allow your Love Author to explain.

A relationship is never 100 percent smooooooooth sailing (sorry, couldn't resist a little cow humor thrown on top of some fish imagery). There will be times within every human relationship where differences of opinion will occur and gripes shall arise. When these inevitable things take place, both partners will be called upon to either confront or debate over the contentious matters at hand in order to work things out.

Except for the Taurus.

Should the person born beneath the sign of the bull have a fishbone to pick with its Piscean partner, it more often than not won't say a word. Because of its planetary ruler's influence, many a Taurean will stifle whatever is bothering him or her in order to maintain the peace and not rock the fishing boat.

Similarly, Pisces' planetary ruler of Neptune not only deals with unconditional love and fantasy, it also oversees the unevolved traits of self-sacrifice and self-imposed martyrdom as well. The watery planet's negative influence can make many a fish person feel it must suffer through relationships of the most unhealthy kind without so much as uttering a Piscean peep of complaint.

It's in the best interest for the children of both Venus and Neptune to be as upfront and vocal with their gripes and differences as often as possible, and even more importantly, when it occurs.

Communication is necessary for a relationship to not just thrive but survive, Taurus and Pisces. And just to inform both of you non-offending ones, every relationship on this green earth needs to have an argument, debate, and yes, even a good old fashioned fight now and then in order to remain healthy and stable.

The best way the Taurus and the Pisces can ensure their romantic shelf life together is for both signs to consistently work at vocally expressing its gripes and fears just as much as their romantic declarations of impassioned love for each other.

Should the bull and the fish successfully avoid any kind of avoidance behavior within their relationship, the grounded stability and emotional well-being naturally created by their love union will strengthen over time.

Additionally, should the Taurus and Pisces rock their own boat of romance by immediately addressing whatever problems or grievances should arise within their relationship, the stronger their bond of complementary energies will merge and flow together like the waters of a freshly drawn, heated to perfection bath mixed with the most intoxicatingly fragrant of bath salts.

Gemini-Gemini

Did either twin know that every sign of the zodiac is archetypally represented within those mystical cards of divination, otherwise known as the tarot?

Gemini's archetypal tarot card is far from obvious yet quite apropos for this particular chapter, given its entire focus being dedicated solely to the Chatty Chads and Cathys of the zodiac: the lovers.

Many of mankind's earliest cultures believed everyone was born with merely half a soul and that each person has a spiritual twin with whom it was separated from upon entering this plane of existence at the time of its birth.

The tarot card of the lovers is assigned to the sign of Gemini due it representing the particular moment when one's soul is made complete upon being reunited with its spiritual twin.

The search for a romantic partner may not be as cosmically melodramatic a concept as being reunited with one's soul twin, but the process can seem like quite the daunting quest for the typical Gemini all the same. This is due to the twinish person's romantic needs extending beyond the standard requirements the rest of the zodiac uses when looking for a significant other.

In their quest for romance, those born beneath the sign of the twins inherently hope to find both a best friend as well as a romantic partner.

The optimal romantic relationship for the Gemini can be likened to a particular kind of close knit companionship many of us experienced with our childhood best friend during the elementary school years.

In other air-signed words, a love interest who on top of everything else the Gemini can regularly joke and giggle with, as well as constantly yak with non-stop as it did with its best buddy back in the fifth grade.

Along with the classic imagery of the lovers tarot card, a more modernized example comes to mind that also succinctly represents the dynamic when two sets of twins become one romantic couple: the Weasley twins from *Harry Potter*.

Although the Weasley brothers visually match the first representative of air's symbol by being twins in the most obvious of ways, there's far more beneath the surface as to why this particular pair embodies the magical atmosphere that's whipped up whenever two Geminis join romantic forces.

For starters, the Weasley twins set themselves apart from the entire motley magical crew of *Harry Potter* land. How so? Both brothers make the conscious decision to discontinue their studies and not graduate from Hogwarts School of Magic.

There will be more on those two in just a bit, but additional trivia of the twinish kind is required right about now. Just so both of you identical gene holders are up to date, astrologically it's generally frowned upon whenever two people of the same sign date each other. But there is one major exception.

Any of those born beneath the sign of the trivia monger care to guess which resident of the zodiac is immune to this same signed dating rule? YOUR SIBLING'D SELVES, AKA the sign of Gemini!

The sign of the twins breaks free from the rest of the astrological bunch by being the only resident of the zodiac that can freely date itself.

Same-sign dating can be quite problematic for the rest of the zodiac due to certain core personality traits immediately rising to the surface, such as being openly (Aries) or covertly (Capricorn, Virgo) competitive; too uncompromisingly headstrong (Leo, Scorpio, Aquarius); or too idealistic about love in general (Libra, Taurus).

However, when two Geminis date each other, a world of inquisitive wonder unfolds due to their intellectually curious personalities revving each other into a heightened state of near-constant mental stimulation.

Still scarred by those mind-numbing first dates where all evening not a single question was even directed towards your air-signed self? Or just as painful, the evening's flow of conversation felt like you were extracting every molar from your date from hell's barely moving mouth.

The only lapses in conversation between two Geminis upon first meeting will most likely occur due to one twin set interrupting the other while in the midst of lively discussion, or from both air signs having the same thought and simultaneously saying it out loud.

In fact, it's highly recommended the Mercurial couple not invite others along on their first few dates due to the remainder of the planet's population barely being able to contribute a syllable's worth to the evening's conversation. The gabbing will be THAT fast and furiously paced between both air signs while becoming better romantically acquainted with each other.

But just as there are key advantages to this uniquely exceptional union of astrological similarity, the sign of duality must be made aware there are pitfalls as well. The two themes of the most problematic potential for the joining of two sets of twins are abundance and speed.

With your sign being the wordsmith of the zodiac, how about we use the first term of problematic potential in a game of grammar.

A Gemini is truly a social creature and being as such, is known for having an "abundance" of acquaintances.

While reading the above, were you expecting the use of another word implying social familiarity?

The statement didn't end with the word "friends," if for the implication of time and attention needed to cultivate and upkeep that very same word. The typical Gemini may enjoy chatting a lot of people up but doesn't necessarily want to get tied down with commitment to those it gabs with.

In order for any relationship between two people to bond and grow, there must be time and effort invested by all romantic parties involved. Spreading one's air-signed self too thin or having sparse slots of time in between social engagements simply won't cut it if the two social butterflies (Gemini creature) of the zodiac wish to develop a romantic union.

Keeping in mind the aforementioned concept of abundance gone out of whack, let's throw another monkey (Gemini animal) wrench into the machine by adding the concept of speed to the mix of problematic potential. Some golden words of relationship advice to both participating Geminis: "Slow down, shut up, and BREATHE!"

Despite being air signs, a vast majority of those born beneath the element that incites breathing barely ever do so. The worst repercussion for never taking in the very stuff of its own elemental foundation results in many a Gemini buzzing about from one bit of mental stimulation to the next without fully absorbing or appreciating whatever it was it has just previously experienced.

Take that barely breathing concept that affects many an air sign, apply it to the twins' social hummingbird (yet another Gemini animal) behavior displayed amongst its numerous social acquaintances, and quite often the result is one or both Geminis being in a near constant state of distraction, along with the strong likelihood of one or both eventually cheating on the other.

Returning once more to our *Harry Potter* analogy, upon being expelled from Hogwarts, the Weasley twins didn't merely goof off and play pointless pranks forever afterward.

This dynamic duo of twins pooled their resources together by establishing their own company. A place of magical business that had within its title, a best friendish word that implies uncontrollable snorting brought about from too many peals of wild laughter: Weasley Wizard Wheezes.

Noble goals that every team of twins might want to consider when dating one of its astrological own, right down to any and all activities of the romantically wheezing kind.

So after all that, the only thing left to say to both best friends of the astrological and romantic kind is go outside and play!

Gemini-Cancer

You both must have heard that old but wise adage that still applies in the modern day, right Gemini and Cancer? A person can choose his or her friends, but not his or her neighbors.

This neighborly concept applies astrologically, yet at the same time is completely irrelevant when it comes to playing the zodiac dating game.

Take you two for example. Nothing can change the astrological fact the signs of Gemini and Cancer are next-door neighbors on that big wheel of life, otherwise known as the zodiac. Yet that inalterable information is neither karmic apples nor cosmic oranges during those not so common times when the twins and the crab decide to join romantic forces.

Moving from old adages to more contemporary rules of cosmic thumb, it's generally understood the signs that border each other are categorized beneath a most unexciting descriptor of astrological compatibility: neutral.

(A solitary cough can be heard in the far off, remote distance.)

Every sign has the potential to work together. Some combinations take a lot more work than others to achieve a state of equilibrium. With the joining of the signs considered to be neutral of each other, the state of equilibrium is something very much like the solid borderline that naturally forms whenever oil and vinegar are put into the same container. In other words, mixing the two isn't a bad thing, but a whole lot of shaking is needed for there to be any kind of blend. For the most part, the core differences within this neutral astrological duo all boils down to their brains.

Gemini is an air sign. Cancer is a water sign. The air signs initially react to the outside world via the functions of the left hemisphere of its brain. The water signs initially react to the outside world via the brain's right hemisphere.

The left hemisphere of the brain is otherwise known as the rational mind. The right hemisphere is otherwise known as the emotional or intuitive mind.

A left-hemisphered person is motivated most to exercise the processes of the rational mind, which are the following mental functions: thought and communication. A right-hemisphered person is motivated most by what resides beneath the domain of the non-rational mind, namely one's emotions and intuition.

Sounds easy enough, right? One last rule of mental play regarding all this geographical brain matter must be mentioned. We humans have total control over the functions of our left hemispheres and no control whatsoever over the functions of our right hemispheres.

Being the first representative of the element of air, the functions of thought and communication bear the strongest influence for those born beneath the sign of the twins.

The Gemini doesn't just like to talk. In order to optimally function, those born beneath the first of the air signs NEED to talk.

The air signs in general avoid the emotional realm altogether due to the rational mind having no control over those messy and scary things that are generated from the brain's non-rational hemisphere (aka emotions).

In fact, the mental muscles of many a twin-born person are so inherently strong, its left hemisphere will quite often wrestle its feelings into submission by rationalizing them a far distance from the surface of its conscious mind, and as often as possible.

As already mentioned, those born beneath the element of water primarily operate from the brain's right hemisphere. The water sign person will literally see how something makes it FEEL before any of its actions are put into effect.

Non-water signs like to think feelings fit in custom-made gift boxes where each emotion sits in a little compartment and waits to be called out at some point in the very distant future.

The water signs know better. They know all too well that human emotion is a force much like Mother Nature herself. We cannot MAKE the weather happen. We live with it and adjust accordingly whenever it chooses to change.

The best way a Cancer expresses its emotionally-based element of water is by nurturing others. If a crab person is emotionally connected to another, it will literally mother that person in order to express its emotional state, regardless if they're related by blood or not.

Based on differences of astrological foundation, many times it'll seem as if the twins and the crab lived on the opposite ends of town versus being astrological next-door neighbors.

Airy Gemini is a social butterfly and likes to be out and about as often as its booked social calendar will allow. Watery Cancer likes nothing better than shacking up in the cozy comfort of its own home.

The Gemini is naturally attuned to the latest styles and likes to be on top of what's hot, especially when it comes to computer and communication gadgetry. The Cancer turns to the past for its inspiration, deriving security from what has already been. Things tied to the past hold the strongest allure for this most sentimental of signs.

Most Geminis are inept in the kitchen and can barely handle the task of boiling water. Most Cancerians are naturally skilled in the kitchen and thoroughly enjoy making good food for themselves and nourishing those they care for.

Adjustments of astrological temperament are required of both signs if this romantic union wishes to have a pulse, let alone last. By far the biggest problems potentially pose themselves during the earliest stages when the Gemini and the Cancer begin the dating process.

The Gemini tends to initially warm up to love's domain with a laid-back and light-hearted attitude akin to a slowly simmering Crock Pot. The Cancer usually proceeds down that same path with an emotional heat that's fast and thoroughly all encompassing, much like a microwave running at the highest derivative of heating power.

Crustacean case in point. In the beginning stages of dating, nothing makes a Gemini run in the opposite direction faster than a Cancer immediately smothering it with emotional clinginess. If a Gemini makes a crab's shell go bright red with passionate longing, the best initial approach the Cancer can take is one that mirrors the twins' airy element: easy breezy.

Conversely, nothing steams a crab's shell more than a Gemini spreading itself too socially thin and its lack of availability. One of the best indications of romantic commitment a twinish person can make is purposefully toning down its social calendar of seemingly nonstop activity. The first of the air signs will also need to incorporate external displays of affection from the earliest stages of the relationship if it wishes the Crab to stay put in its love cage.

Both signs will need to be especially patient with each other whenever adjusting to the changes made to either's environment should things become more romantically intimate.

The Gemini will need to overlook the Cancer's bouts of awkward quietness when first introducing him or her to the overwhelming social network otherwise known as the twins' many friends and social acquaintances. In turn, the Cancer will need to show the Gemini how to breathe with its head between its legs from the hyperventilation that may occur during its first attempts at being quiet while in a watery atmosphere of domestic non-distraction.

If both signs are willing to make some major adjustments to their core senses of self, these astrological next-door neighbors stand a good chance of transforming their domestic compatibility rating of neutral to something altogether romantically new.

Gemini-Leo

Did you lovebirds know the most damaging forest fires occur in areas that don't necessarily have the most flammable material but are susceptible to high winds?

Flame, unto its solitary self, doesn't make a fire burn fast and furiously. Take said flame and infuse it with the oxygen from the windy air and you have one serious scorcher. Kind of like when the Gemini and the Leo date each other.

In astrology, the four elements of earth, air, fire, and water are naturally paired off. Each grouping consists of two elements that are cohesive or naturally work well together, otherwise known as being complementary. Hence, the elements of earth and water complement each other, but more important for this particular pairing, the elements of fire and air are complementary.

Returning once more to our romantic forest fire analogy, when speedy, airy Gemini joins romantic forces with fiery fixed Leo, the erratic nature of the burning wildfire is made more constant and tempered down to a slow and steadily burning flame.

The element of air has the mental functions of rational thought and communication at its foundational core. Being the first of the airy representatives, one needn't be Albert Einstein to observe the role communication plays with anyone born beneath the sign of the twins.

Behold! The jabberjaws/Chatty Chads and Cathys/motor mouths of the zodiac!

Since the sign of the twins is ruled by Mercury, the planet of communication, it must be emphasized the average Gemini doesn't just like to talk, it NEEDS to if it wants to optimally function.

The fire signs (Aries, Leo, Sagittarius) are action oriented and most members of the family of flame like as much of their action to be as fast-paced as possible. The exception is the fixed member of the fire sign family: Leo, the lion.

Leo stands apart from the other fast-paced, constantly on the go fire signs by virtue of its fixed astrological quality.

The fixed signs are positioned at the mid-point of each of the four seasons. The sign of the lion takes place when summer is at the height of its dog days.

Leo's fixed nature gives this sign a very different dynamic from the rest of the fiery family. Amongst the fixed, nothing is ever rushed or approached with a fast and furious pace. Slow and steady wins the race with these heavy hitting signs.

Combining the air sign of speed talking with the fixed sign of the fiery feline may sound like a union of polar opposites due to the Gemini and the Leo working from such differing dynamics.

However, joining the romantic energies of the twins with the lion more often than not results in a serious romance of long-lasting potential versus a burning ball of passion that extinguishes itself as quickly as when it first combusted.

In fact, both signs' core differences of dynamic tend to be seen as refreshingly fun by the other versus any kind of obstacle that could potentially get in the way of the Gemini's and Leo's budding intimacy upon first dating each other.

The Gemini's lively and upbeat skills of conversation has a way of keeping the lion sign, known for its theatrical flair, thoroughly entertained. While the Leo's passionate approach to life is so naturally dramatic and heartfelt, it can easily captivate the attentions of the twin, leaving the motor mouth of the zodiac agog with wonder and stunned to silence.

The best advice your Love Author can give the Gemini when first dating its Leo love interest? Flattery will get you EVERYWHERE with your lion lover! A backup of flowers, refined chocolates (preferably of the non-American variety), along with handwritten declarations of love certainly won't hurt either.

In other words, the best way to trap a lion in its love cage is by courting him or her. And Gemini, that doesn't mean pursuing your Leonine lover in a court of law or challenging it to a vigorous round of hoops on the b-ball court.

Courting (noun and gerund for those truly hardcore wordsmiths of the zodiac,): a way of getting to know a person through gradual stages of increased intimacy by incorporating romance with social activities.

Lions, the best way to have your twin jumping through your love hoops from the very onset? Ask the Gemini questions.

Asking an air sign questions keeps it mentally stimulated and more importantly wards off a particular state of being air signs dread most: BOREDOM.

For you lazy Leos who just whined aloud, "But I don't know what to ask," here are a few romantic inquiries your Love Author guarantees will generate some kind of twinish response: Where are you originally from? What do you currently do for work? How many brothers and sisters do you have? What's your favorite movie/color/car/day of the week/Beatle/Chinese Dynasty?

And to romantically enlighten those born beneath the sign of big hair and even bigger egos, "QUESTIONS ABOUT YOURSELVES ARE NOT VALID AND THEREFORE DO NOT COUNT, LEO!"

Asking your Gemini date what he or she thinks about your Leonine choice of evening apparel or if it noticed an entire half inch was cut from the bangs of your big-haired mane is romantically null and void due to the conversation being reverted away from him or her and back upon your spotlight-loving self.

Just as the Leo would take heartfelt offense with the twinish person avoiding the courting process altogether, the lion should also duly note the Gemini would interpret an absence of questions as its date not having a shred of interest in its mentally inquisitive self as a whole.

Whereas Leo's fixed quality is steadfast and lion-heartedly loyal, Gemini's quality is one of varied changeability, otherwise known as mutable.

This mutable nature instills within many a Gemini a wandering eye that many times can lead the twinish person to cheat for the sheer sake of variety, which is almost always based in the accursed source of every air sign's troubles. The Gemini was bored.

The best advice your Love Author can give the Leo on how to make sure its Gemini love interest stays loyal and true? The faithful Gemini is one who is mentally stimulated.

Moving onward to other key differences of romantic dynamics between the lion and the twins, doing things off the cuff or from a randomly spontaneous angle is totally radical for the Gemini and radically insane for the fixed sign of royalty, Leo, who likes to have as much control over every aspect of the monarchy that is its world as possible.

Problems emerge when the monarchy turns into an absolutist dictatorship of Leonine control, where all activities are pre-scheduled agendas, and any kind of twinish last minute changes or fickle impulses are strictly forbidden.

For the love of Mercury, Gemini, NEVER do the surprise thing with your Leo love interest, especially showing up to its lair unannounced.

Despite the twins being stunned to silence upon walking in on its lion lover and finding it with (I almost can't say it) UNPRIMPED HAIR, the Gemini most likely won't utter a word due to an unprepared lion roaring it right out of its den.

Even with the above said, if these two complementary signs take the time to initially adjust to each other's differences of dynamic and overall personality, then let the good times roll and burst into long-lasting, air-stoked flame!

Gemini-Virgo

Sit down, Gemini and Virgo. We need to talk.

Given the fact you both are ruled by Mercury, the planet of communication, there's no point in wasting everyone's time babbling a lot of superfluous fluff regarding the twins and the virgin joining romantic forces. In fact, your Love Author shall attempt to communicate in the most direct and non-sugar coated of ways to both of you as if my words were heaping spoonfuls of cod liver love oil.

For starters, the two of you are SURE you're dating each other, right?

I should preface things by stating every sign has the potential to work together in a romantically involved way. It's just that some signs take a lot more work to achieve a state of equilibrium than others. And just to inform all romantic parties currently involved, you two are WORK!

The inherent energies and overall personalities of the Gemini and the Virgo operate so differently that combining these two signs in any kind of one-on-one partnership requires a consistent level of hard work. So much so, your Love Author will be the first to admit the work needed to keep the Gemini Virgo romantic union up and running can be downright back breaking at times!

Of the twelve signs, Gemini and Virgo are each other's biggest challenge to relate with naturally due to each sign's placement on the zodiac wheel. They are positioned at the harshest astrological angle possible of 90 degrees, which is better known as the square.

When two signs square each other, a consistently high probability exists for either sign to easily rub the other the wrong way usually because either or both signs are simply being their natural selves.

In order to fully grasp their vast differences of temperament, Mercury, the planetary ruler that the twins and the virgin share, needs to be examined with further detail.

Those who are Mercury-ruled are mentally driven and function best through thought and communication, which are the areas of life the planet named after the divine messenger of the gods oversees.

The sign of the twins is the power talker of the zodiac. Those born beneath the sign of the virgin are the analytical thinkers equipped with minds that are incredibly precise and detail-oriented.

Because their shared planetary ruler is the fastest moving heavenly body throughout the solar system, it stands to reason the Mercurial signs of Gemini and Virgo possess the fastest minds, mouths, and overall dispositions of the zodiac. Their mentally driven nature never allows either to slow down, even if to simply breathe.

With that in mind, both the virgin and the twins are equally susceptible to a particular curse commonly shared amongst the Mercury-ruled. A mental malady that almost always can be blamed for those choice times whenever the Gemini or the Virgo has gotten themselves into trouble or hot water: BOREDOM.

The best form of mental stimulation for Mercury's children is duality, or the joining of polar opposites. Despite Gemini and Virgo sharing the mental affliction of becoming bored in less than five nanoseconds if their minds aren't kept immediately engaged, the two signs greatly diverge on how their Mercurial energies are utilized on a daily basis.

Because Mercury's influence makes its mind so highly analytical, Virgo is also known as the detail-driven sign. Those born beneath the sign of the virgin have a natural ability to focus their attention with laser beam-like precision on the tiniest of fine points. However, there are times when the Virgo can become SO detail driven, he or she will often miss the forest for the trees due to its analytical mind becoming overtaken with the most nitpicky of technicalities.

Conversely, the Gemini's Mercurial nature can make it so starved for mental stimulation, details are often either totally overlooked or not even considered at all. Whereas the Virgo can lose itself within the most fine lined of details, the Gemini can become so easily distracted and scatter brained, its lack of attention to detail can be viewed as being just downright sloppy.

If this Mercurial love union wants to have a pulse, let alone last, the mutual flow of open communication is crucial. Should either sign fail to contribute its fair share of communicative effort, this meeting of the two Mercurial signs will proceed to immediately disintegrate.

Once that occurs, both Mercurial parties will begin to question the foundation of its relationship, with each feeling as if it can't relay a single thought to the other without a constant stream of distracted misunderstanding and/or reactions of oversensitive resistance attached to every word.

The Gemini and the Virgo usually don't mix, let alone mingle together. Much like the planet that rules over both signs, the reasoning behind this astrological segregation is both two-sided and Mercurial to the core.

Despite being associated with its verbal powers of communication, there almost always is an imbalance of communicative timing when the Gemini and Virgo first meet.

In other word-discussing words, when these two Mercury ruled signs first encounter each other, it's practically a guarantee one will be jabber-jawing in overdrive, leaving the other in a quietly subdued state of resentful annoyance, mostly due to not being able to get a word in edgewise. Or worse, the few bits of communication that actually manages to escape one Mercurial's lips were never even heard by being either completely ignored or spoken over by the other.

This in turn usually results in one side of the Mercurial fence thinking what a vapidly rude windbag the other is for talking too much, while dualistically rendering the other side into thinking what a stuck up snob the other is for barely saying a word all night.

From there things usually crescendo into the worst kind of Mercurial mess of misunderstanding where the two signs known for being the Chatty Chads and Cathys of the zodiac silently glare in opposite visual directions from each other, and ne'er a word is said for the remainder of the first meeting.

With those misunderstood first impressions in mind, this next piece of astrological information should neither shock nor surprise those who are Mercury ruled: The most deafening silence occurs whenever a Gemini or a Virgo is purposely not talking. Good times.

Okay, so the above was not romantic ticker tape parade material, but as stated in the beginning of this chapter, which your Love Author is compelled to once again repeat that you two ARE WORK!

If this meeting of the Mercurial minds wants to survive and avoid succumbing to an immediate mayhem of misunderstanding, both signs will need to gauge their words, and just as importantly, their listening powers, so that neither is made to feel as if its communications is being overlooked, ignored, or is in any way (shuddering) interrupted.

It's worth a shot, you two. So how about giving your Mercurial best at making the good times, as well as the open outlets of communication freely flow, Gemini and Virgo?

No matter the outcome, all romantic parties will be relieved to know its love union will at least never result in either sign being left in that most dreaded of mental states for the Mercury-ruled: Boredom.

Gemini-Libra

Welcome aboard, Gemini and Libra!

Please be sure the buckle portion of your seat belts of our romantic first–class, extra-cushioned passenger seats are firmly adjusted because we'll be reaching some seriously high altitudes on this air-signed love trip!

Astrologically, the best love unions are made of two people born beneath the same element. Since Gemini and Libra are both air signs, it doesn't get much better than when these two members of the house of easy breezes lift off into romantic flight.

Did either of you lovebirds know that the element both your signs foundationally share is unique amongst all the other elements of the zodiac? Of the four elements, the three signs that make up the element of air are each represented by non-animal symbols. The signs of Gemini, Libra, and Aquarius aren't associated with any kind of animal imagery due to their unifying element of air being firmly based within the functions of the rational mind.

Whereas an animal's first reaction to the outside world is purely instinctual and without planning or thought, an air sign taps into the processes of the rational mind whenever initially reacting to stimuli from its environment.

And in case either of your voraciously curious air-signed minds were wondering, the main processes of the rational mind are thought and communication.

The role communication plays for those born beneath the element of air is especially important since the breezy signs not only enjoy talking and conversing as often as possible, you Chatty Chads and Cathys of the zodiac NEED to do both on a regular basis in order to optimally function.

Mental stimulation is crucial for those born beneath the element of air. And since duality, or the joining of opposites, is the best form of mental stimulation for the family of fast talkers, it stands to follow that the state of being that an air sign loathes most is boredom.

With Gemini and Libra both being air-based, the mental stimulation factor flies up and away when these two signs begin dating. Neither will be able to learn enough about the other upon first meeting, nor will either be lacking in questions to ask about the other's history, background, likes, and just as important, dislikes.

Probably the best reason why the signs of Gemini and Libra are so romantically compatible is because this astrological combo has one of the highest statistical probabilities against either air sign from becoming bored.

While further explaining the differing natures between your signs, do enjoy our newly converted cedar wood Finnish sauna flight cabin, Gemini and Libra, and be sure to have a member of our love crew stimulate the blood flow to your open pores with our newly purchased L.L.Bean birch branches.

Air signed romantic first class does have its privileges. So far we've described the Gemini Libra dating process after it has already been put into full effect. A trait shared by many an air sign that has yet to be mentioned is the pleasure it derives from the social act of flirting. Many times the twins and the scales will delay officially dating if only for the purpose of prolonging the sweet anticipation and romantic innuendo created when either sign flirts with the other.

Both signs need to keep in mind the possible drawbacks regarding the art of flirtation's delicate nature, as well as its limited range of romantic freshness. Hopefully the Libra won't put the romantic idealism into overdrive by never knowing when the flirting ends and the dating begins. Just as hopefully, the Gemini doesn't drive the overall dating process into a crashing halt by steering its words of playful innuendo into any kind of hardcore talk bordering on verbal porno.

Now, this zephyr-like match up of air signs isn't comprised solely of romantic easy breezes. Let's begin the parlay of romantically perishable potential that could give possible cause to any kind of turbulence during the course of your air-signed love flight.

Truth be told, the first representatives of the windy element have a tendency to bend the truth. Said another way, the twins expand upon their words with exaggeration or omission or dare it be said, at times can speak of things with only partial veracity. In other words, Geminis, especially of the unevolved kind, have a penchant to lie.

Most certainly not everyone born beneath the first of the air signs are truth-benders, but the portion of the twinish population that does have a propensity for honesty alteration needs to get that trait out of its astrological system if it plans on committing itself with a romantic partner born beneath the sign whose astrological symbol are the scales of TRUTH, AKA Libra.

Even what's considered a harmless white lie by most has the potential to offend a scales person to high-minded heaven. Tampering with the truth in any degree can put your relationship with your Libran lover in serious jeopardy if not verbally kept under wraps, twin boys and girls.

While speaking the raw and naked truth, since we're discussing the inherent flaws associated with each air sign's astrological character, your Love Author must be as equally upfront and honest with the middle representatives of the talking headed element (Pssst. This means you, Libra).

Despite being adamant purveyors of truth, the sign of the scales isn't necessarily associated with the most aggressive kind of rational thought processes: decisiveness.

Waiting for the typical Libran to make any kind of non-life threatening decision can be likened to watching the seasons change or listening to one's hair grow. The weighing of choices back and forth is often THAT drawn out and time consuming.

For the rest of the zodiac, waiting for the middle representative of air to make a definite decision can be a drawn out nuisance, but for the sign inherently lacking even the slightest bit of patience (Psssst. This means you, Gemini), standing on the sidelines while the Libra's scales hem and haw over and over can be downright life threatening.

In order to keep things romantically running as smoothly and as non-life threatening as possible, your Love Author cannot strongly enough suggest the Libran allow its Gemini love interest to pre-decide the following before every date: which movie to be seen and which restaurant to go to eat.

Should the Gemini pre-determine those little romantic decisions ahead of time, it may be pleasantly surprised to hear the Libran's relief-filled thanks for sparing it the mentally torturous burden that would have taken up nearly half of the evening's allotted dating time.

Lastly, if both air signs want to keep their love union flying high, they'll each need to gauge themselves from spreading their air currents too thin. Gemini and Libra are two of the most sociable signs of the zodiac. Both air signs tend to have an extremely wide network of friends and acquaintances, and their social calendars are usually solidly booked well before the dating process even commences.

Tone down the social engagements and be mindful of overextending yourselves, especially when first dating, Gemini and Libra. Focus your attentions on your air-signed love interest so as to keep him or her from being dropped to distraction even before your airy union is given the chance to take off the romantic runway and soar.

To bring us back on flying track, as you two breezy lovers were about to be reminded about the Gemini Libra love union having one of the highest levels of harmonious compatibility amongst all other astrological combinations, your Love Author would like to announce the air-signed VIP first-class love trip has simultaneously reached its highest altitude of flight.

If the twins and the scales manage to keep their social selves securely grounded, then the sky's the limit for you airy ones to soar to romantic heights never before seen or experienced.

Gemini–Scorpio

Let me guess, you two. Upon informing your closest friends and relations that the Gemini was joining romantic forces with the Scorpio, the reaction rendered by many could only be described as odd at best. Correct?

A reaction of catching one's facial self, comprised of covered-up surprise with just as quickly covered-up confusion, results in a furrowed-brow half-smile similar to when one chomps down on the side periphery of the tongue in the middle of a formal dinner.

To be frank, Twins and Scorpion, there's no set reaction, nor even a standard proper response. While we're at it, there are no generally accepted rules of mannered etiquette as to how one should react whenever being informed the Gemini and the Scorpio have begun dating.

Most of the outside world's weirdness of reaction upon first being informed of the twins scorpion love union is actually based in the following: The romantic joining of the Gemini with the Scorpio wins first prize for the astrological pairing that's the most unobvious!

Tell the confusion-rendering couple what they've won, Johnny!

Johnny?

(The camera pans away from our Love Author, across the studio audience, to a headphoned Johnny, whose face has just contorted into a strange, brow-furrowed half-smile, as if orally encountering a slice of aluminum foil while in mid-hamburger bite.)

So Gemini, Scorpio. How's about we make things even more romantically confusing by getting hyper-astrologically technical!

When looking at the prototypical wheel of the zodiac, the sign of Scorpio lies at a 150 degree angle to the sign of Gemini. The proper astrological term for this very particular angle is the quincunx.

Say it along with me, audience: Ku-win-kwunx. Very good!

The quincunx is also known by the much easier pronounced astrological reference word "inconjunct." When two signs are placed at an inconjunct angle of each other, nothing remotely matches, and every inherent aspect of one sign is square pegged against the natural energies of the other.

Some keywords associated with the inconjunct are: redirection, challenge, diversion, and requires adjustment.

As stated earlier, matching up the Gemini with the Scorpio is an astrological combination that most of the outside world has a hard time picturing due to the union's high factor of unobviousness. When viewed individually, one would think the person born beneath the sign of the twins and the individual born under the sign of the desert deadly were hardcore polar opposites. Each sign's inherent energies seem that diametrically different when compared to each other.

Airy Gemini is considered one of if not the lightest sign of the zodiac. Those born beneath the twins tend to have an easy breezy, light hearted approach to things and don't enjoy getting bogged down by anything too deep or intense.

Intensity is the middle name of the Scorpio. The middle representative of water probes its world with such depth of feeling that an ever intense approach is its sign's standard for living life at large, which makes the sign of the Scorpion one of the heaviest of all the Zodiac.

Gemini is ruled by Mercury, the planet that oversees the rational mind and all that is conscious. Scorpio is ruled by Pluto, the planet that oversees the irrational mind and all that is subconscious.

The Gemini loves to gab on the phone and can engage in small talk for hours! The Scorpio secretly desires non-necessity small talk be made an illegal offense, and the only variation of gabbing it allows would be the kind reserved for emergencies.

A Scorpio can keep a secret until the grave. Many will wish a Gemini an early grave for its inability to keep a secret for more than five minutes.

Change is openly embraced by the Gemini. So much that its openness to change can lead to nothing ever being brought to full completion due to the twinish person dropping whatever it's doing in order to begin a newer, cooler thing. Change for the Scorpio is one of the dirtiest words in its all-controlling vocabulary. So much that the Scorpio will go to the greatest lengths possible just to resist the forces of change, all the while never getting anything started, let alone completed.

Romantically, the Gemini loves the touch and go playfulness of flirting, tends to hold off on getting too serious with any one love interest, and likes to feel as if it always has the option of playing the field. Romantically, the Scorpio takes no prisoners when in love and hunts to kill. It loves with such intensity it's only natural for the Scorpio to commit soon after meeting the object of its most intense affections. And Pluto have mercy on its lover's soul should the Scorpio's love interest attempt to cheat or romantically play the field.

As you can clearly see, touch, taste, and whatever other senses there are, this is not the most cut and dry of romantic setups. The nature of the quincunx relationship is so vacillating, there is no standardized best approach a Gemini and Scorpio can reliably take when dating each other. Every combination of twin and tail zinger will be drastically unique in its unobviousness.

Since this duo is so uncommonly unique, it's highly recommended both signs will at some point need to display its most Nietzsche-like behavior traits in order to assure any kind of relationship longevity.

Nietzsche is a German philosopher dude who more or less (much less than more) said the following to a bunch of other German dudes, "That which does not kill the Gemini, nor the Scorpio, makes them stronger."

Those born beneath the sign of the twins may risk spontaneously combusting, but the air-signed portion of this love union will need to exercise great patience while all romantic parties adjust to each other's very different energies. That and the Gemini's Tazmanian devil self will be required to slow down to an acceptable level of unblurry visibility if it wishes to have its Scorpio partner's intensely loving nature be directed towards its general direction.

That's quite the breeze when compared to the Nietzschian advice for those born beneath the sign of the desert deadly. You want this most unobvious of love duos to not just survive but thrive, Scorpio?

It all comes down to five words for you intense ones: LIGHTEN UP AND LAUGH OFTEN.

Whoa! Keep your distance, tail zingers! Your sign prefers the flow of communication to be direct and simple, am I right? Your Love Author will proceed to move backwards very quickly from all of the ever-approaching poisonous appendages as he begs those born beneath the most intense of signs to romantically ponder things.

Despite all the inconjunct talk about how unobvious those born beneath the twins and the scorpion inherently are, the two signs share a unique bond that once again is far from obvious and based on their planetary rulers when viewing both from a mythological perspective.

Gemini's planetary ruler is Mercury, the mythological Messenger of the Gods, and Scorpio's is Pluto, the mythological ruler of the Underworld. In the land of ancient myth, both mortal and immortal alike were forbidden to ever set foot in Pluto's dark realm, with one exception—Mercury, the deity with the lightest of winged feet.

Go ahead, Gemini and Scorpio. Give it a go. The romantic rewards may be just as unobvious as the nature of your love union but may turn out to be quite worth it in the long run if both sides put its best foot forward, be it heavy or light.

Gemini–Sagittarius

(Entering room.) Oh, hey! Gemini. Sagittarius.

(Casually strolling past, stopping mid-step to give each of you a prolonged glancing over.)

If I didn't know any better, my view upon entering the room just now of the two of you sitting all relaxed and casually hanging out usually wouldn't give me cause to wonder if anything out of the ordinary was going on.

But I do know better. Much, much better.

I just happen to know the astrological fact that the twins and the centaur are polar opposites of each other, and not to be trite in a nasal Paula Abdul way, but opposites attract.

And when two astrological opposites are within close physical proximity of each other, the attraction factor turns into an all-out starved shark feeding frenzy of kissing touchy feely!

Hey, lighten up you two! There's nothing wrong with the romantic fact that your Love Author is astrologically savvy enough to deduce that just a few moments ago, you both were groping for each other like wild primates.

Some would say you oppositely attracted lovebirds were merely obeying an inalterable law of both astrology and science.

Remember those magnet experiments used in junior high to demonstrate the law of attraction? Take those same oppositely charged pieces of metal that slammed into each other whenever one was within remote proximity of the other, except now one of the magnets is called Gemini and the other Sagittarius.

(Uncomfortable silence.)

Okay then! Let's skip the magnet talk and give both of you an overview of each other's individual astrological backgrounds to see just how different, as well as similar, you two are together.

For starters, Gemini is ruled by Mercury, the smallest planet in all the solar system, and Sagittarius is ruled by Jupiter, the biggest space ball of them all. That one juxtaposition of difference between your signs should always be kept in mind whenever your energies are compared, contrasted, or bound together in either wedded bliss or tongue-blistering divorce court.

Mercury's influence makes the Gemini mentally curious about every subject within the known universe, motivating the twins to learn a little something about everything. Jupiter's massive influence provides enough motivational pull for the Sagittarius to move way, way back from the fine print of its world in order for it to see the overall big picture, many times without a single detail in its far reaching sight.

Gemini, your naturally ruling house is the third, which oversees a person's local area or overall neighborhood of residence. Sagittarius, your naturally ruling house is the ninth, which oversees any kind of long distance travel; the more exotic and further away from what one is familiar with, the better.

Even with all of the above differences mentioned, the rule with polar opposites is they share just as many similarities as oppositions. Gemini and Sagittarius are both mutable signs by quality, thus they share the same mutable traits dealing with the theme of variety.

These two signs are the multitaskers of the zodiac. Both the Gemini and the Sagittarius function best doing as many things as they can simultaneously. So much that if forced to do one task at a time, either sign would most likely screw it up. Why? The dreaded curse prevalent amongst those born beneath any of the mutable signs: Boredom.

Both signs get into their fair share of trouble due to making any attempts necessary just to avoid being bored at all costs.

When applied to the actual dating process, the mutable signed theme of variety dualistically can become either highly positive or negative as the Gemini and Sagittarius become better romantically acquainted with each other.

Both signs are talkers and can chat anyone up at any time. Thus, people born beneath the sign of the twins and the centaur tend to individually have a slew of friends and acquaintances. Pair these two highly social creatures romantically together and the network of friends and acquaintances covers at least a third of the local population.

The extended social circles alone should safeguard either sign from ever experiencing any kind of encroaching boredom. Additional forms of protection from the dreaded B-word are the twins and the centaur's wide range of interests and activities, along with the enjoyment of becoming better familiar with what was previously untried or not yet known. But even with that said, variety does have its down sides.

With both signs so powerfully attracted to one another, and with so many things to do and people to see, the Gemini and Sagittarius will naturally want to spend every hyper busy moment together in the early phases of dating. However, if not monitored, both signs will busy themselves right into an extensive period of illness from burning themselves out after being oblivious to their body's warning signs of oncoming physical exhaustion.

This leaves us with the most detrimental of potential pitfalls that could plague the Gemini Sagittarius love union. With the signs of the twins and the centaur both being a mutable astrological quality, and since mutable energy craves regular doses of variety and change as often as possible, the Gemini and the Sagittarian commonly share the following personality flaw. They cheat.

The above statement does not refer to either sign possessing a natural proclivity of breaking the rules of play associated with any standard parlor game, twins and centaurs.

Said another way, many Geminis and Sagittarians of the unevolved kind tend to be cheaters/philanderers/make with the bed creaks behind their lovers' back. You get the adulterous picture.

Certainly not every twin and centaur sins against relationships by way of being unfaithful, mind you. And more times than not, those zodiacal carbon copies and pony boys and girls that actually do commit their lustful deeds of lasciviousness consistently do so for the same reoccurring reason. Which is what, class?

"Because they were bored, Mr. Love Author."

'Nuff said.

One final factor in giving the astrological law of polar opposites full scope to the two fastest moving (and groping) of multitasking signs. Attraction is what brings the polar opposites together, which in turn, yields some fast and furious bed creaking. At a bare minimum, some heavy pawing as your Love Author almost uncomfortably witnessed firsthand with his unknowing entrance upon the Gemini-Sagittarius version of *Wild Thing Kingdom*.

Even with that blushingly said, if there is nothing more other than a few fast and furious bed creaks, or nothing of binding common interest beyond the initial attraction, the polarized spark will be snuffed out just as quickly as it blowtorched began. Why?

Many times the flames of opposing desire are quickly doused due to both signs driving each other naturally crazy after the passing of five post-bed creaking minutes, give or take.

Ah, but if the polar opposites can stand each other's presence for more than five minutes post-you know, and have a thing or two they like about the other or share a few things in common, then here is where we find those keeper relationships that stay together.

In fact, when there are binding ties that extend beyond the initial animal attraction, many of these dualistic duos literally last until death do they polar opposite part.

Gemini–Capricorn

(Shhhhh! Here they come!)

Oh, hi, Gemini. Capricorn.

Don't you two look, ummmmm (coached whisper hissed from distant corner of room—"NICE!") NICE! That's right! (Nervously giggling.) You two as a couple sure do look super nice ... and stuff.

And by nice, I mean romantically normal nice! Not different from the rest nice or far from typical nice. Just nice, as in nice and normal!

What other word is there that could better describe the black sheep couple of the zodiac?

DARN IT! Not even a few pages of this chapter have fully turned before the false bubble of romantic niceties got blown to bits!

My apologies, Gemini and Capricorn. At this uncomfortable blurting-out-loud point, your Love Author may as well just say what needs to be said regarding the romantic teaming up between your signs.

Coupling a person born beneath the sign of the twins with another born under the sign of the mountain goat is anything BUT romantically normal or nice. This particular pairing of signs is about as different and non-normal as one can romantically imagine. So what's with all the non-normal talk, twins and goats? In a word, the quincunx. Ask a non-normal question, get a non-normal answer.

When looking at the prototypical wheel of the zodiac, the sign of Gemini lies at a 150 degree to the sign of Capricorn. The proper astrological term for this very particular and peculiar angle is the quincunx.

Everyone repeat along with me. Ready? Ku-win-kwunx. Very good!

The quincunx is also known by the much easier pronounced, astrological reference word, "inconjunct." When two signs are placed at an inconjunct angle of each other, nothing remotely matches, and every inherent aspect of one sign is square pegged against the natural energies of the other. Some keywords associated with the inconjunct are: redirection, challenge, diversion, and requires adjustment.

Matching up the Gemini with the Capricorn is an astrological combination that most of the outside world has a hard time picturing due to the union's high factor of unobviousness. Hence, the rest of the world makes a surface pre-judgment of the twins goat romantic union as anything but typical or normal.

When viewed individually, one would think the person born beneath the sign of the twins and the individual born under the sign of the mystic mountain goat were polar opposites. Each sign's inherent energies seem that diametrically different when compared to each other.

The Gemini's inner child is always on call and readily available, as evidenced by its spontaneous bouts of silliness or laughter. The Capricorn has no inner child, even when it was a child, due to being given adult responsibilities early on in life which left them no time for being spontaneous, let alone for silliness or laughter.

The Capricorn is all about status and is hyper sensitive on how it comes across to the public. The Gemini, not so much.

The Gemini loves to chit chat and can spark up a conversation with just about anybody. The Capricorn won't converse with just anybody, especially those it doesn't know well.

The Capricorn is all about being discreet. Look up the word indiscreet in the dictionary and you'll find an image of Gemini, the blabbermouth of the zodiac.

The Gemini communicates as fast and furious as a teenager. The Capricorn communicates as detached and formal as a bank teller.

The Capricorn usually chooses a goal early on in life and will work ceaselessly to eventually achieve it. The Gemini may choose a goal early on in the day, but it'll eventually cease being its first choice by the end of it.

The Capricorn usually hones its work or trade skills in order to become a master specialist in a choice area of its career. The Gemini's vacillating mental state usually makes it a jack of all trades and master of none.

From an early age, the Gemini has a lightning fast sense of humor that's evident by its ability to crack jokes and mimic impressions of others. The Capricorn's sense of humor is non-existent before the age of forty, which is evident by its inability to barely crack a smile before that age, and will often mimic wild laughter in response to the many jokes it doesn't get.

The Gemini loves being around people its own age. The Capricorn loves being around people who are significantly older or younger, and almost never its own age.

The essence of the quincunx relationship is so non-normal there isn't any kind of standardized approach a Gemini and Capricorn can reliably take when dating each other.

Every combination of twin and goat will be drastically unique in its unobviousness.

Since this duo is so uncommonly unique, it's highly recommended both signs will at some point need to display its most Nietzsche-like behavior traits in order to assure any kind of relationship longevity.

Nietzsche was a German philosopher dude who more or less (much less than more) said the following to a bunch of other German dudes, "That which does not kill the Gemini or the Capricorn, makes them stronger."

Those born beneath the sign of the twins may risk the dangerous repercussion of spontaneously combusting, but the air-signed portion of this love union will need to exercise great patience while all romantic parties adjust to each other's very different energies. That, and the Gemini's Tasmanian devil self will be required to slow down to an acceptable level of visibility if it wishes to have its Capricorn love interest's grounded and pragmatic attentions be directed towards its general direction.

Cappies, your love advice is far more challenging, but it's not like your sign's ever had things handed to them on a silver platter. Am I right?

Want this most unobvious of duos to not just survive but thrive, goat guys and girls? Then the Capricorn mustn't allow itself to worry about what anyone else says or thinks about your Gemini love union.

A fuller phrasing of worry or care was originally used in the previous sentence, but I then realized your sign is great at working hard, not working miracles.

So go ahead, twins and goats. Give it your best romantic shot together!

If the Gemini manages to slow its speedy self down enough for the Capricorn to gradually develop a "devil may care" attitude about its unobvious love union, then the black sheep couple of the zodiac has the potential of transforming into a blue ribbon winner of a romantic partnership.

Gemini-Aquarius

Welcome aboard, Gemini and Aquarius!

Please be sure the buckle portion of your seat belts of our romantic first class extra-cushioned passenger seats are firmly adjusted, because we'll be reaching some seriously high altitudes on this air-signed love trip!

Astrologically, the best couplings are those made of two people born beneath the same element. Since Gemini and Aquarius are both air signs, it really doesn't get much better than when these two members of the house of easy breezes lift off into romantic flight together.

Did either of you lovebirds know that the element both your signs foundationally share is unique amongst all the other elements of the zodiac?

The three signs that make up the element of air are each represented by non-animal symbols. The signs of Gemini, Libra, and Aquarius aren't associated with any kind of animal imagery due to their unifying element of air being based within the functions of the rational mind.

Whereas an animal's first reaction to the outside world is purely instinctual, an air sign chooses from the processes of the rational mind whenever initially reacting to any given stimuli from its environment.

In case your air-signed curiosities were wondering, the processes of the rational mind are thought and communication

Being mentally stimulated is of utmost importance to those born beneath the element of air. And since duality, or the joining of opposites, is the best form of mental stimulation for the family of fast talkers, it stands to follow the state of being the air sign loathes most is boredom.

With Gemini and Aquarius both being air based, the mental stimulation factor goes through the proverbial roof when these two signs first begin dating. Neither will be able to learn enough about the other upon first meeting, nor will either be lacking in questions to ask about the other's history, background, likes, and (just as dualistically important) dislikes.

Probably the best reason why the signs of twins and the water bearer are so romantically compatible is due to this particular coupling having one of the highest probabilities against either airy person from becoming bored. Both signs' inherent traits of needing to be in a near constant state of heightened mental stimulation, along with a voracious hunger to learn, should keep things romantically fresh and intellectually interesting for all air-signed parties involved.

Even with that said, it must be noted this zephyr-like match-up between the first and the last of the air elementals isn't comprised strictly of romantic easy breezes.

Despite both signs belonging to the element of communication, the twins and the water bearer each has its own unique set of communicative challenges that exist within each other's inherent personalities.

While explaining the different communicative natures between your signs, go enjoy our newly converted cedar wood Finnish sauna flight cabin, Gemini and Aquarius, and be sure to have a member of our love crew stimulate the blood flow to your skin with our newly purchased L.L.Bean birch branches.

Air signed romantic first class does have its privileges.

With Gemini being the first zodiacal representative of the element of air, the twins' need to communicate is at its most pure and concentrated. It's not simply that a Gemini likes to talk, it astrologically NEEDS to talk.

If too much time passes where the Gemini is denied the opportunity to share the countless thoughts that crosses its inquisitively curious mind, or if the twinish person goes for too long without a conversational outlet to socially chit chat with, it dangerously runs the risk of succumbing to Gemini power babble.

The typical twins' need to gab makes its mouth move fast and furiously in the presence of any given stranger off the street, but when in power babble mode, many a Gemini's revved-up chatter will fire off involuntarily, often without the presence of any other breathing life forms nearby.

The first representatives of each of the four elements display its element's essence at its most pure and concentrated form. When that elemental essence is observed through a lens of negativity, the sign of the twins becomes the air sign most susceptible to the darkest form of communication known to modern man: gossip.

The Gemini who gossips is, in reality, an air sign who doubts its own sense of intelligence and self-worth. The more the first of the air signs refuses to look within, the more its mutable energies will be spent nosily probing into the affairs of others, where every petty particle of dirt it digs up is broadcasted to the outside world via the communicative sin of gossip.

It would behoove the first of the air signs to keep this golden Gemini rule regarding the power communication holds in its life: The more evolved the twinish person, the more selectively efficient its cleverly witty words shall be.

Breezily blowing forward to the mental workings of the last of the airy bunch...

The sprawling intellectual landscape that is the mental home turf of the typical Aquarian is impressively vast. Yet for many a water bearer, it can be distantly lonely. The tower of the Aquarian mind tends to soar above the mental structures of all the other residents of the zodiac, yet its stratospheric altitude can make it quite a cold place.

The last representative of each of the four elements makes its element's essence the most far reaching to affect entire groups and the masses at large. With the foundation of air being human intellect, it's no wonder the vast majority of the world's most innovative thinkers, composers, and inventors were born beneath the sign of the water bearer.

Yet even with that said, those born beneath this most intellectual of signs tend to be lone wolves who spend a majority of their thinking time locked within their own ivory towers of high intellect.

Unfortunately for many a twenty-first century Aquarian, the challenges experienced in relating to popular culture and those who readily partake in it seem to get more and more difficult with each passing year, given the pervasive dumbing down of nearly every aspect of today's society.

When further applying the aspect of duality to the most cerebral sign of the airy family, the more intellectually elite the mind of the water bearer is, the less common the Aquarian's social skills and ability to relate to others shall be.

The best weapon an Aquarian can wield whenever sensing the air becoming heavy with unrelated misunderstanding? Breathing.

Despite the elemental foundation of both Gemini and Aquarius consisting of the very stuff we breathe in, every member of the airy family has a tendency to barely breathe throughout most of its mentally active day. Taking the time to breathe is the most effective option the air sign has at keeping its mind and energy as light as the element that rules over them.

Now that we've gotten the communicative down sides of both your signs discussed and out of the way, every set of twins and water bearer should prepare to revel with bated breath regarding each other's airy traits that are of a thoroughly positive nature.

The brain of the brilliant Aquarian will gladly follow the Gemini's brightly bouncing lead as the twinish person gives its water bearer love interest a multifaceted show-and-tell of the myriad of things that interests its mentally voracious mind.

Likewise, the Gemini will be stunned to silence upon hearing every unique thought of inventive genius and innovative originality that springs forth from the futuristic mind of its Aquarian significant other.

Your Love Author would like to announce to our VIP first class that your air-signed love trip has now reached its highest altitude of flight.

It must also be mentioned if both the twins and the water bearer manage to stay mindful of each other's specific communicative challenges, then the sky's the limit for you airy ones to soar to heights never before seen or experienced.

Gemini-Pisces

Hold up, Gemini and Pisces. I need to step out for a bit and find me a Red Bull and any cheap excuse of an energy bar 'cause you two are WORK.

Alrighty then! Now that I've done what's humanly best to crank my energies up to as maximum a non-illegal level as I can, allow your Love Author to start by being brutally blunt: The two of you are SURE you're dating each other, right?

I should preface things by stating that every sign has the potential to work together in a romantically involved way, it's just that some signs take a lot more work to achieve a state of equilibrium than others. And just to repeat what I stated earlier, you two are WORK!

The inherent energies and overall personalities of the Gemini and the Pisces operate from such vastly different foundational points that combining these two signs in any kind of one-on-one partnership requires a consistent level of hard work from both parties. So much that your Love Author will be the first to admit the work needed to keep the Gemini Pisces union romantically solvent can be downright back breaking at times!

Of the twelves signs, Gemini and Pisces are each other's biggest challenge to relate with naturally due to each sign's placement on the zodiac wheel. They are positioned from each other at the harshest astrological angle possible of 90 degrees, which is better known as the square.

When two signs square each other, a consistently high probability exists for either sign to easily rub the other the wrong way, quite often because either or both signs are simply being its natural self. For the most part, the core differences within this astrological duo all boils down to their brains.

Allow your Love Author to physically explain quite literally.

Gemini is an air sign. Pisces is a water sign. The air signs initially react to the outside world via the functions of the left hemisphere of their brain. The water signs initially react to the outside world via their brain's right hemisphere.

The left hemisphere of the brain is otherwise known as the rational mind. The right hemisphere of the brain is otherwise known as the emotional and intuitive mind.

A left hemisphered person is motivated to exercise the processes of the rational mind, which are thought and communication.

For those who still may be unsure as to the exact nature of these rational processes, the latter of the two can be given further elaborate description. Communication can also be categorized as talking, speaking, blabbing, yakking, chatting, and jabberjawing.

A right hemisphered person is motivated most by its emotions and/or intuition.

Sounds easy enough, right? Ah, but one last rule of mental play regarding all this brain matter must be mentioned.

We humans have total control over the functions of our left hemispheres and no control whatsoever over the functions of our brain's right hemispheres.

Air signs generally avoid the emotional realm altogether due to the rational mind having no control over those messy things that are generated from the brain's non-rational hemisphere. Hence, most Geminis function from an overall environment that's "emotions lite" with many a twins person opting more towards an "emotions free" structure of living.

In fact, the mental muscles of those born beneath the element of air are so inherently strong, their left hemispheres will quite often wrestle their feelings into submission by rationalizing them far from the surface of their conscious minds as often as possible.

Conversely, since they operate from their right hemispheres, the water signs will initially sense how something makes them feel at first before any kind of thinking is done and prior to any first actions being taken.

Human feelings may be the astrological foundation for every member of the family of wet, but for the last representatives of the watery element, emotions hold a bit more influence besides merely being a first reaction to stimuli from the outside world.

Imagine if you can the Pisces as a radar station that picks up all energies intuitive and/or emotional from the general atmosphere that surrounds them. The typical Piscean will by default naturally tune into whatever emotional energies are present within its environment at any given time, be those energies from the past, present, or future.

The tricky part is the Pisces always has its emotional radar on.

Due to its emotional radar working 24/7, the world for the typical Piscean is often perceived as a very overwhelming place, rendering a goodly portion of the fish community speechless or very quiet for the better part of their day.

The typical fish person's reactive state of being is an environment where words simply don't cut it most of the intuitive time.

Verbal communication usually doesn't suffice in relaying all the feeling-sensitive energies most fish folk take in on a daily basis whether they're operating from the conscious or subconscious mind or functioning with awake alertness or from the deepest of dream states.

Returning once more to the inherent challenges with romantically pairing the Gemini with the Pisces, one part of this dynamic astrological duo identifies its core sense of self through the act of verbal communication (Gemini), and the other half finds that very same act to be a distractive nuisance, which often falls short of adequately expressing its natural state of emotional being (Pisces).

Fun, huh?

Even when these two signs first meet, misinterpreted misunderstandings usually run rampant from the get go. The Gemini will often initially misinterpret the Piscean's silent nature as either being stuck-up, standoffish, or disapproving. The Pisces will often misinterpret the Gemini as an overbearing windbag that's utterly self-possessed. Good times.

Okay, so the above was not ticker tape parade material, but as I've said earlier before in this chapter, and as I am compelled to once again repeat, you two ARE WORK!

Gemini and Pisces, more often than not there will be choice moments over the course of your relationship where neither of you will even remotely be near the other on the same page of understanding, resulting in both romantic parties having not the slightest clue where the other is coming from.

Fortunately, the twins and the fish are both mutable signs. Of all the astrological qualities, signs that are mutable adapt to change the quickest. Rather than dropping the relationship ball should an impasse occur as two cardinal signs are prone to do, or hold grudges against each other after an uncompromising stalemate of stubbornness has taken place as with two fixed signs, the mutables are naturally equipped with a personality trait that could be the saving grace to allow their relationship to withstand any given gridlock of mutual misunderstanding.

The mutable signs are able to let go and move on. Should the Gemini and the Pisces experience a standoff of mutual misunderstanding, it's highly recommended both signs get out of each other's way and allow a little time to pass. The twins' and fish's mutable ability to adapt can allow either sign to let go of whatever differences there were, which hopefully will prevent said differences from eventually becoming the cause of their love union's overall demise.

It all comes down to whether both mutables are willing to contribute each other's fair share of the adapting and adjusting work necessary for their partnership to not just thrive but survive. Should that not be the case, this particular astrological pairing is doomed to crash and burn as quickly as it shakily started.

But hey, you never know unless you try, Gemini and Pisces. So roll up those sleeves and get cracking! Your mutual efforts could very well pay off in the romantic long run.

Cancer-Cancer

Since all romantic parties were born beneath a sign where the past plays a major force of influence, your Love Author asks both crabs to take one of his hands into each of your respective claws, GENTLY AND NO SQUEEZING, in order to journey with him back through times of old.

Actually, it's only to the year 1991, and strictly for comic commercial purposes. In November of that year, *Saturday Night Live* added another gem to its treasure chest of commercial parodies. This particular jewel of advertising buffoonery was entitled, "The Love Toilet."

The pseudo-sponsor presented Victoria Jackson and Kevin Nealon portraying lovers who are utterly enamored with each other. The infatuated pair is at first shown partaking in various outside activities together while an announcer's voice can be heard in the background: "You dine together. You play together. You sleep together. You even bathe together."

The visuals then move indoors as the camera zooms in on Victoria and Kevin lovingly staring into each other's eyes while sitting next to but facing each other on what appears to be some sort of ceramic, backless couch.

The announcer then purrs, "So why not share the most intimate moment of them all? With ... The Love Toilet."

Hopefully everyone got the waste product punchline since the details regarding this powder room parody needn't be discussed any further. The overall purpose behind partially describing such potty pranks, you crabs may be pondering?

When two Cancers join romantic forces, there is a higher than usual probability of an environment being mutually made as scarily similar as the aforementioned "Love Toilet" scenario.

If the same signed couple wishes to avoid having its budding bloom of a romantic relationship from immediately going straight down the love toilet, the overall traits of the Cancerian personality must be analyzed with a crab-clawed comb.

The flow of human emotion is at the core of every water sign, and what many humans, including many a water-based one, tend to forget is that emotions are non-rational things.

The rational mind resides strictly within the left hemisphere of the human brain. Anything emotional or intuitive is housed within the brain's right hemisphere.

When dealing with any and all stimuli from the outside world, those born beneath the element of water will utilize their emotions first and foremost. The water sign will literally determine how something makes it FEEL before going into any kind of action or subsequent reaction.

Non-water signs like to think their feelings fit in custom-made gift-boxes where each emotion resides in a nice little compartment while waiting to be called out at some point in the distant future.

The water signs know better. They know all too well that human emotion is a force much like Mother Nature herself. We cannot MAKE the weather happen; we live with it and adjust accordingly whenever it chooses to change. Those born beneath the element of wet naturally understand they have no control over true emotion when it hits their radar.

When two Cancers begin dating, they're more than likely to develop an innately intuitive sense of the other's presence without either crab needing to analytically discuss how or why it has come about. Nor will one water sign necessarily have to explain to the other what is being mutually felt together.

In spite of the aforementioned world of wordless wonder created whenever two water signs emotionally bond, in order for every human relationship on this planet to not only thrive but survive, communication must be regularly and mutually exercised.

Once an emotional bond has been firmly established, all romantically wet parties will need to guard against a particular form of communication killing behavior utilized by many an unevolved water sign: passive aggression.

Passive aggression is a non-confrontational tactic where one states its case, displays its willfulness, or attempts to get one's way through behavior that is both non-active and non-communicative that's never direct but always undermining.

Your Love Author likes to believe that open communication is the solution for any kind of deep-seeded problem in a relationship, but not so in the case of passive aggression.

Should one water sign experience a constant and relentless show of passive aggressiveness over time from its water-signed lover, the best thing it can do is run.

At least the energy exerted will be put to good use versus the vast amount wasted in trying to directly confront the most non-direct of confrontational tactics.

Should open and clear communication not be implemented on a regular basis, it's almost an absolute guarantee the tacitly (AKA not spoken but understood) placid romantic waters two Cancers dive into together upon initially meeting will become dark and turbulent in no time soon thereafter.

Continuing with the basic astrological foundation behind the first of the Water signs, picture a crab as it sidles along the beach near the lapping waves of the ocean. The sea creature never runs freely forward. A crab's motion is always tentative. What gives this caution-filled animal the allowance for movement of any kind is the security and shelter the crab's hardened shell provides.

Now picture the Cancerian. The crab person functions best when it has the security of a home base. This is NOT the type of sign that can live out of a suitcase or on a friend's couch for an indefinite period of time.

Because the sign of Cancer is the first representative of its watery element, the two things that motivate those born beneath the sign of the crab most and provide it with the best sense of security are the two core aspects to human life: home and family.

When two Cancers join romantic forces, the aspects of home and family become even more influential from both the positive and negative spectrums.

Should two Cancers end up cohabitating in the same sand castle, it'll be one of the most comfortably inviting homes in the neighborhood. Not only will the casa de crab feel cozy and comfy, the crustacean home cooking will be second to none!

Where did you think the term "comfort food" came from? Two Capricorns shacking up together? Yeah, right.

But even Cancerian comfort has a downside if left unmonitored. Crab clutter. Cancer is also known as the sign of the pack rat. Partaking in such domestically efficient activities as regularly throwing things out and consolidating to make the most of its living space are traits that do not come naturally to the typical crustacean. Why? Everything in the crib o' crab holds sentimental value.

Take one Cancerian who has been consistently challenged by this concept, add another crustacean into the mix, and the casa de crab clutter becomes the hoarder house in no time.

I'll be honest with the two of you. It's not highly recommended for two people of the same sign to date each other. A double Cancer love union in particular risks the romantic danger of becoming a mutual crab cage of emotional co-dependency reminiscent of "The Love Toilet" where both wet ones are joined at the hip and hardly ever leave the confines of their sand castle.

Both Cancers will need to gauge the flow of feelings to ensure neither's emotions ever block vital aspects to their relationship's survival, such as open communication and mutual compromise.

Because if either water sign allows its emotions to rule the roost and uncontrollably run rampant, the casa de crab will quickly morph into the hoarder house with a leaking love toilet in no time flat.

Cancer-Leo

Come on in, Cancer and Leo!

Your Love Author whipped himself up a scrumptious meal which, by food group, marks the joining of romantic forces between your signs.

A combo plate consisting of succulent sushi placed atop the juiciest slab of prime rib.

My food has also been slathered with far too much wasabi, an observable detail that only now I am just noticing, given my tongue is currently morphing into a ballistic missile testing ground of burning heat.

(Eyes watering.) If you both would excuse me for just a moment? Many thanks.

(Sprinting into kitchen to douse entire face in water-filled sink of soaking dishes.)

My apologies, cats and crabs! I simply didn't foresee how downright sensitive things would become. Kind of like when the Cancer and the Leo begin dating each other.

Just so everyone is on the same astrological page, the signs of Cancer and Leo border each other on the big wheel of the zodiac. Despite the ocean waves washing directly upon the shores of the wild jungle, the crab and the lion are two very different astrological creatures that exist in two distinctly unique environments.

Technically the signs that border each other are categorized beneath a most unexciting descriptor of astrological compatibility: neutral.

(A solitary cough can be heard in the far off distance.)

Every sign has the potential to work together. Some combinations take a lot more work than others to achieve a state of equilibrium. With the joining of the signs considered to be neutral of each other, the state of equilibrium is something much like the solid borderline that naturally forms whenever oil and vinegar are put into the same container. In other words, mixing the two isn't a bad thing, but a whole lot of shaking is needed for there to be any kind of blend.

At their core, Cancer and Leo function from very different perspectives, making it seem as if these two signs lived on opposite sides of the globe versus being astrological next door neighbors.

Watery Cancer loves the comforting glow of its home and prefers being there over any kind of social engagement. Fiery Leo loves the glaring glow of the spotlight and prefers being at any kind of social engagement rather than at home.

A Cancer is motivated into action predominantly by two things in life, home and family, and tends to put itself and its own needs on the back burner whenever activated by either factor. What predominantly motivates a Leo into action is itself, and will often put the needs of others on the backburner in order to have its noticed.

When a Cancer is stressed or upset, not many notice at first due to it keeping things to itself, or by expecting others to figure things out by employing passively aggressive tactics. Many can't help but notice when a Leo is stressed or upset due to its seeming inability to not keep a thing to themselves, along with employing attention grabbing tactics of hyper-dramatics where nothing is left to figure out.

The Cancer wants nothing more than to have a baby. The Leo is nothing short of a big ol' baby when it doesn't get its way.

Even with the above core differences, the crab and the lion share a key common bond of a personality trait that happens to be one of the strongest components of either signs' core sense of self.

This chapter began with your Love Author attempting to emphasize this trait's importance by means of gustatory detail, since it will most likely determine the overall longevity of the Cancer Leo love union.

Each romantic party will need to be consistently mindful of this trait within the other if it wishes its partnership to have any kind of shelf life. And just as important, each will need to be consistently mindful of keeping this trait at bay within itself: SENSITIVITY.

Leo and Cancer share the distinction of being the two most sensitive signs of the zodiac. However, the way both signs express its heightened level of sensitivity differs just as much as its natural habitat.

Being a water sign, the Cancer expresses itself best through emotions. Since the sign of the crab is the first representative of the watery element, the most pure and unadulterated way a Cancer expresses its emotions is by nurturing others. If a Cancer is emotionally connected to someone, it literally will "mommy" that person in order to best express its emotional state, regardless if they are related by blood or not.

Want to make a Cancerian happy? Give full attention and thanks to its nurturing actions and energies.

Want to have a Cancerian turn into one big crab of hyper-sensitivity? Ignore its attempts to nurture.

Similar to when the feelings of an overly sensitive mom are hurt, the Cancer will wield the two most effective weapons that harness its sign's heightened sensitivity best, but through the most indirect of means: guilt and passive aggression.

The more the Cancerian removes the focus away from itself, the more those with whom it has issues with will squirm, eventually caving in to the immense pressure created by the Crab's passive aggression or guilt-heavy environment.

Whereas dear old mom is the best example of choice in comprehending the highly sensitive side of the Cancer, the Lion of both the actual jungle and fairy tale should be kept in mind whenever analyzing the acute level of sensitivity that lies within the personality of those born beneath the fire sign of Leo.

Unlike its moon-ruled neighbor who internalizes, the solar-ruled Leo likes to outwardly shine and is as externally expressive a sign as you'll ever hope to find.

The typical Leo is uber-sensitive to garnering the attentions of others, as well as possesses an intense awareness of how high it is placed on the pedestal of its partner's adoring affections.

Remember the fable of the lion who turns into a teary eyed kitten after having a thorn penetrate its paw? The roar of the astrological lion becomes even more ear-shatteringly sensitive should one downplay or worse, completely ignore a Leo, regardless if it is amorous or ill.

Now, let's take a Leo in an especially self-centered frame of mind and place it next to a Cancerian partner who is feeling a tad insecure at that exact same moment in romantic space and time. The Cancer will begin showering all of its nurturing energies towards the Leo, who at that time, just happens to be totally immersed in self-focused thought.

The Cancerian will then immediately proceed to interpret the Leo's self-concerned obliviousness as a response of rejection to its nurturing actions. It is only then that the solar-ruled Leo will emerge from its egocentric world by virtue of the temperature passive aggressively plummeting.

The Leo will then ask the Cancer if anything is wrong, to which the chill shall then become even more pronounced by the crab's arctic response of "no." Followed by all romantic parties being left to solitarily sink or swim in each of its self-imposed seas of sensitivity and self-defensive touchiness.

And the key for this love union of astrological next-door neighbors to have any kind of lasting romantic shelf life, Cancer and Leo? The two most sensitive signs of the zodiac are required to lighten up by not taking anything too personally or sensitively.

Sounds like a snap of the crab claw or an ease-filled lionly leap through romantic hoops, but is it? I'll let you two hyper-sensitive ones decide.

Cancer–Virgo

Crustaceans and Virgins, your Love Author presents before you one of the greatest examples of man's ingenuity known today: the Neolithic wooden water wells of Leipzig!

They may not sound like much, but Leipzig's wooden water wells hold a most unique distinction within man's history on this planet, given they are the oldest of their kind ever unearthed.

Scientists were able to determine the exact moment as to when these well-designed pieces of human innovation were created through the dendro-chronological process, a system of time measurement that determines the age of a piece of wood by the number of tree rings located within it.

Upon completing the testing process, the scientific community was stunned to discover the wells were constructed with wood that had fallen, been cleared, and masterfully constructed, nearly 7,000 years ago, which was some 2,000 years prior to the forging of metal tools in Europe.

Not only are these wooden artifacts the oldest of their kind ever made, your Love Author thought he'd go out on his own tree limb by theorizing these truly ancient inventions also tangibly represent the combined energies of the Cancer and the Virgo when joining romantic forces.

In astrology, the four elements of earth, air, fire, and water are naturally paired off. Each grouping consists of two elements that are cohesive, or naturally work well together, otherwise known as being complementary. Hence, the elements of fire and air, but more importantly for this particular pairing, the elements of earth and water are complementary to each other.

When looking at the basic natures of the Cancer and the Virgo by virtue of their elemental foundations, they share a central core trait: Security.

Picture a crab as it sidles along the beach near the lapping waves of the ocean. The sea creature never freely runs forward. A crab's motion is always tentative. What gives this caution-filled animal the allowance for movement of any kind is the security and shelter the crab's hardened shell provides.

Now, picture the Cancerian. The crab person functions best when it has the security of a home base. This is NOT the type of sign that can live out of a suitcase or on a friend's couch for an indefinite period of time.

The earth signs, including Virgo, are based in the tangible. Said in more modern terms, an earth sign is made to feel secure by the possessions it owns, how much money it has in the bank, and its work output.

Not only does Virgo belong to the element of earth, the sign of the harvest maiden is categorized as one of the three karmic signs, whose overall goal is to be of service to others. When combining the core traits of Virgo's earthy foundation of deriving security from the tangible, along with its karmic status of being a sign of service, the end result is work, work, and hmmm, what's that last one? Oh yeah. Work.

A Virgo can try doing one thing at a time, but most likely it will take longer than usual pursuing that dynamic of a route, due to the sheer drudgery of it all since it is astrologically designed to juggle vast numbers of tasks, assignments, and chores all at the same time.

Besides ancient water wells that are older than the hills themselves, the complementary dynamic between the elements of earth with water can also be likened to something much more modern and concrete: a river dam.

The key to a dam's effectiveness is its foundation. Thus, let us imagine communication to be the binding cement that holds the foundation of the Cancer Virgo relationship securely into place.

Open communication is a critical component for any given relationship between two humans to not only survive but thrive by virtue of it dispelling any erroneous assumptions being made between either/all parties.

Returning once more to those really old well thingies, since Cancer is the sign most influenced by the past and Virgo is the sign that functions best with any kind of detail, your Love Author would like to make this pairing's complementary nature as tangible as possible by providing details behind the Neolithic water wells' very distant beginnings.

Astrologically, the categorization of time and the evolutionary stages of humankind's development on this planet are known as the ages of man." Each age is assigned to one of the twelve signs of the zodiac and lasts anywhere from 1,500 to 2,000 years.

The age of Cancer is said to have occurred during the years of 8,600 B.C. to 6,450 B.C. and is known as the Neolithic revolution, since this is the era when the concept of civilized society officially began.

A new world was emerging from the Ice Age's retreating glaciers during the Neolithic revolution. However, those living on the planet at that time were forced to move to higher ground due to a good portion of the Earth's coastal regions being submerged beneath the rising sea levels caused by the deglaciation or melting process.

Upon reaching higher ground, the people of the post-Ice Age who had previously been nomadic wanderers found themselves in the general vicinity of other humans and began to form history's first villages and towns.

Also during this time, man's focus on home life became enhanced with the domestication of the first farm animals of pigs, goats, cows, and bees, along with the construction of society's first city, Jericho, which stands to this very day on the west bank of modern Palestine.

Given the themes of the ocean and the security derived from one's home, it's easy to see how the Neolithic revolution relates to the sign of the Crab, let alone this age of man being categorized as thoroughly Cancerian.

Additionally, Leipzig's wooden water wells not only display the influences of the sign of Virgo taking place during the Neolithic revolution, its construction as a whole embodies the solid cohesion created when the elements of water and earth join complementary forces.

The wells are tangible proof that our ancient ancestors were quite the hard working multi-taskers since the discovery shows those who settled down from a nomadic way of life during the post Ice Age were society's first farmers and carpenters.

The wooden structures not only survived for millennia, they also avoided the decaying process by being buried in waterlogged soil and even more fascinatingly, by being comprised of a variety of materials besides timber wood.

The wells managed to stay intact through the passage of the centuries by having layers of waterlogging organic materials, such as plant remains, bark, and bast fiber cords added to the wood's foundation.

Multi-tasking. Earth. Variety. They all sound like Virgo buzzwords to me.

Moving to higher ground wasn't enough for the post Ice Age population to survive. As they foraged into a strange and glacier-less world, these pioneering people needed to be innovative, adaptable, and most importantly, they needed each other to better their chances of survival.

A Cancer Virgo union doesn't create the dynamic of a thrill-based, roller coaster ride of a relationship with sudden surprises waiting at every turn. Given how both the crab and the virgin deeply crave security, the biggest pitfall these two signs will need to be mindful of is allowing their regimen of the routine to make their worlds unchangingly static and easily anticipated over time.

However, much like Leipzig's wooden water wells, the solid sense of home the Cancer can offer, added to the Virgo's earnest ethic of hard work, can provide the sought after security needed for this particular pairing to have the potential wear with all to last the passage of time.

Cancer-Libra

What's next on the agenda, Ms. Zodiac? An official meeting of student reprimand with the threat of possible expulsion?

Indeed. And the names of today's degenerates?

Cancer and who? Libra?

Very witty. Is this your way of getting even for last administrative assistant day's IOU note, Ms. Zodiac?

What? You weren't being in any way droll? Very well then. You may send both signs in, Ms. Zodiac.

Good day, Cancer and Libra. You both may be seated. First, I must say how shocking it is seeing either of you in my office.

When Ms. Zodiac came in to enlighten me of precisely which students were being officially reprimanded today, I thought she was joking.

And it must be noted that Ms. Zodiac has not a comical bone throughout the entirety of her exceptionally bony body!

So exactly WHY is Principal Love Author currently in such a state of shocked stupor?

Cancer and Libra are two of the most rule abiding, non-troublemaking signs, and individually the crab and the scales have both been known to display behavior of the most exemplary and non-delinquent kind.

Cancer, you're reputed for being the nurturer of the zodiacal bunch that's inherently devoted to its home and family.

Libra, your inherent charm and social graces naturally create an atmosphere of peace and harmony around yourself and everyone else within your sign's vicinity.

With Cancer's planetary ruler of the moon being associated with emotional security as well as any/all comforts of the homey, domesticated kind; and with Libra's planetary ruler of Venus dealing with the concepts of love and beauty, the two of you seem programmed to be prototypes of the perfect astrological student. But that was until you decided to date each other.

Of the twelve signs, Cancer and Libra are each other's biggest challenge to relate with due to their placement on the zodiac wheel. They are positioned from each other at the harshest astrological angle possible of 90 degrees, better known as the square.

When two signs square each other, a consistently high probability exists for either sign to easily rub the other the wrong way, quite often because either or both signs are simply being its natural self.

The inherent energies and overall personalities of the crab and the scales operate from such vastly different foundational points that combining these squaring signs in any kind of one-on-one partnership requires a consistent level of hard work from both parties. So much that Principal Love Author will be the first to admit the work needed to keep the Cancer-Libra union romantically solvent can be downright back breaking at times!

The core differences within this astrological duo all boils down to brains. And this next section WILL be included on your Love Squares 101 test.

Libra is an air sign. Cancer is a water sign. The air signs initially react to the outside world via the functions of the left hemisphere of the brain. The water signs initially react to the outside world via the right hemisphere.

The left hemisphere of the brain is known as the rational mind. The right hemisphere of the brain is known as the emotional/intuitive mind.

A left hemisphered person is motivated the most to exercise the processes of the rational mind, which mainly consist of thought and communication.

A right hemisphered person is motivated most by emotions and/or intuition.

Sounds easy enough, right? But one last rule regarding all this brain matter must be mentioned.

We humans have total control over the functions of our left hemispheres and no control whatsoever over the functions of our right hemispheres.

Air signs in general avoid the emotional realm altogether due to the rational mind having no control over those messy things that are generated from the brain's non-rational hemisphere. Hence, most Libras function from an overall environment that's "emotions lite," with many a scales person opting more towards an "emotions free" structure of living.

In fact, the mental muscles of those born beneath the element of air are so inherently strong, their left hemispheres will quite often wrestle their feelings into submission by rationalizing them far from the surface of their conscious minds.

Conversely, since they initially operate from their right hemispheres, the water signs will initially sense how something makes them feel at first before any kind of initial thinking is done and prior to any actions being taken.

With Cancer being the first representative of the watery element, emotional energies are felt to the core. Those born beneath the sign of the crab naturally understand they have no control over true emotion when it hits their radar.

One part of this astrological duo identifies itself through the act of verbal communication (Libra), the other half finds too much of that same act to be a distractive nuisance that often falls short of adequately expressing its natural state of emotional being (Cancer).

Even when these two signs first meet, misinterpreted misunderstandings usually run rampant from the get go.

The Libra will often initially misinterpret the Cancer's quiet nature as either being stuck up, standoffish, or disapproving. The Cancer will often initially misinterpret the Libra as being a shallow chatterbox that's utterly self-possessed. Good times.

Stepping back to look at how both signs inherently operate, the squaring differences become even more glaring.

Cancer loves to stay at home and enjoys being the king/queen of its sand castle. Libra enjoys being the king/queen of small talk and rarely stays at home due to its many social engagements.

The Cancer is a pack rat that can't throw anything out because of its sentimental face value. The Libra would rather be thrown face first to a pack of rats if it couldn't throw every unnecessary thing out or were forced to use any kind of sentimental décor.

Ask a Cancer to complete the phrase, "Baby's…?", and it more than likely responds with the word "diaper." Ask a Libra to complete the same phrase, and its reply will more than likely be the word "breath."

Ask the typical Cancer what you should make for dinner, and it can't say its favorite recipes fast enough. Ask the typical Libra what you should make for dinner, and it can't say, "Reservations" fast enough.

Ask the typical Cancer what it wants for dinner and the decision is made based on what is seasonal and fresh. Ask the typical Libra what it wants for dinner, and a fresh, new season will have passed before any kind of definite decision is made.

Comparing the inherent nature of the crab and the scales isn't strictly about contrasting differences. Both signs are strongly motivated to be in a committed romantic relationship. Many born beneath either sign can develop issues with co-dependency, along with an inability to voice their gripes and differences to their romantic partners.

Cancer has a tendency to internalize and repress anything considered highly stressful or negative, and Libra's need for peace and harmony gives it a proclivity to be non-confrontational at all costs.

Difficulties don't immediately arise when these two signs first meet. The squaring challenges between the crab and the scales usually don't become prominently problematic until well after they initially commit to each other.

If neither sign openly communicates its gripes or issues, the Cancer and Libra will remain committed to each other but bonded together by resentful misery versus any kind of romantic attachment.

Care to not flunk your romance test of Love Squares 101, Cancer and Libra? Nurture yourselves individually by first finding peace and harmony from within before seeking any kind of romantic fulfillment from an outside source. Class dismissed!

Cancer-Scorpio

Imagine if you will, Cancer and Scorpio, a futuristic fantasy land weaved within the plots of some of the best examples of twentieth-century science fiction.

Case in point, the 1967 sci-fi novel turned 1976 cult classic film by the same name, *Logan's Run* (LR for short), and the 1931 futuristic work elevated to literary classic, *Brave New World* (BNW for short), by the British satirist Aldous Huxley.

In both stories not of this time or place, hedonistic pursuits of pleasure are the main focal points for all literary parties involved. Whether one loses itself in mental ecstasy after taking soma, BNW's hallucinogenic pill like no other, or excitedly enters LR's government-sponsored orgy center with wild abandon, the stratospheric self-satisfaction in either sci-fi story creates an almost zen-like state where words can't adequately describe the barrage of pleasure-causing endorphins experienced. It's kind of like when the Cancer and the Scorpio begin dating each other.

Astrologically, the best love unions are those made of two people born beneath the same element. Since Cancer and Scorpio are both watery to their core, it really doesn't get much better than when these two members of the element of wet meet and romantically mingle!

The flow of human emotion is at the core of every water sign, and what many humans, including many a water-based one, tend to forget is that emotions are non-rational things. The rational mind resides strictly within the left hemisphere of the human brain. Anything emotional or intuitive is housed within the brain's right hemisphere.

If you want to speak to your partner, your brain oversees that task by having its left hemisphere send impulses to your mouth, which makes it move in order to say what needs to be said. Speech is a function of the rational mind and hence, is under the domain of the left hemisphere.

Now let's theoretically say you still need to speak to your partner, and rather desperately this time around, I might add. The only difference is your partner is nowhere physically near you. Just then, your phone rings. You pick it up to hear your water-signed partner say, "Hi, honey. I just felt a strong sensation that you needed to speak to me." The right hemisphere of your partner's brain has just been engaged and put to full use.

When dealing with any and all stimuli from the outside world, those born beneath the element of water will utilize their emotions first before anything else. The water sign will literally see how something makes them "Feel" before going into any kind of action or subsequent reaction.

Non-water signs like to think their feelings fit in custom-made giftboxes where each emotion resides in a nice little compartment waiting for its name to be called out at some point in the distant future.

The water signs know better. They know all too well that human emotion is a force much like Mother Nature herself. We cannot make the weather happen. We live with it and adjust accordingly whenever it chooses to change.

Those born beneath the element of wet naturally understand they have no control over true emotion when it hits their radar. When in touch with its emotions, the water sign flows with them.

Returning once more to our current love scenario, the duo in question isn't comprised of merely one astrologically wet one. The romantic pairing of the Cancer with the Scorpio is truly harmonious since it involves the union of two water signs.

An interesting phenomenon tends to occur after two water signs have initially joined romantic forces and an emotional bond has been formed between them. Overall things get quieter.

Because both parties share a watery astrological foundation, the Cancer and the Scorpio are more than likely to develop an innately intuitive sense of the other's presence without either sign needing to analytically discuss how or why it has come about. Nor will one water sign necessarily have to explain to the other what is being mutually felt.

This non-verbal, intuitive bond that forms whenever two water signs become emotionally close is, for the most part, a glorious thing much along the romantic lines of the pleasure experienced by the characters from LR and BNW whenever venturing on their pursuits of self-satisfaction.

But this emotional bond of the water-signed kind does have its downsides too. Inherently Cancers tend to be naturally sensitive and Scorpios tend to be naturally intense. What both watery parties need to be mindful of once their emotional bond has formed is for neither to become so super sensitive about things that every slightest hurt is retained. Nor for either to let things get so emotionally intense that one water sign ends up scarily jealous and/or hyper-possessive of the other.

Should the Cancer or the Scorpio see any of these negative trends beginning to form, it is highly recommended either of the following options be implemented: lightening things up and openly communicating.

Nothing dispels an atmosphere of heavy emotion faster than a little laughter, and a change of scenery never hurts either. In spite of the aforementioned world of wordless wonder created when two water signs emotionally bond, in order for every human relationship on this planet to not only thrive but survive, communication must be regularly exercised and perceived to always be accessible by all romantic parties involved.

Once an emotional bond has been firmly established, all watery parties will need to avoid two forms of behavior that specialize in breaking down the flow of open communication between each other: passive aggression and assuming.

The former of the two just so happens to be the relationship-killing weapon of choice employed by many an unevolved water sign.

Passive aggression is a non-confrontational tactic where one states its case, displays its willfulness, or attempts to get one's way through non-active and non-communicative behavior that's never direct but always undermining. Your Love Author likes to believe open communication is the solution for any kind of deep seeded problem in a relationship, but not so in the case of passive aggression.

Should one water sign experience a constant and relentless show of passive aggressiveness over time from its water-signed lover, the best thing it can do is, in a word, run. At least the energy exerted will be put to good use versus the vast amounts that'll be wasted in trying to directly confront the most indirect of non-confrontational tactics.

The next form of emotional bond-breaking behavior expressed by many an unevolved water sign is a tendency to assume those around automatically know what it is thinking and/or needing without having to verbally express itself.

To quote my fourth grade teacher, Sister Rita Stoneface, "When one assumes, one makes an ASS of U and ME."

At its core, assuming is a behavior tactic where one wishes to avoid having to deal or speak with others. It provides a person with a false license to avoid all forms of clear communication such as asking questions outright or specifying details so that all parties are on the same page.

Swimming back into a much warmer love current, regularly implementing open communication without the presence of either passive aggression or assuming will only make the waters of your emotional bond even more crystal clear, Cancer and Scorpio. Doing so creates the best chances for both of you watery ones to be swept away to romantic shores more blissful than any pleasure seeking sci-fi novel could ever hope to present.

Cancer-Sagittarius

Seriously, Cancer and Sagittarius. I need to throw this one out there. Are you two SURE you're dating each other?

Maybe you both have other romantic partners who either got lost or separated while all parties foraged their way to this particular chapter of the book? Close but no cupid doll, huh?

So both of you are unshakably sure in your convictions that one half of this newly budding romance is a Cancerian and the other a Sagittarian, correct? Okay, then. Boldly forward we go.

Sorry for the obnoxious obviousness just then, crabs and centaurs, but the two of you romantically joining forces is definitely NOT a common occurrence one hears about every day. Nor is your astrological union considered to be in any way obvious.

When looking at the prototypical wheel of the zodiac, the sign of Sagittarius lies at a 150 degree angle from the sign of Cancer. The proper astrological term for this very particular angle is the quincunx. Everyone repeat along with me. Ready? "Ku-win-kwunx." Very good!

The quincunx is also known by the much easier pronounced, astrological reference word, inconjunct. When two signs are placed at an inconjunct angle of each other, nothing remotely matches, and every inherent aspect of one sign is square pegged against the natural energies of the other.

Some keywords associated with the inconjunct or quincunx: are re-direction, challenge, diversion, and requires adjustment.

The quincunx is quite the tricky thing, especially when applied to the relationship dynamics created between two signs that are naturally positioned from each other at that 150 degree, inconjunct angle. The astrological rule of thumb about the signs that border either side of a person's sun sign create an overall "oil and vinegar" relationship dynamic. The signs that are quincunx of each other tend to create a similar effect but with a more intense, all or nothing edge.

Most of the outside world has a hard time picturing the signs of the crab and the centaur romantically together due to this particular coupling's high factor of unobviousness. When viewed individually, one would think the Cancer and the Sag were hardcore polar opposites. Both signs' energies and overall personalities seem THAT inherently different from each other.

Being the domestic sign of the zodiac, Cancer loves nothing more than staying at home. Sagittarius would rather be anywhere else than at home since this non-domestic sign loves nothing more than travelling to the most exotic of locales.

Because it loves to stay at home so much, the Cancer can become sedentary from too much sitting, which can result in the crab experiencing ebbs of low energy. The natural energy of the Sagittarius is usually revved so high, it barely has the ability to sit, let alone be sedentary.

The two main things in life that motivate a Cancer into action are home and family. Because the Sag is almost always motivated to be in a near constant state of action, those rare times when it is at home or with family are usually due to sleep or sickness.

Cancer's love of home often gives it the inclination to sit around the house, and if unmonitored, its shell will spread enough for it to eventually be sitting around the house quite literally. Sagittarius' love of partying gives it the inclination to invite every friend and stranger over should they host a party at its house that, if unmonitored, will find it sitting around the jail house for the duration of the evening or longer.

With the above said, one (and certainly not the only) of the biggest challenges this particular combo of the first of the water signs with the last of the fire signs will need to face, especially upon first meeting, will determine how much longevity the Cancer-Sagittarius union inherently has: ADJUSTMENT.

Because their energies and motivations run and move at such differing levels and speeds, adjustments will need to be made by both signs in order for this love union to even have a pulse. Namely, the crab will need to pick up its usual sideways sidle to more of a straightforward stroll, and the centaur will need to lurch the brakes on its usual racing gallop to more of a trot. A brisk trot, but a trot nonetheless, pony boys and girls.

Crustaceans and centaurs, your Love Author has both good and bad news accompanying this whole adjustment thing. Sag, I know you're the see-the-glass-half-full optimist of the zodiacal bunch but we're going to get the bad stuff out of the romantic way.

The bad news is that each sign's inherent flaws could easily interrupt things, or worse, drive your budding new relationship straight off the romantic cliff.

Cancer, your inherent moodiness may get so stoked while initially adjusting that the Sag may start wondering if your middle name could possibly be "Jekyll" and whether your last name really is "Hyde." Sagittarius, your inherent energies are so consistently high revved and level of patience so naturally low, the Cancer may begin to think if Ritalin was designed specifically with your sign in mind given your inability to sit still for more than five minutes, along with nearly spontaneously combusting whenever having to wait more than a few nanoseconds longer than expected.

The good news is if the bad news occurs throughout the adjustment process, the crab pony love union will proceed to immediately crash and burn during the earliest stages of your relationship.

The actual good news is the crab and the centaur share a special astrological bond that's truly unique. Along with their love union being considered highly unobvious, the signs of Cancer and Sagittarius possess a common tie of an even more unobvious nature that's not readily known even by most astrologers.

The heavenly body called the great benefic, better known as Jupiter, is the planetary ruler of the sign of Sagittarius. By virtue of it being the most gargantuan planet of all the solar system, Jupiter is associated with the themes of expansion, luck, and optimism to name a fortuitous few.

The great benefic naturally rules over the sign of the centaur, but the lucky planet's energies and influences function best in or are exalted in the lunar-ruled sign of Cancer. Why?

With the first of the water signs being the natural nurturers of the zodiac and otherwise known as "the mommy sign," who better than mom to best share the bounty of Jupiter's abundance?

I won't kid either of you, Cancer and Sagittarius. The romantic pairing of your signs won't be any kind of crab cake walk or fun-filled pony ride given your extreme differences of temperament and personality. But when considering the Jupiterian bond shared between your signs, if the Crab and the Centaur approach each other's differences of dynamic with a consistently positive approach, your luck factor as a couple may stand a chance of hitting it romantically big together.

So throw caution to the unobvious wind and take a romantic roll of the dice together, Cancer and Sagittarius, for as they say in those lottery commercials, "You gotta be in it to win it."

Cancer-Capricorn

(Entering room.) Oh, hey! Cancer. Capricorn.

(Casually strolling past, then stopping to give each of you a prolonged glancing over.)

If I didn't know any better, my view upon entering the room just now of the two of you sitting all relaxed and casually hanging out usually wouldn't give me cause to wonder if anything out of the ordinary was going on.

But I do know better. Much, much better.

I happen to know the astrological fact that the crab and the mystic mountain goat are polar opposites of each other. Not to be trite in a nasal Paula Abdul way, but opposites attract.

And when two opposites are within close physical proximity of each other, the attraction factor turns into an all-out starved shark feeding frenzy of kissing touchy-feely!

Hey, lighten up, you two! There's nothing wrong with your Love Author being so astrologically savvy as to correctly deduce that just a few moments before coming in here, you two were pawing at each other like wild primates.

Some would say you oppositely attracted love birds were merely obeying an inalterable law of both astrology and science.

Remember those magnet experiments they used back in junior high to demonstrate the law of attraction? Take those same, oppositely charged pieces of metal that slammed into each other whenever within remote proximity together, except now one of the magnets is called Cancer and the other Capricorn.

Cancer and Capricorn are polar opposites. Being as such, polar opposites naturally attract! And by naturally attract, they're hot for each other/warm for each other's form. You get the lustfully arousing general picture.

For every sign in the zodiac, the universe counterbalances that sign's energies through its polar opposite. Just as it sounds, the polar opposite pairing of signs couldn't be any more diametrically different on many levels. However, equally as important, the polar opposites share just as many similarities as they do differences.

How about we skip all the technical talk and provide both romantic parties an overview of each other's individual astrological backgrounds to see just how different and similar the crab and the goat are together.

Cancer, the influence of the moon, your planetary ruler that oversees the heightened sensitivity of human emotion, tends to make you openly cry upon seeing any given Hallmark commercial or variation of baby animal. Capricorn, your ruler is Saturn, the planet of hardship and pain, which is the astrological taskmaster whose cosmic motto is "The more you cry, the less I care."

Cancer is the domestic sign and having a comfortable home base is very important. Capricorn is the sign of status and achieving material gain and recognition through work is most important.

Having a watery or emotionally based foundation, the Cancerian best expresses its feelings by mothering or nurturing those with whom it feels emotionally close. Having a planetary ruler somberly called the Lord of Karma, the Capricorn's emotionally detached demeanor tends to be both stoic and stern, leaving even its own mother to wonder if it possesses any feelings whatsoever.

Cancer is one of if not the most personalized signs of the zodiac given the two things in life that motivate it most are home and family. Thus, the Cancerian will speak to those whom it is emotionally attached to with a sense of warm familiarity as if that person were family. The Saturnine nature of the Capricorn makes it one of if not the most depersonalized signs of the zodiac. Aside from friends and family, the typical Cappie will speak to others with the politely distant formality of either a bank teller or unamused librarian.

Even with all of the above differences mentioned, the rule with polar opposites is they share just as many similarities as oppositions. Cancer and Capricorn are both cardinal signs. The cardinal signs take place at the commencement of each of the four seasons and thus are naturally good at beginning/initiating/starting things from scratch. By virtue of its cardinal quality, Cancer and Capricorn share a unifying tie that motivates both signs to begin its actions, start its projects, and build anew— SECURITY.

Being the first representative of the watery element, the Cancer seeks security from a perspective of deeply held emotion. Being the last representative of the earth signs, the Capricorn seeks security from a tangible perspective that is thoroughly entrenched within the material plane.

Both signs are willing to do whatever it takes in order for its sense of security to be maintained, assured, and established.

As stated earlier, the Capricorn relies upon its fierce work ethic like no other to garner, protect, and find security with its tangible possessions and assets. The Cancer needs to rely upon being fierce, period.

Not sure what that last sentence could possibly mean? Surprisingly, many a Cancerian doesn't realize that being fierce is a quality that inherently lies within the core of every individual born beneath the sign of the crab. Your Love Author will further clarify this generalized term by providing a concrete example from within the deepest wilds of the animal kingdom.

From the perspective of motivational action, what is the most deadly "force" on this planet amongst living creatures? A mother protecting her young. Be it Mrs. Moose or Mamma Hippopotamus, the animal mothers of the wild will kill a person ten times before it hits the ground if it so much as gets in between her visual path with, let alone attempts to harm, her offspring.

It would behoove every crustacean to remember should anyone it cares for urgently needs its help or is directly in harm's way, its inner mom has the ability to hear and heed the Cancerian call of the wild. This maternal instinct of the most emotionally fierce kind applies to all crabs regardless of gender or whether its young is related to them by blood or not.

The converging of polar opposite signs has an all or nothing effect. There almost never is a middle of the road or wishy washy end result whenever two polar opposites meet, especially after they initially paw at each other like sharks in a feeding frenzy.

Attraction is what brings the polar opposites together, which in turn, yields some initial and immediate, ummm, shark-like behavior.

Even with that blushingly said, if there is nothing more other than a few fast and furious bed creaks, or in other words, nothing of binding common interest beyond the initial attraction, the polarized spark will be snuffed out just as quickly as it began. Why?

Many times the flames of opposing desire are quickly doused due to both signs driving each other naturally crazy after the passing of five post-bed creaking minutes, give or take.

But conversely, if the polar opposites can stand each other's presence for more than five minutes post you know and have a thing or two they like about the other, or even better, share a few things in common, then here is where we find those fairy tale relationships that stay together.

In fact, when there are binding factors beyond the initial animal attraction, many of these dualistic duos literally last until death do they polar opposite part.

Cancer-Aquarius

A Cancer with who? An Aquarius? You're joking, right? According to cosmic law, combining the energies of a water elemental with that of air in and of itself is not only considered to be unacceptable on a karmic level, but the romantic notion of the Cancer dating the Aquarius should be viewed as an astrological abomination and must be prevented from occurring at all costs.

JUST KIDDING, you two!

None of the above is even the slightest bit true about your signs dating each other, crabs and water bearers, especially the whole "astrological abomination" part! But truth be told, the Cancer romantically joining forces with the Aquarius is definitely NOT a common occurrence one hears about every day.

To repeat, the coupling of the crab with the water bearer is in no way considered to be any kind of desecration to the cosmic order of the universe. Putting all fatalistic jokes that fall flat aside, it still must be said the Cancer and the Aquarius teaming up as a love duo is about as unobvious an astrological combo as one could ever hope to find.

When looking at the prototypical wheel of the zodiac, the sign of Cancer lies at a 150 degree angle from the sign of Aquarius. The proper astrological term for this very particular angle is the quincunx. Everyone repeat along with me. Ready? "Ku-win-kwunx." Very good!

The quincunx is also known by the much easier pronounced astrological reference word, "inconjunct." When two signs are placed at an inconjunct angle of each other, nothing remotely matches, and every inherent aspect of one sign is square pegged against the natural energies of the other. Some keywords associated with the inconjunct are: redirection, challenge, diversion, and requires adjustment.

The quincunx is quite the tricky thing, especially when applied to the relationship dynamics created between two signs that are naturally positioned from each other at that 150 degree angle. The astrological rule of thumb about the signs that border either side of a person's sun sign create an overall "oil and vinegar" relationship dynamic. The signs that are quincunx of each other tend to create a similar effect but with a more intense, all or nothing edge.

I won't kid either of you, Cancer and Aquarius. Most of the outside world has a hard time picturing the two of you together due to your union's high factor of unobviousness. When viewed individually, one would think the Cancerian and the Aquarian were hardcore polar opposites since both signs' energies and overall personalities seem THAT inherently different from each other.

Being the first representative of its element, the Cancer's emotions are the most pure and uncomplicated of all the water signs, and thus those born beneath the sign of the crab are in a constant state of "feeling" nearly most of the time.

Despite many erroneously thinking the sign of the water bearer is an actual water sign, (including many a water bearer, itself), Aquarius is the last representative of the element of air, and its approach to everything can be so purely cerebral that many born beneath this most intellectual of signs can easily fall out of touch with its feelings altogether.

The past is a potent force of influence for the Cancer since it derives a sense of security from what has already been. Things that have a sense of history have quite the allure for this most sentimental of signs.

Sentimentality is about as alluring as a last minute root canal minus the Novocaine for the typical Aquarian. Because its inventive mind cranks out so many ahead of its time thoughts, the future is the force of influence that stimulates he or she most, and usually without a shred of attachment to anything connected to the past.

Having an elemental foundation that's watery or emotionally based, the Cancerian best expresses its feelings by mothering or nurturing those with whom it has close emotional attachments. Having an elemental foundation that's airy or rationally based, the Aquarian can be so emotionally detached its own mother will sometimes wonder if it possesses any feelings in any capacity whatsoever.

When hearing of the Cancer's love of home and its love of staying at home, one would think its lack of being out and about would make it a reclusive lone wolf. In actuality, the Cancer's abode is usually abuzz with various relatives and friends.

When hearing of Aquarius being the sign of both friendship and groups, one would think the water bearer would be quite the social animal with never a moment alone. In actuality, the water bearer's inherent sense of fierce individualism and non-conformity result in many Aquarians becoming lone wolves that keep mostly to themselves.

Cancer is one of if not the most personalized signs of the zodiac given the two things in life that motivates it most into action are home and family. Thus, the Cancerian will speak to those whom it is emotionally attached to with a sense of warm familiarity as if that person were family.

The intellectual nature of the Aquarius makes it one of if not the most depersonalized signs of the zodiac. Aside from close friends and family, the typical water bearer will speak to others with the distant formality of either a bank teller or unamused college professor.

Cancer is all about the tried and true. Aquarius is all about the untried and brand-spanking new.

Inherently infused with a sense of pride for its home area and homeland, Cancer is one of the most patriotic signs. Inherently infused with a sense of rebellion, the sign of Aquarius naturally goes against any kind of established norm, making the water bearer one of the most patriotically derisive of signs.

With the above said, one (and certainly not the only) of the biggest challenges this particular combo will need to face, especially upon first meeting, will determine the overall longevity of this most unobvious of unions: ADJUSTMENT.

Because their foundational energies and motivations vary and differ so greatly, adjustments will need to be made by both signs. Namely the Cancer needs to not be so inherently touchy and sensitive, and the Aquarian needs to not be so inherently distant and detached.

Crabs and water bearers, your Love Author has both good and bad news accompanying this whole adjustment thing between your signs.

The bad news to the adjustment phase when getting to know each other is that each sign's inherent flaws of character could easily interrupt things or drive your budding new relationship straight off the romantic cliff.

Cancer, your inherent moodiness may fluctuate so much while initially adjusting, the Aquarius may begin to wonder if your middle name could possibly be "Jekyll" and whether your last name is really "Hyde." Aquarius, your naturally chilly and detached demeanor could have the Cancer nervously pondering if your middle name is really "Serial" and your last name "Killer."

And now for the good news! The good news is that if the bad news occurs throughout the adjustment process, the crab water bearer love union will proceed to immediately crash and burn during the earliest stages of your relationship, which at least will be better than having to sever your bond when there are things like jointly held assets or pets involved.

JUST KIDDING!

Actually, that last time I wasn't.

Cancer-Pisces

Dive in, Cancer and Pisces! Grab your noses, close your eyes, and proceed to splash bomb your best cannonball or belly flop in the love pool!

Astrologically, the best romantic unions are those made of two people born beneath the same element. Since Cancer and Pisces are both water signs, it really doesn't get much better when these two members of the house of wet jump into the same emotional waves and proceed to astrologically body surf together.

The flow of human emotion is at the core of every water sign, and what many humans, including many a water-based one, tend to forget is that emotions are non-rational things.

The rational mind resides strictly within the left hemisphere of the human brain. Anything emotional or intuitive is housed within the brain's right hemisphere. For a rational example, if you want to speak to your partner, your brain oversees that task by having its left hemisphere send impulses to your mouth, which tell it to move in order to say what needs to be said. Speech is a function of the rational mind and is housed under the domain of the left hemisphere.

Let's theoretically say you still need to speak to your partner rather desperately this time around. The only difference is your partner is nowhere physically near you. Just then your phone rings. You pick it up to hear your water-signed partner on the other end say, "Hi, honey. I just felt a strong sensation that you needed to speak to me." The right hemisphere of your partner's brain had just been engaged and put to full use.

When dealing with any and all stimuli from the outside world, those born beneath the element of water will utilize their emotions first before anything else. The water sign will literally see how something makes them feel before going into any kind of action or subsequent reaction.

Non-water signs like to think their feelings fit in custom made gift-boxes where each emotion resides in a nice little compartment while waiting for its name to be called out at some point in the distant future.

The water signs know better. They know all too well that human emotion is a force much like Mother Nature herself. We cannot make the weather happen. We live with it and adjust accordingly whenever it chooses to change.

The water signs inherently know they have no control over true emotion when it hits their radar. When in touch with its feelings, the water sign flows with them.

An interesting phenomenon occurs when two water signs emotionally first commit to each other and join romantic forces. Overall things get quieter.

Because both parties share an astrological foundation that is watery, the Cancer and the Pisces are more than likely to develop an innately intuitive sense of the other's presence without either sign needing to analytically discuss how or why it has come about. Nor will one water sign necessarily have to explain to the other what is being mutually felt.

This non-verbal, intuitive bond that forms whenever two water signs become emotionally close and/or romantically intimate is for the most part a glorious thing!

But this emotional bond of the water-signed kind does have its down sides. Inherently Cancers tend to be naturally sensitive. The same can be equally if not more said of Pisceans. Those born beneath the sign of the crab possess an inherent need to escape the brash reality of the day to day world by the comfort and security they derive from their homes.

This same watery need to retreat from the harsh world of reality naturally motivates those born beneath the sign of the cosmic fish as well with the Pisces' need to lose their sense of self altogether in various activities.

What both water signs need to be mindful of once the emotional bond has started to form is for neither to become so super sensitive about things that every slightest hurt is retained. Nor is it cosmically okay for one water sign to use the other as its excuse from having to deal with the realities of the outside world regardless of how harsh they may appear to seem.

Should the Cancer or the Pisces observe any of these negative trends starting to form, it's highly recommended one or both of the following options are implemented by either water sign: lightening things up and openly communicating. Nothing dispels an atmosphere of heavy emotion faster than a little laughter. Getting out of the house for a change of scenery never hurts either.

In spite of the aforementioned world of wordless wonder created whenever two water signs emotionally bond, communication must be regularly exercised and perceived to always be accessible by all romantic parties involved.

Once an emotional bond has been firmly established, both water signs must avoid two forms of behavior that focus on breaking down the flow of open communication: passive aggression and assuming.

Passive Aggression is a non-confrontational tactic where one states its case, displays its willfulness, or attempts to get its way through non-active and non-communicative behavior that's never direct but always undermining.

Your Love Author likes to believe that open communication is the solution for any kind of deep-seated problem in a relationship but not so in the case of passive aggression.

Should one water sign experience a constant and relentless show of passive aggressiveness over time from its water-signed lover, the best thing it can do is, in a word, run.

At least the energy exerted will be put to good use versus the vast amounts that'll be wasted in trying to directly confront the most non-direct of confrontational tactics.

This next form of communication avoiding behavior is often utilized by every unevolved member of the water-signed family, but most especially is a favorite form of emotional bond breaker utilized by many a non-evolved Piscean.

Because of its non-verbal tendency, a Piscean pitfall expressed by many a fish person and/or water sign is a tendency to assume. The person will assume those around will automatically know what he or she is thinking and/or needing without having to verbally express itself.

To quote my fourth grade teacher, Sister Rita Stoneface, "When one assumes, one makes an ASS of U and ME."

At its core, assuming is a behavior tactic where one wishes to avoid having to deal or speak with others. It provides a person with a false license to avoid all forms of clear communication such as asking questions outright or specifying details so that all parties are on the same page.

Regularly implementing open communication without the presence of either passive aggression or assuming will only make the waters of your emotional bond even more crystal clear and allow the best chances for the crab and the cosmic fish to surf and swim the most blissful of romantic waves together.

So jump in, Cancer and Pisces! The astrological water's fine and ready to whisk both of you romantically away!

Leo-Leo

Good evening, Leonine violators.

Welcome to lion probation class. Everyone should be well aware why they're here tonight, but Officer Love Author shall now further elaborate on that point, none the Leo less.

Each of you has committed the civic transgression of allowing persons born beneath the sign of the lion to romantically join forces with other persons of the same astrological persuasion.

As part of your community service, you are required by cosmic law to attend this evening's lion probation class, whose goal is to reinforce the notion that romantically pairing two Leos together should only be done under professional supervision.

If everyone can now focus their attentions on the slide projector located at the front of the room. (Classroom overhead lights switch off.)

Slide #1: Madonna and Sean Penn. Bennifer. Monica and Bill.

What do these arrangements of names represent? (Audience mumbles a response)

The notorious pairings of one famous Leo with another of equal fame is correct.

Does anyone know how each of these double feline famous couples ended up faring? (More mumbling)

Sad but true. Every one of the double Leo love unions listed on slide number one failed, some quite miserably. It must be noted when two Lions of famed stature marry, the resulting divorce will often draw as much public attention as the feline fiasco of a marriage.

If you all will now turn to the flow charts located on each of your desks, everyone should see an astrological breakdown further detailing why two Leos dating is considered a dangerous threat to society at large.

The Royalty Sign: Leo is symbolically represented by the animal euphemistically called the king of the jungle, and the sign of the lion is otherwise known as the royalty sign. To put it simply, you can't have two kings ruling one castle. Moving right along.

The Sun: Every sign has a planetary ruler. Despite being the center of our solar system, the sun is categorized as an astrological planet. Why? To handle being Leo's planetary ruler.

Having the Sun as its ruler, the typical Leo loves to shine and be noticed in the spotlight of other people's attention. But what's a lion to do if there's competition? And worse! What if the competition loves to bask in the spotlight and be noticed just as much given its of the same astrological making?

As with any high-stakes competition with two equally matched contenders, the end result is one winner who dominates and takes all. With two Leos, it usually boils down to which lion gains total control over hogging the spotlight while managing to keep the competition out of it, regardless if they are dating or married to each other.

The Battle of the Fixed Dating the Fixed: Leo is a fixed sign by astrological quality, and two fixed signs dating is one of the most challenging combinations to maintain due to the following fixed traits: a natural tendency to resist change; a proclivity to see things as one dimensional, or distinctly black or white; an inherent inclination to not compromise; or a consistent knack for being obstinate, which is a polite way of saying "pig-headed stubborn."

Many believe putting two Leos together results in an immediate cat fight, but this could not be further from the romantic truth. If anything, when two lions first begin dating, things couldn't be more feline fantastic! Given their sign's solar need to shine, along with naturally being romantic to a fault, when two Leos commence the dating process, both Lions put every effort into looking their best and being on their best behavior.

A great looking date with hair as big as mine who is just as hopelessly romantic as my big hearted self? What could possibly go wrong?

If everyone would repeat the following in their best CatWoman voice, "Purrrrrrrrrrrrrrrrrrr-fectly EVERYTHING."

Officer Love Author now asks that all writing utensils be put down in order to partake in tonight's final exercise of visualizing the dating process between two Leos as if it were a *Godzilla* movie.

Much like the standard plot found in the typical *Godzilla* movie, the overall atmosphere needs to be picture postcard perfect when two Leos first begin dating.

As in the Japanese fright flick, everything has to be going feline fantastic in order to juxtapose the truly horrific nature of what lies above or below, which soon shall volcanically descend upon the film's idyllic surroundings and peaceful townsfolk.

Just as in the *Godzilla* movie where the film's lead lovers walk hand in hand down the promenade, past the school as the closing bell rings. The teacher stands in the entrance waving in slow motion, mouthing "Goodbye, children!" to her happily exiting students before the camera pans up and away allowing the audience to see the churning volcano or bubbling ocean's surface far off in the distance.

Terror is about to descend upon Romanceville!

In other words (dramatic orchestral chords while a woman hysterically screams), the two Leos are about to have their first difference of opinion!

Picture these lionly lovers jumping through romantic hoops, otherwise known as the initial courtship phase, and then a disagreement or difference of opinion occurs.

Instantaneously both Lions will dig their heels into the ground, determined never to budge a millimeter for the duration of their lionly lives! Upon seeing its fixed sign partner doing the aforementioned heel digging, the other fixed sign will become even MORE inflexibly unrelenting, stupefied at how obviously wrong its fixed sign partner is about everything.

Like the townspeople from the celluloid Japanese seaside town of placid perfection, everyone is taken completely off guard. No one sees it coming when Godzilla emerges from the ocean's depths, while the three-headed dragon, Ghidora, simultaneously swoops down from the sky to have a screaming showdown of monster-sized proportions with the gargantuan lizard.

But just like the dapper and well-suited male lead whose mouth moves well before the audience hears his dubbed in English voice, Officer Love Author would like to inform his captive viewing audience, "There may just be a way."

Plug your ears everybody because this one's gonna be a real screamer: COMPROMISE.

It's Romanceville's only hope, Leo-san!

Not just one but both fixed signs will need to regularly compromise with its fixed sign partner in order for this relationship to not have a horror flick ending of romantic armageddon. Leo is one of the most stubborn signs in the known universe, and many seasons shall pass over this monster scene of opposing opinion before either feline realizes its lionly lover is just as stubborn as itself.

Does anybody recall Godzilla ever relaxing, or even exhaling a flaming sigh of relief? If Ghidorah was strongarmed out of the picture, Rhodan or Mothra soon took its screaming place and the monster wars of inflexible will raged on and on.

The film's lead lovers may have gotten separated while Ghidorah was deflecting that flying school bus hand-flung by Godzilla, but they always manage to find each other in a tearful hug right before the movie's end. Just as the camera pans up and away, displaying the smoking carnage as peace once again returns to the town of Romanceville. Or does it? (Overhead lights switch back on.)

This concludes tonight's lion probation class. Officer Love Author thanks everyone for their required presence and would like to leave a final thought as each of you exits the building in single file form: "Only YOU can prevent fixed fire signs from dating each other."

Leo-Virgo

Come on in, Virgo! Thanks so much for making it to my annual neighborhood potluck fondue soiree. Before blowtorching your fondue stick to an acceptable sanitary state, Virgo, there's someone here I'd like you to meet.

Leo, this is my good acquaintance and neighbor of many years, Virgo. Virgo, this is my good acquaintance and neighbor of many years, Leo.

Now how is it possible you two haven't met yet given both of you are astrological neighbors of yours truly, but also next door to each other?

The following soiree scenario was presented in order to emphasize the astrological fact the signs of Leo and Virgo are next door neighbors on that big wheel of the cosmos, otherwise known as the zodiac.

Despite the wild growth of the Leonine jungle bordering the meticulously manicured Virgoan front lawn, this particular astrological combination deals with two distinctly different personalities that exist in two distinctly different worlds.

Technically the signs that border either side of a person's sun sign are categorized beneath a not so exciting descriptor of astrological compatibility: neutral.

(A solitary cough can be heard about four or five houses further down the block.)

Every sign has the potential to work together. Some combinations take a lot more work than others just to achieve a state of equilibrium. With the joining of the signs considered to be neutral of each other, the state of equilibrium is something very much like that solid borderline that naturally forms whenever oil and vinegar are put into the same container. In other words, mixing the two isn't a bad thing, but a whole lot of shaking is needed for there to be any kind of blend.

At their core, the Lion and the Virgin function from very dissimilar perspectives, making it seem in many ways as if these two signs lived on opposite ends of the globe versus being astrological next door neighbors.

Being one of the three karmic signs, the Virgo derives the most fulfillment in serving others. Being the only solar sign, the Leo derives the most fulfillment being noticed by others.

The Virgo's demure sense of earth-signed humility tends to make it uncomfortable with crowds and shun the spotlight. The Leo's strong sense of fire-signed ego tends to make it stand out in a crowd and bask in the spotlight.

Fiery Leo is a highly romantic creature that's willing to forego everything for love! Earthy Virgo is a creature of habit that's anything but romantic. And who's got time to forego things when there's work to be done?

The Leo's natural sense of authoritative leadership makes it suitable to being its own superior and not so suitable to a superior giving it tasks or telling him or her what to do. The Virgo's dutiful sense of dedication makes it most suitable to being given tasks and successfully completing what it's told to do.

Things will often go unnoticed when a Virgo is upset, hurt, or sick, due to its tendency to put its own needs last. The last thing anyone would want is to ignore a Leo when it is upset, hurt, or sick due to its tendency to put its own needs first by dramatically broadcasting each and every one of them to anyone within earshot.

Moving away from opposing characteristic camps, the lion and the virgin actually share two key personality assets that are central to both signs' core sense of self.

Intriguingly, these commonly shared character strengths will determine the overall longevity of the romantic union between these two very different astrological personalities.

And look Virgo! An easy to remember formula that's just as neat and tidy as the immaculately kept flagstone walkway on your side of the yard! D-Squared = Diligence and Dedication

The fixed nature of the Leo and the Virgo's need to be of service to others endows both signs with the willpower and tenacity to roll up their sleeves and work tirelessly, provided there is an aspired goal to mutually work towards.

When both signs' inherent sense of diligence and dedication focus on a mutually aspired goal (like their relationship, maybe?), the efforts of the lion and the virgin can give their love union the potential to be consistently long lasting.

It's when either sign's sense of diligence or dedication becomes muted or re-routed, as to include goals that aren't jointly shared, the Leo Virgo relationship stands to quickly dissolve soon thereafter.

Regardless of gender, the dynamic this very particular partnership functions best in is one where it's understood by all romantic parties that the Leo wears the pants in the family. Leonine energy prefers being in control and Virgoan energy prefers to dutifully serve to near perfection.

When a Leo Virgo coupling calls it quits, there will be a tendency for others around them to put all of the breakup blame on the Virginal half of the partnership. This is often based on the wrong assumption of the Virgo criticizing and hen pecking its lionly lover to such extremes that the Leo had no choice but to sever the romantic ties for good.

In romantic reality, this is often not the case. The Virgo may criticize others, but those who are the hardest hit by detail-driven criticisms is its perfection seeking self.

Instead, many a Leo Virgo love union will end due to the lionly portion of the romantic pair refusing to relinquish even the slightest bit of control with not only its Virgoan lover, but with the world at large. This is due to Leo's fixed astrological quality.

As a whole, the fixed signs do not have the easiest time seeing other people's perspectives that aren't their own. Other fixed characteristics that are anything but easy are: a natural tendency to resist change; a mental proclivity to see things in a one dimensional, black or white way; an inherent inclination to not compromise; or a consistent knack for being obstinate, which is a polite way of saying "pig-headed stubborn."

Along with those tricky character traits, the fixed signs also tend to be control freaks of the highest order, with many believing they have total dominion over every aspect of their tightly controlled lives.

It's only when such uncontrollable factors as fate, illness, the aging process, and death make their presences known to that the fixed personality is forced into submission to think otherwise.

Unfortunately for this particular pairing, should any kind of life-altering change enter the lion's life while it is romantically bonded to a Virgo, the energies of many a Leo will be spent not only stubbornly resisting said change, but also in blaming its earth-signed partner by making it feel completely at fault for everything going wrong during that challenging time.

Many service-oriented Virgos will accept projected guilt and blame, falsely believing they can work at making things better.

If the inflexibly resistant Leo had applied its diligence in working with the Virgo's sense of dedication instead of against it, not only would the lion smoothly adjust to the changes happening, but the emotional bond shared with its Virgoan lover would have become much stronger as well.

So go ahead, Leo and Virgo. Diligently reach for the stars together as a dedicated romantic team. But it's highly recommended all parties do so while their toes are firmly planted in the ground AND with as relaxed and non-controlling a grip as possible.

Leo-Libra

Did you lovebirds know the most damaging forest fires occur in areas that don't necessarily have the most flammable material but are susceptible to high winds?

Flame, unto its solitary self, doesn't make a fire burn fast and furiously. Take said flame and infuse it with the oxygen from the windy air and the result is one serious scorcher, kind of like when the Leo and the Libra begin dating each other.

In astrology, the four elements of earth, air, fire, and water are naturally paired off. Each grouping consists of two elements that are cohesive or naturally work well together, otherwise known as being complementary. Hence, the elements of earth and water complement each other, but more important for this particular pairing, the elements of fire and air are complementary.

Returning once more to our romantic forest fire analogy, when fiery Leo joins romantic forces with airy Libra, the erratic nature of the furiously fast burning wildfire is made more constant and simmered down to that of a slow and steady flame. This is due to both signs being the tempered middle representatives of each of its respective elements.

Being the middle representative of the element of air, those born beneath the sign of the scales mainly function through the mental processes of thought and communication. With its planetary ruler of Venus being the heavenly body that oversees such mmmm mmmm good things as love, harmony, and charm, the Libra's communications are filtered through a Venusian lens of grace and manners.

Unlike its air-signed relatives, Gemini and Aquarius, which each have the potential to take its communication down an imbalanced path of either too much or too little, the Libra interacts with the outside world with an innate sense of balanced decorum. Its skills of conversation can charm nearly anyone from any walk of life, and its inherent sense of tactful manners and discretion provides it with a keen awareness of when to speak and just as importantly when to not say a word.

The fire signs are action oriented, and most members of the family of flame prefer the majority of its actions to be as fast paced as possible with the exception of the fixed member of the fire signs: Leo.

Unlike the other spitfire signs that make up the element of fire, the sign of the lion differs from the rest of the flaming family if for the simple reason that amongst the fixed, nothing is ever rushed, spontaneous, or frantically fast-paced. Slow and steady wins the race with these heavy hitting signs!

The Leo's fixed dynamic and overall approach to things can be most easily observed by its animal counterpart in its natural habitat. In the wild, a lion or lioness will tap into the high levels of energy needed to move quickly, only if it determines it is necessary to do so. Otherwise, the kings and queens of the jungle move about with a gradual, relaxed pace and rush for no one!

More often than not, pairing up the highly polished (Libra) and royally regal (Leo) middle representatives of the elements of fire and air together usually results in a serious romance of long-lasting potential versus a burning ball of passion that extinguishes itself just as quickly as when it first combusted.

Even the key character flaws of one sign can be counterbalanced in a most complementary way by the inherent personality strengths of the other. The Libra's mild mannered graces can act as a calming counterpoint should the Leo perform one of its over-dramatic displays of attention-getting fireworks, and the Leo's leader-like sense of direct forwardness can assist with finding a defined course of resolution whenever a bout of chronic Libran indecision should occur.

Take heed, Leos! Should a Libran be asked to make any kind of noncritical decision, the lion risks the possibility of either listening to the locks of its big haired mane grow or witness any of the four seasons change before its eyes due to its scale-signed lover weighing every possible option back and forth, over and over, before approaching any kind of decisive resolve.

If your Love Author be so bold as to humbly offer a piece of invaluable advice to your fiery majesty. If you fixed cats wish to avoid losing your mind as well as temper by reactively roaring yourselves back to being single, the two things the Leo should always decide IN ADVANCE before going on a date with a Libran love interest are: what movie will be seen and what style of food will be eaten at which restaurant.

The signs of the lion and the scales aren't always about having regal and dignified bearings at all times. These two signs can be real pigs. SO sorry, Leos and Libras! My deepest apologies for even using the word pig! That simply wasn't right. Hog fits far better. The two biggest romance hogs in the zodiac? You found 'em!

Both Leo and Libra are diehard romantics of the most hardcore kind you will EVER find. Romance junkies born beneath either sign live and breathe for the love stuff throughout nearly every minute of its waking day.

With the scales' planetary ruler being named after the goddess of romance and the lion's natural house of rulership being the fifth, otherwise known as the house of romance, the R-word isn't important for both the Leo and the Libra. It's vital.

Unfortunately the world is currently quite the unromantic place. Mention the word courting nowadays and most people will think you're either talking about the latest basketball stats or your plans to actively sue someone. Because of this, most Leos and Librans are almost fully convinced chivalry is currently dead and romance went out of style long ago.

Even with such romantic restriction mentioned, the signs of the lion and the scales optimally respond to and interact best through the process of courting.

Courting (noun) is a way of getting to know a person through gradual stages of increased intimacy by incorporating romance with social activities.

With both sign's inherent sense of heightened romance being properly fulfilled by each other, the romance hogs of the zodiac will feel more ecstatic than a hog in mud. But as every junkie knows, the better something makes you feel, the higher a price there is to pay.

Both romance hog signs must be wary of their love fix becoming too all-encompassing during the courting process, where the icky, unromantic world of the day to day becomes nearly impossible to deal with over time. Should that take effect, the love union of the romance hogs will dissolve soon there afterwards due to the rose-colored glasses of romantically addictive idealism distorting the overall view of things and each other.

So go hog wild and date away, Leo and Libra! It's about time both romance hogs' long starved need for high romance receive its proper nourishment with the two of you joining forces. Just try to not get all piggy about it.

Leo-Scorpio

This chapter has barely begun and already you both have put me in quite a pickle, Leo and Scorpio! Your Love Author planned on generalizing the positive and negative dynamics when the lion and the scorpion join romantic forces under the format of "I have good news and bad news," but even THERE we have issues. When asked to choose, I can already see both signs instantly responding with opposing answers at the same time.

Being solar-ruled and the sign known for its sunny disposition, the good news is the only way to initially go for the Leo. Scorpio is intense and no nonsense. If there's any pain to be addressed a Scorpio would rather tear off that bandage of bad news in one swift and painful motion, regardless if any hair follicles or patches of skin he ripped off right along with it.

So what to do you two? How about we start over from satirical scratch.

Here's a question for you, Leo and Scorpio. Are both of you familiar with the concept of non-beginner chili sauce? Rather, I should ask are either of you knowledgeable about the range of specialized chili sauces that cater to a very specific portion of the consumer population, namely advanced chili sauce lovers to the extreme?

Only one solitary factor determines the variety of range with these extreme chili sauces not made for beginners: heat, be it oral, esophageal, or gastro-intestinal.

The variations of heat for the advanced chili sauce lover come in three selections: super hot, deadly hot, and HF, which stands for human flamethrower. Since we're dealing with a portion of the consumer population already well versed with gustatory discomfort, heat is the unifying factor within every variety of extreme chili sauce. It all boils down to how much heat the consumer is willing to internally handle.

The same can be likened to when the Leo and the Scorpio join romantic forces, but instead of heat, a similar concept of discomfort used for variation will be present anytime the lion and the scorpion interact together: challenge. It all boils down to how much challenge these two love consumers are willing to handle together. What, you both may be wondering, nails the concept of challenge so firmly into the foundation of the Leo Scorpio love union?

The signs of the lion and the scorpion both are of the same astrological quality: fixed. Far more than any of the other astrological qualities, the fixed signs experience the most challenge getting along with one another and maintaining a state of equilibrium as a couple.

As a whole, the fixed signs do not have the easiest time seeing other people's perspectives that aren't their own. Other fixed characteristics that are anything but easy are as follows: a natural tendency to resist change; a mental proclivity to see things in a one dimensional, black or white way; an inherent inclination to not want to compromise; or a consistent knack for being obstinate, which is a polite way of saying "pig-headed stubborn."

I'm sure all fixed parties are currently saying to themselves, "Wow, those people sound really difficult. I'm glad I'm not one of them," due to the fixed involuntarily knee-jerk response of initially saying no for the sake of saying no. But no matter, besides extreme chili sauces, your Love Author has deduced yet another example of challenging comparison that adequately describes the Leo Scorpio love union. The dating process between these two fixed signed powerhouses can also be compared to a *Godzilla* movie.

Much like the standard plot found in the typical *Godzilla* movie, the overall atmosphere needs to be picture postcard perfect when the Leo and the Scorpio first begin dating.

As in the Japanese fright flick, everything has to be fixed sign fantastic in order to juxtapose the truly horrific nature of what lies above or below, which soon shall volcanically descend upon the film's idyllic surroundings and peaceful townsfolk, much like in the *Godzilla* movie when the film's lead lovers walk hand in hand down the promenade, past the school as the closing bell rings. The teacher stands in the entrance, waving in slow motion and mouthing, "Goodbye, children!" to her happily exiting students. The camera pans up and away allowing the audience to see the churning volcano or bubbling ocean's surface far off in the distance.

Terror is about to descend upon Romanceville!

In other words (dramatic orchestral chords while a woman hysterically screams), the Leo and the Scorpio are about to have their first difference of opinion!!

Picture the lion and the scorpion walking paw and stinger together amidst the puffy clouds of honeymoon phase bliss, and then a disagreement or difference of opinion occurs. Instantly, both fixed signs will dig their heels into the ground, determined to never budge a millimeter for the duration of their lionly and scorpionic lives!

Upon seeing its fixed sign partner doing the aforementioned heel digging, the other fixed sign will become even MORE inflexibly unrelenting, stupefied at how obviously wrong its fixed sign partner is about everything.

Like the townspeople from the celluloid Japanese seaside town of placid perfection, everyone is taken completely off guard. No one sees it coming when Godzilla emerges from the ocean's depths, while Ghidora, the three-headed dragon, swoops down from the sky to have a screaming showdown of monster-sized proportions with the gargantuan lizard.

But just like the dapper and well-suited male lead whose mouth moves well before the audience hears his dubbed in English voice, your Love Author would like to inform all feuding fixed signed parties there may just be a way.

Plug your ears everybody because this one's gonna be a real screamer: COMPROMISE.

It's Romanceville's only hope, Leo and Scorpio-san!

Not just one, but both fixed signs will need to regularly compromise with its fixed sign partner in order for this relationship to NOT have a horror flick ending of romantic armageddon. Leo and Scorpio are two of the most stubborn signs in the known universe, and many seasons shall pass over this monster scene of ultimate obstinance before either side realizes its fixed sign partner is just as stubborn as itself.

Does anybody recall Godzilla ever relaxing or even exhaling a flaming sigh of relief? If Ghidorah was strong armed out of the picture, Rhodan or Mothra soon took its screaming place and the monster wars of inflexible will raged on and on.

The film's lead lovers may have gotten separated while Ghidorah was deflecting that flying school bus hand-flung by Godzilla, but they always manage to find each other in a tearful hug right before the movie's end just as the camera pans up and away to display the smoking carnage as peace once again returns to the town of Romanceville. Or does it?

I won't kid either of you, Leo and Scorpio. The love union between your signs won't be a simple matter of jumping through romantic hoops together. Much like how the concept of heat is a constant component with the various renditions of extreme chili sauce, the aspect of challenge will always be an ongoing factor within the Leo Scorpio love union.

But that's not to say all is gloom and doom regarding the astrological pairing of the lion with the scorpion! Should both fixed parties actively participate in the art of compromise, as well as accept the notion that challenge will be a regular feature of their relationship, this love union should be well equipped to romantically handle the heat no matter how extreme.

Leo-Sagittarius

(Blaring alarms. Flashing lights. Computer-generated voice repeating, "WINNER! We have a WINNER, FOLKS! WINNER! We have a WINNER, FOLKS!")

(Yell talking.) HELLO, LEO AND SAGITTARIUS! WOULD YOU BOTH PLEASE COME WITH ME!

(Passing through heavily curtained door, briskly walking down a long hall, and swiftly ducking into a quiet, dimly lit room.)

PLEASE COME IN AND HAVE A ... Excuse me. Please come in and have a seat.

Sorry for screaming in your faces. My ears were still ringing from all that racket!

As a precautionary measure, anytime the jackpot is hit on one of our machines, the lucky winners are escorted here following the happy, yet-to-be-determined, non-rigged event.

And that's just regarding your cash winnings. Upon observing the astrological fact our jackpot takers are born beneath the signs of Leo and Sagittarius and have just begun dating, the casino sent me ahead to ... I'm sorry, what was the question? How do we know you're a newly dating Leo and Sagittarius couple? Well, all I can say on the record is if you're going to take our money, we're going to know who is walking out the door with it.

Before being informed of just how much the government will be taking from your prize money before either of you see even a penny of it, I will be debriefing both of you regarding your actual love winnings.

Astrologically, the best romantic unions are those made up of two people born beneath the same element. Since Leo and Sagittarius are both fire signs, it really doesn't get much better than when these two members of the family of flame join romantic forces. Since the Fire signs are action oriented, romantically combining the Leo with the Sagittarius will feel as if every night of the initial dating process were an action packed carnival, or as reality dictates, a jackpot winning casino!

On the astrological surface of things, Leo and Sagittarius, you've both hit the romantic jackpot as far as pairing up with each other's best possible choice of zodiacal sign. But don't go cashing in all those love chips just quite yet.

Because both signs' astrological qualities are so dynamically different, the Leo and the Sagittarius are highly advised to give their budding new romance a longer than usual period of adjustment if they hope to achieve any kind of long-lasting romantic success.

These two signs may be housed under the same elemental roof, but when comparing the lion's and the centaur's astrological qualities, many times it'll seem as if the fixed nature of the Leo and the mutable quality of the Sagittarius emerged from opposite reaches of the solar system. Their overall approaches to things will inherently differ that greatly from each other.

The four fixed signs (Leo, Aquarius, Taurus, Scorpio) take place smack dab in the middle of each of the four seasons. The four mutable signs (Sagittarius, Gemini, Virgo, Pisces) occur at the tail end of a season.

As a whole, the fixed signs do not have the easiest time seeing other people's perspectives that aren't its own. Other fixed characteristics that are anything but easy are as follows: a natural tendency to resist change; a mental proclivity to see things in a one dimensional, black or white way; an inherent inclination to not want to compromise; or a consistent knack for being obstinate, which is a polite way of saying, "pig-headed stubborn."

The fixed signs hold on to what they know and resist the forces of change with a tightly fisted grip that would give even the multi-armed Hindu god Shiva immediate circulation problems. The mutable signs not only embrace the concept of change, they thrive on it. The fixed signs function best when their energies are concentrated on one dimension. The mutable signs are the multitaskers of the zodiac.

A mutable sign person CAN, in theory, attempt doing the slow and steady fixed sign approach of accomplishing one thing at a time, but it's practically a guarantee it will screw things up if it actively chooses that intensely focused dynamic. This is due to the traits shared amongst all the mutables of possessing not even the slightest shred of patience, as well as being susceptible to mind numbing boredom after sitting down for no longer than five minutes.

If the non-existent patience or driven to tears boredom doesn't do them in, then variety, the other driving force of motivation for the mutable signs, will. The mutable signs need the forces of change and variety to optimally function, but problems quickly arise when the need for those very needs can distract them from concentrating on any kind of follow through.

The fixed signs are known for their tenacity and focus by following things through to completion, but they are also known for their lack of motivation at getting those same things initially started. The mutable signs are known for doing as many simultaneous actions as physically possible, but are just as known for dropping said actions at choice times due to their susceptibility of being easily distracted.

Now, let's take the overall essence behind the qualities of fixed and mutable and apply them specifically to the fixed and mutable members of the fire-signed family. Leo has a slow and steady approach to life. Sagittarius' is fast and furious. Leo likes to have a sense of regimented routine in its day to day life. The only kind of routine a Sagittarian likes involves regular doses of variety and change in its day to day life as often as possible.

Leo prefers being in total control by planning things in advance. Hence, it's practically a guarantee the lion will arrive at any scheduled activity on time, every time. Sagittarius prefers things being spontaneous and tends to procrastinate to the last possible minute. Hence, it's practically a guarantee that most of the time the Sag is never on time.

Leo has the patience of a saint. Sagittarius can be a saint's worst nightmare if it has to wait more than half a microsecond longer than expected for anything.

The Leo's fixed quality makes its overall temperament steadily ground-ed and even keeled, as evidenced by the time the typical lion takes to slowly chew and fully savor its food whenever eating. The Sagittarian's mutable quality makes its overall temperament fast paced and high strung, as evi-denced by the milliseconds it takes for the typical centaur to power vacuum down its food and barely tasting any of it whenever eating.

The lion and the centaur stand to benefit a great deal from dating each other by virtue of the evolved aspects of one's astrological quality positively influencing the other. If the Sagittarius can refrain from being its usual Tasmanian devil self of frantically paced activity, it may just let the Leo teach it a thing or two about the art of relaxing.

Similarly, the Leo's sense of regimented routine may get a breath of much needed fresh air after following the Sagittarius around on one of its typical days, which is usually anything but typical. The centaur's varied and numerous interests can transport the lion far from its daily beaten path to unexplored, never-before-experienced activities.

If these two dynamically different fire signs take the time to adjust to each other's variations of speed and overall energies, the initial flames sparked by the Leo Sagittarius dating process stand to stoke themselves into a bonfire love union of long-lasting potential.

And should the Leo and Sagittarius absorb any of each other's posi-tive personality traits, the initial love winnings will break the bank by hitting the grand jackpot of romance.

Leo-Capricorn

You saw Leo at a what? Tag sale? GET OUT!

Capricorn was spotted where? The Salvation Army? NO WAY!

Granted everyone should have access to finding a bargain at a local tag sale, as well as freely be able to nab a deal at the community thrift store, but the false sightings mentioned above were meant to illustrate how UN-obvious either environment is for both the signs of Leo and Capricorn. It's kind of like when these two signs decide to date each other.

When looking at the prototypical wheel of the zodiac, the sign of Capricorn lies at a 150 degree angle from the sign of Leo. The proper astrological term for this very particular angle is the quincunx.

Everyone repeat along with me. Ready? "Ku-win-kwunx." Very good!

The quincunx is also known by the much easier pronounced, astrological reference word, inconjunct. When two signs are placed at an inconjunct angle of each other, nothing remotely matches and every inherent aspect of one sign is square pegged against the natural energies of the other.

Some keywords associated with the inconjunct are: redirection, challenge, diversion, and requires adjustment.

Even with the above said, there are glad tidings of the inconjunct kind for the lion and the goat romantically bonding together. Of all the astrological quincunx sign combos, the Leo Capricorn union is the least unobvious!

(A solitary tumbleweed blows past both the jungle and the mountains ...)

The outside world has a hard time picturing together the signs that are inconjunct of each other due to the high factor of unobviousness.

To reiterate, this inconjunct unobviousness is the least obvious with the Leo Capricorn love union.

Less is much more when it comes to standing beneath the spotlight of unobviousness, especially for signs who care a great deal about their public image, such as the lion and the goat.

The inconjunct differences between the Leo and the Capricorn may not be as overtly noticeable as the rest of the quincunx combos, but they are there in less subtle and more internalized ways.

Being a cardinal sign, the Capricorn's energies function best whenever building from the ground level up or starting from scratch. Initially putting things into motion may be the Cappie commodity, but having the follow through to see the start-up things reach completion is a major goat glitch.

Making the initial effort to start something from scratch can be a major challenge for the fixed sign Leo. However, once the Lion has begun, it's assumed the king of the jungle didn't exert itself for something to be dropped midway through or done half-heartedly. Follow through is a trademark of the feline fixed sign.

The Capricorn is the work horse of the zodiac and has a labor ethic unlike any other sign. The optimal work environment for the typical Cappie is a structured setting where the goat can steadily climb Mt. Status by gaining recognition whenever achieving its goat-like goals.

Much like the king of the jungle, the Leo will exert itself only when overtly necessary. Given its royal status, the lion doesn't take orders well and cannot be told what to do. After clashing with enough bosses and superiors, it should dawn on the naturally bossy types that its best work environment is working for itself or where it is boss and rule supreme.

The Leo is a creature of high romance that dreams of true love and of being married. The Capricorn is a creature of habit and hard work that's not at all romantic due to already being married to its job.

Whether finding it in its line of work or through a hobby, the Leo needs an outlet for creative self-expression in order to optimally function. That and the Lion needs to have some amount of fun in its life or it will begin to dramatically dysfunction from the perceived absence of it.

As I already mentioned, the Capricorn works a lot. (Cough.) Not only is there an absence of fun in the lives of many a Cappie, but with their naturally serious temperament, most goats barely crack a smile, let alone laugh out loud at a good joke, which the missing fun factor prevents them from ever understanding anyway.

Fortunately for this particular inconjunct pair, the Leo and the Capricorn do share two core personality traits: prestige and status. Prestige deals with a person's reputation arising from success, rank, or wealth. Status is the position of an individual believed to confer elevated rank or stature.

Prestige and status are two words that primarily have the same meaning. The Leo and the Capricorn converge at the same conclusion for both words, however the two signs differ in their modes of approach as to how they achieve either word's definition.

Otherwise known as the sign of status, the Capricorn, believes the high level of status associated with any kind of substantial material gain is achieved by only one thing: elbow grease (also known as working one's goat hooves to the bone).

The royalty sign, otherwise called Leo, believes that astrological nobility has its privileges. According to the lion's pride, prestige is earned by simply being born a Leo.

With both signs' inherent sense of status and prestige, the Leo and the Capricorn naturally gravitate towards social circles of notoriety, wealth, and power. Whenever they are in the public eye of the rich and powerful, the Lion and the Goat move about with a dignified sense of reserve. Both signs speak to those they are unfamiliar with in a business-formal tone that is detached but accompanied with the most impeccable of manners.

With the above said, it should be no surprise that appearance is of the utmost importance to both the Leo and the Capricorn. Here are two signs that would rather have their heads mounted in a trophy room than be spotted in public donning sweatpants or seen with any exposed body part that's either unmanicured or unshaved. This rule of appearance for both the lion and the goat applies to any kind of public exposure, be it attending a gala charity event in the early evening or stopping at the local convenience store for milk in the early morning.

With the above said and referring back to this chapter's opener, can everyone now perfectly picture the Leo rummaging through a tag sale of bric-a-brac, or the Capricorn clamoring for secondhand bargains at the local thrift store?

(Not one, but two tumbleweeds blow past both the jungle and the mountains while a vulture caws in the far distance ...)

Refraining from any further displays of overdone sarcasm, it can be inferred both signs have rather expensive tastes and are inherently allergic to anything resembling low quality or secondhand.

In order for this union of inconjunct signs to have a romantic pulse, both parties will need to mutually work at changing a core aspect of its astrological personality: expectation.

Leo, you can't expect the Capricorn to be the passionate partner of high romance you've idealistically dreamed about. They simply don't work that way. And speaking of work, Capricorn, you can't expect the Leo to be romantically content with the fact you're equally as committed to your job as you are to your partner. Work time must be sacrificed in some Capricorn capacity in order for personal time to be invested in order to make your lionly lover feel special and adored.

If both the Leo and the Capricorn manage to lower its unrealistically high level of expectations, they stand to raise each other's position in society by gaining noteworthy repute together as a romantic team.

Leo-Aquarius

Polar opposites.

When observing any given array of marketable goods, it's clear to see how the concept of polarization is firmly entrenched within today's consumer culture by attempting to sell itself in every way imaginable: hot/cold, old/new, tall/short, smoking/non-smoking, presweetened/sugar-free, etc.

Stepping back from the surface value of the modern and the marketable, the concept of opposites is what has also made the morality tale so popular from ancient times to the very present day. No matter our level of technological advancement, the polarized concept of opposites where there are good guys versus bad guys has spoken to the heart of humanity's core since the oral tradition of storytelling first began.

Despite the morality tale's unrealistically naïve structure of defined good and evil, they are just as well loved and still very much needed as when they were first told. This could be in the form of the ancient myth, such as Sumeria's Queen of Heaven, Ishtar versus the Queen of the Dead, Ereshkigal; or through the most wildly popular of science fiction, like *Star Wars'* Luke Skywalker versus Darth Vader. Or via that most modern of morality tales where there's no need to ask, "Are you a good witch or a bad witch?"

The answer is more than obvious with Harry Potter versus Lord Voldemort, which leads us to astrology.

Astrology's version of polar opposition is less definitive and far more complex than the telling of a morality tale, or whether one has purchased iced tea made with or without sweetener. The concept of opposites exists astrologically as well, but without a good versus bad basis of judgment, nor any kind of absolute, black or white approach. One of the best examples is the two of you, Leo and Aquarius.

For every sign of the zodiac, the universe counterbalances that sign's energies through its polar opposite. Just as it sounds, the polar opposite pairing of signs couldn't be any more diametrically different on many levels. However, equally as important but not nearly as obvious, polar opposites share as many similarities as they do differences.

Astrological polar opposition follows the same guidelines stipulated by a scientific law bearing the same name that states opposites attract.

Remember those magnet experiments they used back in junior high to demonstrate the law of attraction? Take those same oppositely charged pieces of metal that slammed into each other whenever within remote proximity together, except now one of the magnets is called Leo and the other Aquarius.

Despite all the heady analysis, your Love Author is compelled to say we are currently discussing the union of polar opposite signs, and being as such, they have very specific needs. Burning, barely controllable, loin-centered needs. Polar opposites naturally attract, and by naturally attract I mean they're seriously hot for each other/warm for each other's form. You get the lust-filled picture.

Moving away from the hot and bothered, let's review the individual backgrounds of both the lion and the water bearer to see how different and similar these polar opposites are when considering them as a romantic team.

Being the sign of self-expression, the Leo longs to stand apart from any given crowd. Being the sign of groups, the Aquarius longs to be a part of any given crowd.

High temperature descriptors such as warm, fiery, hot, or burning with desire often describe the Leo's passionate approach to things, which often can make this sign become overheated with hypersensitivity. The Aquarius approaches things with such an emotionally detached rationality, low temperature descriptors such as chilly, icy, frosty, or cool are often used to describe the water bearer's overall temperament.

Being the royal sign, the Leo will tend to give those they care for preferential treatment and will often treat those they don't care for with

blatant disdain. Being the egalitarian sign, the Aquarius is fiercely adamant about treating every person from every walk of life the same and
is just as fiercely against giving preferential treatment to any one individual. The Leo likes things tried and true. The Aquarius likes things
brand-spanking new.

With its sign ruling over the house of romance, the Leo expects to be
put on a pedestal where they are given top priority above all others and
adored whenever dating. With its sign ruling over the house of friendship, an Aquarian's friends are most important, so much so the water
bearer's pals are given equal and often top priority with whomever it is
dating.

The Leo's sense of theatrical dramatics is so heartfelt that others will
often question the lion's need to be so overemotional. The Aquarian's
sense of intellectualism is so emotionally detached that others will often
question if the water bearer actually has a heart, or any emotions whatsoever for that matter.

Being the futuristic sign, Aquarius is the most technologically savvy
of the zodiac and is well versed in the latest gadgetry. Being the sign
associated with traditionalism, the roar of the Leo can loudly be heard
whenever having to deal with any kind of gadgetry. Leo is all about star-
crossed lovers. Aquarius is all about *Star Wars*.

Even with all of the above differences mentioned, the rule with polar
opposites is they share similarities as well. Leo and Aquarius share the
same common quality of being fixed signs. Overall the fixed signs do
not have the easiest time seeing other people's perspectives that aren't
its own, besides being innately and unshakably obstinate, (a nice way of
saying pig-headed stubborn).

When the Leo and the Aquarius first begin dating, things couldn't go
any smoother. It's when these two fixed signs have their first difference
of opinion do they both realize just how immovably stubborn the other
can be.

When the first disagreement or verging of opinion occurs, the lion
and the water bearer will instantaneously dig their heels into the ground,
determined to never move a millimeter for the duration of their Leonine
and Aquarian lives.

Upon seeing its fixed sign partner doing the aforementioned heel digging, the other fixed sign will become even MORE inflexibly unrelenting and stupefied at how obviously wrong its fixed sign partner is about everything.

Allow your Love Author to bestow your fixed sign bond with the biggest of time savers, Leo and Aquarius: COMPROMISE.

Both fixed signs need to regularly compromise in order for this relationship to not just thrive but survive. Attraction is what brings the polar opposites together, which in turn yields some initial and immediate physically attracted behavior.

Even with that said, if there is nothing more other than a few fast and furious bed creaks, or in other words, if nothing lies beyond the initial attraction between the polar opposites, then the starting spark of core attraction will be snuffed out just as quickly as it began.

Why? The flames of opposing desire are almost always quickly doused due to both opposites driving each other naturally crazy after five post-bed creaking minutes.

But conversely, if the polar opposites can stand each other's presence for more than five minutes post you know and share a few things in common, then here is where we find those fairy tale relationships that stay together. Polar opposition is never a middle of the road affair resulting in anything remotely wishy-washy, Leo and Aquarius.

Optimally, the romantic bond between the lion and the water bearer could end up tighter than salt and pepper, but your conjoined energies may repel each other worse than Misters Potter and Voldemort grappling for the same wand in furious disgust.

But have no worries over either polar-opposite party from having to decide. Resisting a force of nature far bigger than either of you is an exercise of total futility.

Leo-Pisces

Seriously, Leo and Pisces, I need to throw this one out there. First and foremost, are you two SURE you're dating each other?

Maybe you both have different partners who either got lost or separated while all parties foraged their way to this particular chapter of the book?

Close, but no Cupid doll, huh?

So you both are unshakably sure in your convictions that one half of this newly budding romance is a Leo, and the other is a Pisces, right? Okay then. Boldly forward we go.

Sorry for all the obnoxious obviousness just then, Leo and Pisces, but your two signs romantically joining forces is definitely NOT a common occurrence one hears about every day, nor is your astrological union in any way, shape, or form obvious.

When looking at the prototypical wheel of the zodiac, the sign of Pisces lies at a 150 degree angle away from the sign of Leo. The proper astrological term for this very particular angle is the quincunx. Everyone repeat along with me. Ready? "Ku-win-kwunx." Very good!

The quincunx is also known by the much easier pronounced astrological reference word, "inconjunct." When two signs are placed at an inconjunct angle of each other, nothing remotely matches and every inherent aspect of one sign is square pegged against the natural energies of the other.

Some keywords associated with the inconjunct are: redirection, challenge, diversion, and requires adjustment.

Most of the outside world has a hard time picturing the two of you together due to your union's high factor of unobviousness. When viewed individually, one would think the lion and the cosmic fish were hardcore polar opposites. Each sign's inherent energies seem THAT different from each other.

Leo is a fire sign, which is an action-oriented element with an energetic dynamic that usually functions aggressively outward. Pisces is a water sign, which is an emotionally oriented element with an energetic dynamic that usually functions passively inward.

Because of its fiery foundation, an unevolved trait associated with the Leonine personality is a tendency to be over-aggressive. This will externally show itself by the Leo giving the impression of having total control over everything through the act of domination.

Because of its Watery foundation, an unevolved aspect to the Piscean personality is a tendency to be passive-aggressive. This will externally show itself by the Pisces giving the impression of having little to no control over anything through the act of victimization.

Being one of the three karmic signs, the Pisces derives the most fulfillment by serving others. Being the only solar sign, the Leo derives the most fulfillment by being noticed by others.

The Piscean's inherent sense of shyness tends to make it uncomfortably quiet with crowds and shun any kind of attention-getting spotlight. The Leo's inherent sense of ego tends to make it loud in crowds and bask beneath any kind of attention-getting spotlight.

The Leo's inborn sense of authoritative leadership makes it most agreeable to being its own superior and not at all agreeable to being given tasks or told what to do. The Piscean's inborn sense of service makes it agreeable to being given tasks and doesn't at all mind being told what to do provided it is asked nicely.

Leo prefers being in total control by planning things in advance. Hence, it's practically a guarantee the lion will arrive at any scheduled activity on time, every time. Pisces prefers things being spontaneous and tends to procrastinate to the last possible minute. Hence, it's practically a guarantee that the Piscean is never on time most of the time,.

The unevolved Leo is often accused of being too selfish to the point of playing the role of martyr by loudly complaining if it has to do something for someone other than itself. The unevolved Pisces is often accused of being too selfless to the point of playing the role of martyr by quietly doing everything for others other than what needs to be done strictly for itself.

The joining of the lion with the cosmic fish may be one of the most unobvious of astrological unions, but these very different signs do share some core similarities that could motivate them to stick together as a functioning love team: romantic inspiration and loyal devotion

With Leo's natural house of rulership being the fifth, otherwise known as the house of romance; and with Pisces' heavenly body of Neptune ruling over romantic poetry as well as the entire romance movement at large, the lion and the cosmic fish aren't just signs that are naturally romantic. These two take romance and make it seriously hardcore!

Unfortunately the world is currently quite the unromantic place. Mention the word courting nowadays and most people will think you're either talking about the latest basketball stats or your plans to actively sue someone. Even with such a romantically restrictive backdrop, the signs of the lion and the fish both respond to and interact best through the process of courting.

Courting (noun): A way of getting to know a person through gradual stages of increased intimacy by incorporating romance with social activities.

Upon first meeting, the Leo and the Piscean should easily make each other's better romantic acquaintance by naturally knowing how to engage in the proper rules of courtship. Both signs will more than likely be shocked by the realization that they TOO will be on the receiving end of amorous actions that meet each other's high romantic standards.

In regards to the people whom they deeply care for, those born beneath the sign of the lion hearted are known for its unfaltering sense of loyalty. Those born with the planet of unconditional love as its ruler are known for its Piscean sense of unfaltering devotion.

Put them together with some favorable love conditions and the result is two people who are loyally devoted by being there for each other no matter the circumstances.

I won't kid either of you, Leo and Pisces. Your love union won't always be the smoothest sailing or a simple matter of jumping through romantic hoops. Joining the natural energies of the lion and the cosmic fish will often give cause for either sign to misinterpret the other's actions. The Pisces' quiet nature may be misinterpreted by the Leo to be judgmentally disapproving, and the lion's sense of straightforwardness could easily offend the cosmic fish without the forward fire sign even knowing it.

It's crucial both signs take their time during the initial courting process in order to adjust to the vast differences of dynamic between each other's natural energies. If not, the romantic flames first generated by this particular fire water partnership stand to douse themselves out far faster versus having any kind of chance of successfully swimming together as long-term lovers.

Virgo-Virgo

Hello and welcome to Virgo Jeopardy! It's the trivia game show where both the studio audience along with its competing contestants are nothing but, you guessed it, VIRGOS!

Give your hard-working humble selves a big round of much needed applause that never seems to be fully allotted to your sign in the non-game show world, virgins!

Before we officially begin, let's check off the first bit of business from our Virgoan list of game rules. All Virgoan answers need to be perfectly put in the form of a question. So come on, all you stationary fanatics! Is everyone ready? Let's VIR-GO!

Virgo Jeopardy Question One: The answer is: The etymological or original source behind the Virgoan mantra, "Cleanliness is next to Godliness." You all have twenty seconds starting NOW!

(Virgo Jeopardy theme music)

Time's Up! Jeesh, could that have been any easier, studio audience? How many of our Virgoan contestants' final answer deals with a particular book placed in every hotel room bureau that's too small to be of the phone variety and too large to be of the black variety?

Did you virgins catch your Love Author's divine drift?

Well those Virgos who replied with the very obvious answer of "What is the bible," you are 100 percent WRONG. At first glance the saintly statement of sanitation seems as if it couldn't be from any other source BUT a biblical one, but detailed truth be told, nowhere within the good book can that particular phrase be found.

Those Virgos currently self-flagellating themselves by responding with, "Who was eighteenth century evangelist and co-founder of Methodism,

John Wesley?" are very much mistaken because that IS the correct answer! On to round two!

Virgo Jeopardy Question Two: The answer is: The astrologically distinct grouping Virgo shares with the zodiacal signs of Pisces and Scorpio.

Those Virgins who responded: "What are the karmic signs?" I have this to say: You're correct! The karmic signs are those residents of the zodiac that enter this plane of existence with an inherent awareness of needing to be of service to others. Onto the last round of Virgo Jeopardy!

While the middle representatives of the earthy element prepare for their last and final round, let's hear a few words from our Virgoan sponsor, Caring Colonics, because we all need a regimen of maintenance, even down there.

Welcome back, everybody!

Virgo Jeopardy Question Three: The answer is: A Virgoan standard where the word "Godliness" can be equally interchanged with or substituted.

All Virgos answer in overwhelming unison: "WHAT IS PERFEC-TION?" Well folks, that's all the stopwatched to the exact nanosecond time we have left! Time for this show to VIR-GO! Cleanliness, details, repetition, self-flagellation, karmic service to others, worry, and perfection are all Virgoan themes that two Virgos must face with itself and its same-signed partner when dating each other.

I won't kid either of you perfection seekers. There are very few exceptions (actually there's only one and it so isn't your sign), but it's generally frowned upon for a person born beneath one sign to date another of its own astrological kind.

This cosmic criticism is based on the astrological theory of each sign's double dated presence bearing a particularly problematic potential specific to every individual resident of the zodiac.

It's kind of like when your Love Author hints every person born beneath the sign of the Virgin pretend as if they're COMPETING in an astrologically fictitious game show. The problematic potential specific to the sign of Virgo whenever dating itself? COMPETITION.

The potential problems each resident of the zodiac faces whenever dating itself varies for every sign. For some, naturally strong qualities become amplified, such as two Aries becoming even MORE fight club-ish when dating each other.

For others, such as the Venus-ruled signs, naturally weak traits come to surface, like when two Taureans become so stringently sedentary or two Librans so uber-indecisive, neither same signed team gets much accomplished whenever together.

It's different for the middle representatives of the earthy element. When two Virgos romantically join forces, their problematic potential involves a trait not even associated with their sign. Despite all enquiring Mercurial minds wanting to know more, a quick overview must be made of the typical Virgoan personality before any further romantic analysis is made.

Speaking of analysis, every sign has a core phrase that begins with the word "I" followed by a verb specific to that sign. The sign of the Virgin's core phrase is: "I ANALYZE." That Virgoan verb packs quite the perfectionist punch, but more on that in just a bit.

Virgo is an earth sign, whose astrological quality is mutable, is planetarily ruled by Mercury, and its naturally ruling house is the sixth of health and daily work. The earth signs process the outside world, in particular what is tangible, first and foremost with its senses.

The mutable signs occur as each of the four seasons draws to a close, right before another begins. The mutables function best in environments containing some level of variety and change and are the multitaskers of the zodiac. Mercury is the fastest moving planet that orbits the sun and astrologically oversees the rational processes of human thought, speech, and communication. Mercurial types tend to be highly intelligent, fast talkers, even faster learners, and are always mentally curious to learn something about everything.

Looking once more at Virgo's core phrase of "I ANALYZE," the verb refers to the Mercurial mind of the Virgo, but within also lies the word "ANAL," a descriptor referring to that sign's precision to detail, as well as its house rulership of health. Thus the Virgo's inherent need for its world to be as hygienically clean as humanly possible.

This is also the only resident of the zodiac whose self-identity is interchangeable with the work they do. Take the Virgo's self-identifying work ethic, add to that the feature of being a karmic sign whose overall cosmic purpose is serving others, and the end result is a person with a near perfect work standard that has no competition except themselves.

So what to do when a person born beneath a sign known for its humility and detail driven work ethic that functions best whenever servicing others romantically gets involved with another of the same astrological ilk? They compete. Not overtly, nor even consciously most times. But when placed next to another who is equally as hard working and detail driven, the naturally non-competitive nature of the individual Virgo can morph into quite the aggressively unspoken competition whenever two people born beneath the perfection seeking sign of the Virgin decide to date each other.

One Virgo's house is neat and tidy. The other Virgo proceeds to make its house immaculate. One Virgo's office is extremely well organized. The other Virgo proceeds to invent its own Dewey Decimal-like system of administrative organization. One Virgo efficiently makes the most of its pantry space. The other Virgo proceeds to rearrange all its canned goods not just by size but alphabetically and by color coordination. The competition is never direct, but it is there, leaving the two earth signs exhausted but unable to put a finger as to exactly why their same signed union leaves them both so energetically wiped out.

This nagging sense of underlying exhaustion eventually puts an end to most double Virgin couplings, many times with neither Virgo figuring out exactly why things romantically had to conclude in the first place.

Double Jeopardy final answer, Virgins. The answer is: Competing indirectly towards a physically exhausted breakup or non-competitively breaking free of the trappings typically posed whenever your sign dates each other? And this time around, nothing whatsoever can be put into the form of a romantic question.

Virgo-Libra

You both must have heard that old adage that still applies in the modern day, right Virgo and Libra? It goes something along the lines of a person can choose its friends, but not its neighbors.

This neighborly concept applies astrologically as well, yet also is completely irrelevant whenever playing the zodiacal dating game. Take you two for example.

Nothing can change the astrological fact the signs of Virgo and Libra are next door neighbors with each other on that big wheel of life, otherwise known as the zodiac. Yet that inalterable information is neither karmic apples nor cosmic oranges during those not so common times when the virgin and the scales decide to join romantic forces.

Moving from old adages to more modern rules of cosmic thumb, it's generally understood the signs that border each other are categorized beneath a most unexciting descriptor of astrological compatibility: neutral.

(A solitary cough can be heard in the far off, remote distance.)

Every sign has the potential to work together. Some combinations take a lot more work than others just to achieve a state of equilibrium. With the joining of the signs considered to be neutral of each other, the state of equilibrium is akin to that solid borderline that naturally forms whenever oil and vinegar are put into the same container. In other words, mixing the two isn't a bad thing, but a whole lot of shaking is needed for there to be any kind of blend.

At their core, the signs of Virgo and Libra function from very different perspectives, which makes it seem as if they lived on the opposite ends of town versus being astrological next door neighbors.

With its sign ruling over the house of daily work, the Virgo identifies its overall self with its job and the work it does. With the planet of beauty being its ruler, and in turn, its sign naturally ruling over the house of marriage and partnership, the Libra identifies itself with its physical appearance and how attractively appealing it is to prospective partners.

As already mentioned, the Virgo is all about the work it does and the productive output of its labors. With its planetary ruler, Venus, overseeing such niceties as pleasure and luxury, the Libra is all about having to do the least amount of work possible if it can help it.

The Virgo believes in the concept of perfection and strives to achieve it, no matter how humanly impossible. The Libra believes in the concept of true love that lasts forever and strives to achieve it, no matter how humanly impossible.

Take the Virgo's need for perfection, project it into physical form, and the result is yet another human impossibility: the ever appreciative boss. Take the Libra's need for true love that lasts forever, project it into physical form, and the result is yet another human impossibility: the soul mate that's a match made in heaven.

Being naturally prudent and despising waste of any kind, the Virgo will make the most of its money by partaking in such cost effective activities as cutting coupons and hunting for bargains. Having the most refined sense of taste and luxury of the Zodiac, the Libra's penchant for expensive things makes it despise such cost effective activities as cutting coupons and hunting for bargains. For the Virgo, it's all about the sweat on one's brow produced by good old fashioned elbow grease. For the Libra, it's all about never breaking a sweat and exfoliating often, even around the elbow area. Romance means everything to the Libra. Romance means next to nothing to the Virgo.

Being the multitasker of the zodiac, the Virgo usually makes numerous decisions each day with lightning speed proficiency. Unless hit by lightning, it usually takes a change of seasons for the Libra to make any kind of definite decision no matter the day.

Adjustments of astrological temperament are required of both signs if this romantic union wishes to have a pulse, let alone last. By far, the biggest problems potentially pose themselves during the earliest stages when the Virgo and the Libra first begin dating.

Hands down, of the two, the Libra will need to do more of the initial adjusting than the Virgo due to romance, a quality that is abundantly inherent in its sign being notably absent in its partner.

Libra, tell yourself from the get go that your Virgo man will not be the romantic knight in shining armor who will properly court you by chivalrously taking the lead with everything. Nor will your Virgo lady be the damsel in distress that'll swoon over each of your romantic gestures and be overcome with amorous feelings every time you meet.

The Libra must be okay with the fact its heightened sense of romanticism will not be addressed and often not even recognized with its Virgoan partner. However, even with that said, the two traits that stand out with a Virgoan love interest, while although not dripping with romantic passion, are still quite admirable: efficiency and earnestness.

This is not a sign you'll hear your Virgo love rattling off a list counting all the ways it loves thee, rather it is the sign that efficiently rattles off a list of what needs to be done while rolling up its sleeves and earnestly standing by your side in the midst of a problem or crisis.

Know this up front too, Libra. It's not in the Virgo's astrological foundation to be overly or overtly complimentary. This is not the sign that will gush over the new outfit you just bought or openly admire your most recent haircut. The Virgo will, in all likelihood, NOTICE these things since this is the sign of details but most likely won't say anything outright about them.

Breezily blowing along, we'll now focus on Libra, the air-signed member of this love union. Virgo, we already know how important work is to your sign. This will, in all likelihood, not be the case with your Libran lover. In fact, when first exposed to the scales' love of luxury and attentiveness to its looks, a particular non-hard-workin" word might at first come to mind—lazy, which the Virgo must never utter aloud if it wishes to keep the affections of its Libran love interest. Accept the fact your Libra does not share the same self-identifying work ethic as you, Virgo, and don't hold it against him or her by acting in an outwardly resentful way.

Usually at this point of the program, your Love Author would expound upon the positive traits shared amongst couples comprised of two signs that are neutral of each other, but not this time around.

If the positive qualities of the Virgo Libra love union are overlooked or hard to identify, this astrological combo won't get off the ground whatsoever. What needs to still be addressed is an aspect of the most unevolved kind associated with the Virgo Libra love union should they operate mainly from the negative spectrum: judgmental prissiness.

When viewed individually, Virgo's ideal of perfection and Libra's ideal of beauty are unrealistically challenging enough. However, when placed within the negative spectrum, the overall perspective of things becomes thoroughly flawed and downright ugly due to both signs being uber-uptight and judgmentally critical together as a romantically unevolved team.

No relationship is perfect, virgins and scales. To help ensure your survival as a romantic couple, both signs will need to get its hands dirty by allowing itself to be vulnerable in the presence of the other, regardless if any blemishes of imperfection should show.

Virgo-Scorpio

If the love union between the virgin and the scorpion had to be reduced to merely one word or solitary phrase, it would be Kodomo-no-Asobi, Virgo and Scorpio. Allow your Love Author to explain.

Kodomo-no-Asobi was a Japanese parlor game played by upper class teenage girls in the late eighteenth and early nineteenth centuries. The game is like Blind Man's Bluff for the most part but with extra rules of play for added maturing measure. Just as in Bluff, one person is designated "it" and is blindfolded in the midst of a large, open space. Like Marco Polo, the rest of the players must call out to the person designated "it" while avoiding being touched by whoever is "it."

Unlike Blind Man's Bluff or Marco Polo, Kodomo-no-Asobi stands apart from the typical parlor game involving blindfolds. It was played amongst young adults, namely Japanese teens on the verge of becoming young ladies of status. With that in mind, this particular game of the blindfolded variety went beyond the chaotic motions and random groping typically displayed amongst little kids.

Kodomo-no-Asobi incorporated the maturing concepts of trust and relaxation through its two additional rules of play: all participants were dressed in her best kimono while playing; and the traditional device of the blindfold was still utilized but the "it" person had to seek and find the rest of the players blindfolded while holding a full cup of tea.

Holding a full cup of tea while blindfolded forced the "it" person to strategize with a relaxed sense of decorum versus impulsively flailing about and randomly groping at the open air. The person designated "it" had to acutely listen in order to ascertain the location of the other players' voices for the purpose of seeking them out with a relaxed motion of intent. That or she stood the risk of staining her best kimono or worse, scalding herself (depending on whether the tea used during the game was heated or at room temperature).

On one level, Kodomo-no-Asobi seems like quite the easy game by virtue of its straightforward rules of play. On another level, the added rules to this coming of age Blind Man's Bluff made it deceptively challenging and socially complex, which is much like when the Virgo and the Scorpio join romantic forces.

On one level, the virgin and the scorpion possess the automatic ease and advantage of astrological cohesion by virtue of the two signs being elementally complementary to each other. On another level, this particular pairing has the potential of never experiencing the natural ease and flow created whenever two complementary signs romantically bond due to both signs' inherently intense natures. More on the intense stuff in just a bit.

In astrology, the four elements of earth, air, fire, and water are naturally paired off. Each grouping consists of two elements that are cohesive, or naturally work well together, which is otherwise known as being complementary. For this particular pairing, the elements of earth and water astrologically complement each other. By virtue of their elemental foundations, the earth and the water signs share a core motivational trait: security.

Representing the element of earth and ruling over the house of daily tasks and chores, the Virgo gains security through its work. So much the majority of those born beneath the sign of the Virgin identify their overall sense of self with their jobs and work output.

Representing the element of water and ruling over the house of death and transformative change, Scorpio is known as the survivor sign where it can outlast the rest of the zodiac by making due with as little or few resources as possible. Those born beneath the sign of the scorpion derive security from its most basic of necessities. Anything additional is considered to be either icing on the cake or totally superfluous.

Both signs approach things with an intensity that's rather, well, intense. The Virgo is usually intensely focused on whatever task needs to be completed next or whichever room, person, or thing needs to be thoroughly scoured and cleansed. The Scorpio's intensity is so all-encompassing it will only bother with things it feels will have complete and total follow through. Anything appearing either half-hearted or -assed won't even register on the Scorpio's radar.

Besides old fashioned parlor games, the cohesion of the complementary elements of earth with water can be likened to something a bit more updated and concrete: a river dam. A constructed obstruction placed directly in the path of a flowing body of water can produce any number of effective results, from a re-routed water supply to a hydro-electric energy source. The key to a dam's effectiveness is its foundation.

The proper positioning of a dam's foundation requires consideration of both the earthy component of the dam itself, as well as the pressure and speed of its watery counterpart. Should either side be overlooked or not taken into full consideration, the dam may stand on its own at first, only to disintegrate a short time after its construction.

More often than not, the union of the Virgo and the Scorpio will begin quite soundly, only to fall apart a short time later due to one half overlooking or not taking into full consideration the needs of the other. This is almost always due to the intense nature of either sign being so powerfully focused on a particular purpose or goal that assumptions will be made without the reinforcement of communication.

But as your Love Author's effective yet thoroughly intimidating fourth grade teacher, Sister Rita Stoneface would often say, "When one assumes, one makes an ASS of U and ME."

Continuing with our river dam imagery, let us imagine communication to be the binding cement that holds the foundation of the dam securely into place by virtue of it dispelling any erroneous assumptions being made between either portion of this intense love duo.

For there to be any semblance of romantic success between the virgin and the scorpion, another love metaphor must be included. Since those born beneath the sign of the virgin are especially fond of repetition, and those fixed-signed Scorpios derive comfort from what they have prior experience with, your Love Author would like to come full circle by re-introducing Kodomo-no-Asobi, our Japanese Blind Man's Bluff game for nineteenth century rich girls.

The game sets itself apart from a bunch of hyperactive tots screamingly flailing about by two factors that the Virgo Scorpio Love union must possess if it wishes to not only thrive, but survive overall: trust and relaxation.

By wearing her best kimono and holding a full cup of tea in her hand, the Japanese teen who is "it" must find within herself the poise to move fluidly in as a relaxed manner as possible, as well as trust in herself that she will eventually no longer be "it."

If our "it" girl became too intense while playing, she risked more than just staining her good clothes. Kodomo-no-Asobi taught by example that one's placement in society was best maintained with a consistently relaxed composure. For where there is trust and relaxation, intensity can never be found.

Virgo and Scorpio, the romantic merger between two complementary signs at first glance sounds like the biggest piece of astrological cake to swallow, but after reading this chapter, both of you now know better.

Virgo-Sagittarius

Hold up, Virgo and Sagittarius. I need to step out for a bit and find me a Red Bull and any excuse of an energy bar 'cause you two are WORK.

Alrighty then! Now that I've done what's humanly best to crank my energies up to as maximum a non-illegal level as I can, allow me to start by being brutally blunt. The two of you are SURE you're dating each other, right?

I should preface things by stating that every sign has the potential to work together in a romantically involved way. It's just that some signs take a lot more work to achieve a state of equilibrium than others. And to repeat what I stated earlier, you two are WORK!

Of the twelve signs, Virgo and Sagittarius are each other's biggest challenge to relate with naturally due to each sign's placement on the zodiac wheel. They are positioned from each other at the harshest astrological angle possible of 90 degrees, which is better known as the square.

When two signs square each other, a consistently high probability exists for one to easily rub the other the wrong way, quite often because either or both signs are simply being their natural selves.

To put things into contrasting perspective, Virgo is ruled by Mercury, the smallest planet in all the solar system, and Sagittarius is ruled by Jupiter, the biggest space ball of them all. That one juxtaposition of difference should always be kept in mind whenever the two signs' energies are compared, contrasted, or bound together in either wedded bliss or tongue-blistering divorce court.

Since Mercury is the smallest planet in the solar system, the Virgo is naturally meticulous over the tiniest of details. So much that there are certain occasions when these detail-driven ones miss the forest altogether due to getting stuck in the nit-picky branches of each individual tree.

Since Jupiter is the most gargantuan heavenly body in the solar system, the Sagittarius sees things from a large scope, big picture perspective. The centaur's far-reaching sight clearly can see the overall forest or end result, but the details on how to realistically get there are either blurred at best or nowhere within its field of vision.

Extrapolating a smidge more on the theme of the smallest and largest planets associated with the virgin and the centaur, the Mercurial mental focus of the Virgo makes it keenly aware of any untidiness, causing it to be clean in a most hygienic manner. The Jupiterian wide vision of the Sagittarius makes it oblivious to most untidiness, causing many a centaur (especially of the college-age dude variety) to be sloppy in a most unhygienic manner.

Along with the extreme juxtaposition of their planetary rulers' space-ball size, the Virgo and Sagittarius' cosmic foundations of existence differ just as drastically as well.

Along with Pisces and Scorpio, Virgo is considered one of the three karmic signs who enter this plane of existence with an inherent awareness to be of service to others.

Many Eastern philosophies theorize the soul of a person born beneath a karmic sign felt not enough was done for others in previous lives, and the needs of the self in this life cycle must now take a backseat as a form of karmic retribution. Hence, the sign of the Virgin's perfectionist work ethic and multitasking responsibilities do not naturally occur strictly from heartfelt good intentions. According to karmic theory, the motivation behind any of the Virgo's hard earned labors is based on its soul's need to rectify cosmic balance.

Along with Jupiter, the largest planet in the solar system is known by another name: the great benefic, which is a grand title referencing Jupiter's energies overflowing with abundance and good luck.

Many Eastern philosophies theorize when one is born with the great benefic as its planetary ruler (this means you, Sag), that person's life will be blessed overall with good timing, good fortune, and incredibly good luck due to its soul amassing good karma in life cycles prior to the one it is currently living.

Although its sign is clearly marked with karmic abundance, many a centaur can become far too accustomed to being a walking four-leaf clover, along with expecting everything to naturally work out. The Sag's approach to life when unevolved can end up being both highly presumptuous and just as highly irresponsible.

From a sheer karmic perspective, the Virgo earns every bit of good karma through its blood, sweat, and elbow grease.

Things work a little differently for the Sagittarian (major lack of emphasis on the word "work"). For the child of Jupiter, its very atypical, constant state of luckiness and near perfect knack for being in the right place at the right time are perks bestowed by the universe just for being born under the sign of Sagittarius. This is not necessarily from any generous deeds done on its part for the good of all mankind, as many an unevolved centaur would often like others to believe.

Things are going to get tense when romantically joining someone working at full capacity to subconsciously pay off its karmic debts with someone who doesn't have to lift a finger for its karmic credit. An ever-growing reserve of resentment will more than likely build up over time between the person born beneath the sign of karmic retribution (hint: Virgo) and the one born under the sign of karmic abundance (pssst! Sagittarius).

Said another way, the more time these two signs spend together, the higher the likelihood the Virgo will end up criticizing the Sag for its lack of planning/overlooking of details/high level of partying/lounging around, and in turn the Sagittarius will highly resent such Virgoan verbal tongue lashings. This leaves not too much room for our couple in question to simply kiss and make up.

In order for this particular pairing to have a pulse, a certain aspect must be shared by both the Virgo and the Sagittarius from the very first moments of their Love union's inception: ACCEPTANCE. Sag, accept your Virgoan partner will allow no more than twelve minutes to pass before the uncontrollable urge hits them to clean, organize, or partake in its favorite pastime: WORK.

Virgo, accept your Sagittarian love interest will have a much more relaxed approach to such things as work and discipline, as well as your pony partner will in no way be nearly as germophobic as your hypoallergenic selves.

Virgins, the key to making any fire sign happy can be reduced to one word, which on the surface sounds like a snap, but in reality can be fiendishly difficult to produce: FUN. If a fire sign feels it's having fun, even the tiniest amount, it can handle any romantic challenge placed before it.

Should the Centaur find itself in the proverbial dog house with its Virgo lover, one word: STATIONERY. It may not be the solution to anything, but stationery is a great tool of distraction given the fact organizational paper products are the Virgo's Achilles heel for remaining angry at someone.

Virgo and Sagittarius, as stated from the get-go, you both have your work cut out for you. Taking precautions such as accepting each other for who you are both naturally and astrologically will be required if this relationship between two such differing personalities as yourselves is to have any chance at romantically succeeding. And a fresh supply of laser beam letterhead at your ready disposal can't hurt either.

Virgo-Capricorn

Lifestyles of the Rich and Famous.

That's what immediately comes to mind when I think of your signs joining romantic forces, Virgo and Capricorn. Perfect, right?

(Crickets.)

I'm guessing many of you have no idea what your Love Author is referring to. Heck, I'll go a step further and bet a good portion of you weren't even born yet when it aired on prime time.

Lifestyles of the Rich and Famous was a television program that debuted in the mid-1980s and lasted for an entire decade until the mid-1990s. Each week the show's cameras would come a knockin' on the front doors of every Richie and Rebecca Rich within the worlds of entertainment and sports.

The premise of the program was for the host to casually drop by on the owners of estates so vast they could have each had their own zip code. Said in more earthy terms, *Lifestyles* showcased the one thing that motivates those born beneath the sign of Capricorn the most: STATUS. So much that the show's hosts, Robin Leach and Shari Belafonte, were both born under Virgo, the sign known for its attention to detail, so that at any given moment, either could spend a good portion of air time describing every fine-lined detail behind each obscenely expensive item of luxury. Things featured on the show were so costly that we viewers at home could never hope to ever own, let alone be physically near, unless we magically hit the lottery jackpot.

Speaking of hitting the jackpot, the best romantic matches are those made between two people born beneath the same element. Since the signs of the virgin and the mystic mountain goat are both earth signs, YOU'VE HIT THE ROMANTIC JACKPOT, VIRGO AND CAPRICORN!

When two signs are of the same element, a strong likelihood exists that both parties will get along harmoniously well, as well as see things eye to eye as partners. The earth signs function first and foremost through the sensual and tangible worlds. In other words, anything considered an actual thing that can be tasted, touched, heard, smelt, or seen registers best with those born under the element of earth.

When put in a more modern perspective, the earth signs garner the most security from the possessions they own, the money and material assets they have, and the work they do.

Hey! Did someone just mention that labor intensive concept otherwise known as WORK? The W-word takes on a whole new meaning whenever dealing with the two signs of the zodiac who most value work matters.

The Virgo is so work oriented its entire sense of self is tied into its job and work. The Capricorn is such a relentless laborer that what the rest of the zodiac considers to be a hard day's work is what the average Cappie gets done on its day off.

Let's put it this earth-signed way. It's practically an absolute guarantee the Virgo and the Capricorn won't be hearing any of the following upon first dating each other:

[start bulleted list]

"I'm in between jobs at the moment."

"For some reason me and the right employment just haven't crossed paths yet."

"I've always lived with my mother."

"I'm a little short on cash. Think you can cover the tab this time around?"

"Hey, you got a 20 spot I can borrow? I'll pay you back on the next date."

[end list]

Besides being naturally hard workers, those born beneath the element of earth are inherently practical, responsible, and of the non-slacking, non-unemployed variety of person.

Work may be of the utmost importance to both signs, but how the Virgo and the Capricorn actually approach the W-word differs quite significantly.

Being ruled by Mercury, the smallest and fastest moving planet in our solar system, the Virgo approaches work with a roll-up-your-sleeves, here and now approach, tackling whichever task has the highest priority first. Being ruled by the life-altering planet known as the lord of karma, Saturn, the Capricorn's work is most productively effective when a particular concept is present: THE GOAL. No matter how high up or far off, the work ethic of the Capricorn functions best when it has an aspired goal in mind.

Can anyone guess the biggest pitfall the Virgo and the Capricorn consistently encounter whenever dating each other? Give that earth sign a valid savings and retirement fund for supplying the correct answer of: A much higher than average chance of never seeing each other. This is due to the two work horses of the zodiac being married already to their jobs!

Because these two signs are SO work oriented, terms such as vacation, recreation, relaxation, and even sleep tend to be absent from each of its individual vocabularies, let alone when they begin dating each other.

For starters, when initially dating, a few hours will need to be shaved off of those fourteen-hour work days with at least one evening per weekend being work-free if you labor intensive ones hope to ever get to know each other better. I can only imagine how much discomfort that last statement must have caused both of you, but the romantic truth hurts sometimes.

The next landslide of negative potential two earth signs are prone to experiencing after becoming romantically involved together lends itself to be far more of a problem (more like an epidemic in these modern times), especially amongst those Capricorns that actively tap into the unevolved behavior patterns of their sign: ABUNDANCE FLAUNTING.

Don't get me wrong, goat guys and girls. Because your sign is astrologically designed to be the uber-worker of the zodiac, many a Cappie has an inherent need to drive the latest model of Mercedes or wear the most frightfully expensive eye gear as an expression of its Saturnine work ethic that is like no astrological other.

In other words, your Love Author fully understands the Capricorn's need to display its level of status as a way of openly declaring to the world: "I EARNED THIS BY WORKING MY GOAT HOOVES TO THE BONE," which unto itself isn't a bad thing. It's when the last of the earth sign's need to display its hard work morphs into the unevolved act of flagrantly flaunting its abundance becomes problematic.

As stated earlier, those born beneath the element of earth like their things. From an individualized perspective, the Capricorn personality is prone to the unevolved act of flaunting its abundance. Add another earth sign into the mix (that means you, Virgo) who just happens to lean towards the unevolved state of being materialistic, and the result is a couple that'll make keeping up with the Jones' look like mere kid's play. Their need to consume the latest/greatest, bigger/better "things" will become all consuming quite literally.

Should both the virgin and the mountain goat keep the abundance flaunting at bay, as well as dedicate their working energies to cover their professional goals individually and their personal goals together as a romantic team, then truly I say unto both earth signs, you'll be richer than Midas and have more abundance than any given episode of *Lifestyles of the Rich and Famous*. Champagne wishes and caviar dreams, Virgo and Capricorn!

Virgo-Aquarius

Seriously, Virgo and Aquarius. I need to throw this one out there. First and foremost, are you two SURE you're dating each other?

Maybe you both have different partners who either got lost or separated while all parties foraged their way to this particular chapter of the book? Close, but no cupid doll, huh?

So both of you are unshakably sure in your convictions that one half of this newly budding romance is a Virgoan and the other an Aquarian, right? Okay, then. Boldly forward we go.

Sorry for all the obnoxious obviousness just then, Virgo and Aquarius, but the two of you romantically joining forces is definitely NOT a common occurrence one hears about every day. Nor is your astrological union in any way, shape, or form obvious. In fact, the union of the virgin with the water bearer is about as unobvious an astrological match as one could ever hope to find.

When looking at the prototypical wheel of the zodiac, the sign of Aquarius lies at a 150 degree angle from the sign of Virgo. The proper astrological term for this very particular angle is the quincunx. Everyone repeat along with me. Ready? "Ku-win-kwunx." Very good!

Now, the quincunx is also known by the much easier pronounced, astrological reference word inconjunct. When two signs are placed at an inconjunct angle of each other, nothing remotely matches and every inherent aspect of one sign is square pegged against the natural energies of the other.

Some keywords associated with the inconjunct are: redirection, challenge, diversion, and requires adjustment.

I won't kid either of you, Virgo and Aquarius. Most of the outside world has a hard time picturing the two of you together due to your union's high factor of unobviousness. When viewed individually, one would think the person born beneath the sign of the virgin and the individual born under the sign of the water bearer were hardcore polar opposites. Both signs' energies and overall personalities seem THAT inherently different from each other.

The element of earth derives security from what is concrete and familiar. Mercury is the planetary ruler of the middle representative of the earth signs (this means you, Virgo) and is the fastest heavenly body in our solar system that clocks in the most elliptical orbits around the sun more than any other planet per year. For the Virgo, the more repetitions of familiarity that is experienced, the more security the person born beneath the sign of the harvest maiden derives overall.

The element of air predominantly functions in and expresses itself best through the workings of the rational mind, namely thought and communication. Uranus is the planetary ruler of the last representative of the air signs (front and center, Aquarius) and is the heavenly body that sets itself as far apart from all the other space balls in our solar system by virtue of its Greek versus Roman name and wholly unique egg-like elliptical orbit around the sun. Thus the typical Aquarian is anything but typical. Its natural quirkiness and fierce sense of individualism gives it an overall disdain for anything everyone else considers to be familiar and/or tried and true.

The Virgo most enjoys working within a pre-established, defined structure. The Aquarius least enjoys working outside of any given structure that isn't of its own making. The Virgo functions best whenever assigned tasks from the authorities above that they can complete to near perfect perfection. The Aquarius functions best when rebelling against the authorities above or against any assignment or task they are told they must complete.

The Virgo's sense of style is downplayed and tends to be of a more conservative nature. With the nature of the Aquarius being so inherently non-conformist, nothing is downplayed or conservative, even if it wanted things that way. The typical Virgoan loves stationery. The typical Aquarian loves serial killers.

The Virgo loves being of service to those closest and dear to them and is willing to assist its loved ones whenever needed. The Aquarius is willing to assist any given group of people whom they deem to exist in a state of unjust inequality and tends to be distant and detached even with those who know him or her well.

Interestingly, with Virgo ruled by Mercury, the planet that oversees the rational mind, and the sign of Aquarius being based in the rationally based element of air, the concept of duality figures prominently for both cerebral signs whenever considering their joining of romantic forces.

Let's take the concept of flexibility. Despite being an earth sign that by its elemental foundation would seem to be inflexibly immobile, Virgo's quality of mutable makes it flexibly open to variety and change, as well as masterfully adept at multitasking.

Despite its sign's elemental foundation being the lightest of air, Aquarius' quality of fixed makes it obstinately inflexible to variety and change, as well as better equipped to unilaterally focus versus any kind of distracting multitasking.

In order for this particular relationship to last, let alone have a pulse, a quality will need to be present from the first moments of this love union's inception: ACCEPTANCE.

Virgo, accept that your Aquarian lover marches to the beat of its own mohawked drummer and will never be in any way normal, average, or typical. It's also best advised for the earth sign person to never compare its Aquarian partner to anyone else they've dated before since this sign is truly like no other.

Aquarius, accept that your Virgoan love interest is humble and hardworking, which in turn causes it to be far more conservative and much less outspoken than you. This is not the sign that'll share your excitement regarding the latest corporate or government protest, nor does it enjoy having its daily sense of regimen consistently upset or disturbed.

There is one final concept yet to be discussed that both signs share and harbor a deep need to possess: BELONGING.

Although not an obvious attribute displayed by either sign, both the Virgo and the Aquarius long to belong to whichever group they relate to most and will strive to achieve this cohesive state. The need to belong can apply to any variation of group, be it family, friends, or those who work for either the same company or global cause.

If the Virgo and the Aquarius can make their relationship feel like its own special group, they'll have the motivation to smooth over their inherent differences and both will be more inspired to mutually work at their union's overall longevity and success.

Conversely, if the inherent differences between the Virgo and the Aquarius cause either sign to view their relationship with an us against them mentality, their romantic bond is sure to unravel and disintegrate fast and furiously.

Prepare yourselves, Virgo and Aquarius. There will be many a choice time when not just a friend or family member, but your own selves will question how it is that the two of you got together. But if each of you accepts the other for who you both are as individuals from the start, then the varied and many differences between the two of you will eventually become that effervescent thing that solidifies your bond, making it truly special and preciously unique.

Virgo-Pisces

(Entering Room) Oh hey! Virgo. Pisces.

(Casually strolling past, then stopping to give each of you a pro-longed glancing over.)

If I didn't know any better, my view upon entering the room just now of the two of you sitting all relaxed and casually hanging out usually wouldn't give me cause to wonder if anything out of the ordinary was going on.

But I do know better. Much, much better.

I just happen to know the astrological fact the signs of the virgin and of the cosmic fish are polar opposites of each other, and not to be trite in a nasal Paula Abdul way, but opposites attract.

And when two opposites are within close physical proximity of each other, the attraction factor turns into an all-out starved shark feeding frenzy of kissing touchy feely!

I also happen to know that polar opposites share as many common traits as they diametrically oppose, and a feature that those born beneath the sign of the virgin and those of the cosmic fish share in common is the ability to move with lightning fast speed at the last possible minute.

Hey, lighten up you two! There's nothing wrong with the fact your Love Author is astrologically savvy enough to deduce that just a few moments ago you both were groping for each other like wild primates.

Some would say you two were merely obeying an inalterable law of astrology and science.

Remember those magnet experiments they used back in junior high to demonstrate the law of attraction? Take those same oppositely charged pieces of metal that slammed into each other whenever within remote proximity together, except now one of the magnets is called Virgo and the other Pisces.

(uncomfortable silence …)

Okay then! Let's skip the magnet talk and give both of you an overview of each other's individual astrological backgrounds to see just how different and similar you two are together.

Virgo, you're the sign that oversees the tiniest of details with a most grounded and practical perspective. Pisces, you're the sign that oversees fantasies and daydreams from an imaginative perspective others might interpret as rather ungrounded or a tad impractical.

Virgo, your sign has a tendency to be SO hyper-realistic at times that your words can be a bit too critically truthful to others but to yourselves the most more often than not. Pisces, your sign has a tendency to be SO unrealistic at times that your words can bend the truth in such a non-critical manner you'll tell untruths to others, but to yourselves the most more often than not.

Virgo, you are the sign of extreme efficiency and meticulous organization. Pisces, you are anything but efficient and organized. Virgo, your tidy nature motivates you to thoroughly clean under every nook and cranny. Pisces, if your giving nature encounters someone you feel to be the underdog, you'll thoroughly untidy everything by searching under every nook and cranny for spare change.

Pisces, your charitable nature allows you to give the shirt off your back to whoever needs it most. Virgo, you'll take that shirt and allow just enough starch so it can be ironed to perfection. Virgo, there is a proper time and place for any activity, including sex. Pisces, you'll do it anytime, anyplace.

Even with all of the above differences mentioned, the rule with polar opposites is they share just as many similarities as oppositions. Virgo and Pisces are both mutable signs by astrological quality, thus they share the same mutable traits dealing with the theme of variety. Both the Virgo and the Piscean function best doing as many things as it can simultaneously, and if forced to do one task at a time, it would probably screw things up. Why? The curse of the mutable sign: Boredom.

Speaking of doing many things at a time, your Love Author would like to refer specifically to either sign's propensity to do a bunch of things and then some when it is in a relationship. In other working words, both the Virgoan and the Piscean have a knack for getting involved in romantic unions where it does all the work.

With that said, both signs share two core behavior traits lodged within the negative spectrum that both must be mindful of and avoid at all costs if they wants their budding romance to evolve into a deeper kind of committed love: playing the role of martyr and passive aggression.

Besides being categorized by element and astrological quality, both Virgo and Pisces are also known as karmic signs. The karmic signs enter this world with their souls or subconscious selves fully aware they best function when they are of service to others.

Despite this purposeful sense of service, the soul or subconscious mind of many an un-evolved Virgoan or Piscean can come to resent the mantle of karmic responsibility. Over time this can trigger the need to play the role of martyr often without even realizing it is doing it.

"Oh hey, Virgo. I REALLY appreciate you doing my term paper and tidying up my never-before-cleaned toilet. You don't mind making sure everything's done by noon, do you?"

"You don't? I didn't think so."

"Pisces, are you upset over the 100 bucks I borrowed that I keep reassuring you I'll pay back every time I ask for a 20 spot each week?"

"What was that? I couldn't differentiate what you were saying through those clenched teeth. You're not upset? Oh good! "

Despite both karmic signs sharing a dynamic in past relationships where they did all the work, this simply cannot be the case when the virgin and the cosmic fish join romantic forces. The best way to prevent that self-sacrificing dynamic from repeating itself is communication.

For the Pisces, the above task will be quite the challenging undertaking. Not only does its natural Neptunian energies give it a propensity for truth bending, those born beneath the sign of the cosmic fish also tend to display another kind of negative behavior trait that avoids communication with others all together: ASSUMING.

Because of its non-verbal tendencies, the Piscean will often assume those around him or her will automatically know what it is thinking and/or needing without having to actually verbally express itself. In other words, the unevolved Piscean will assume instead of asking questions outright or clarifying things so that all parties are on the same page.

One final fact regarding the astrological law of polar opposites is that attraction is what brings the polar opposite signs together, which in turn yields some immediate heavy pawing as I uncomfortably almost witnessed firsthand with my unknowing entrance upon the Virgo Pisces version of Wild Thing Kingdom.

Even with that blushingly said, if there is nothing more other than a few fast and furious bed creaks, or in other words, nothing of binding common interest beyond the initial attraction, the polarized spark will be snuffed out just as quickly as it began. Why?

Many times the flames of opposing desire are quickly doused due to both signs driving each other naturally crazy after the passing of five post-bed creaking minutes, give or take.

But conversely, if the polar opposites can stand each other's presence for more than five minutes post you know and have a thing or two they like about the other, or even better, share a few things in common, then here is where we find those fairy tale relationships that stay together.

In fact, when there are binding factors beyond the initial animal attraction, many of these dualistic duos literally last until death do they polar-opposite part.

Libra–Libra

Love. L'amour. Liebe.

In whatever language you say it, the L-word is pretty darn important to those born beneath the L sign. (Psssst! That means you, Libra.) In order to fully comprehend exactly why the L-word is such a big deal for those born beneath the L sign, the overall traits associated with the sign of the scales must first be weighed and balanced.

The signs belonging to the element of air, namely Gemini, Aquarius, and your scaled selves, are the only residents of the zodiac whose symbols aren't animalistic. Why? Rather than employ instinctual behavior associated with the animal kingdom, the air signs initially react to the outside world by exercising the processes of the rational mind. These rational processes consist of the following mental activities: thought, speech, and communication.

Libra is the middle representative of the element of air. Whereas the first representatives of each of the four elements focus predominantly on themselves as solitary individuals, and the last representatives focus on themselves as members of entire groups of individuals, such as humanity at large, the middle representatives focus on themselves predominantly from the perspective of one on one relationships.

The sign of the scales differentiates itself from the other air signs as well as the rest of the middle representatives of the four elements by one defining thing. You got it, the L-word itself: LOVE.

Actually, that would be telling a little white non-truthful other L-word, which never sits well with the sign symbolized by the scales of truth. The answer isn't exactly love itself. It's Venus, the heavenly body named after the ancient Roman goddess who ruled over it.

Mix Venus into the astrological foundation of a sign that predominantly focuses on one on one relationships, and we get a better inkling as to why the L-word is so important to the L sign.

Your Love Author needs to 'fess up yet again. Using the word important in describing the role love plays in the life of the Libran once again is another little white L- word. A bit more emphasis needs to be stressed, such as most Libran females coming out of the womb knowing exactly which shade of café au lait she'll use for her bridesmaids dresses, along with the perfect locale for their wedding photos, or how the word "single" doesn't exist within the vocabularies of the majority of scale-born people.

Why such extreme Libran behavior regarding love? Blame it on the goddess of gorgeous. In myth, Venus wasn't a pretty priss of a deity who never left her divan while presiding over matters regarding love. She was a totalitarian dictator who enforced her will with an iron fist, which would cause you to fear for your pathetic mortal life if you dared to defy her.

With that image in mind, falling in love for the Venus-ruled is much like a military war games manual, complete with stringent guidelines and defined rules of play. And if one wants to play Venus' game of love with the intention of eventually winning, romance must be actively involved nearly every step of the way.

For the Venus-ruled, love cannot exist without the presence of romance, but did you know the phrase "true romance" is actually another little white untruthful L-word? Historically, the origin of that Venusian thing that motivates a Libran most in life, romance itself, has a fictitious nature, making the phrase "true romance" a contradiction of terms.

The origin of the word "romance" is believed to have come from France in the middle ages and dealt with the Roman Empire. Oddly enough, the word first referred to anything localized or being linguistically said in the local language spoken, since Latin was the language used for anything serious or official across the entire Roman Empire.

A bouquet of roses with a life's supply of baby's breath to the Libra who knows this next one: What do the languages French, Spanish, Italian, Portuguese, and Romanian (you read that right) all have in common? For those Venus-ruled who just replied, "They all sound pretty," try exercising those rational minds just a smidge harder.

Answer: They're all romance languages. The countries of origin of each of the languages listed were all territories where the ancient Roman Empire conquered and oversaw back in its super-powered heyday.

At first, the word "romance" referred to something that was localized or homegrown, but that was until the romance story came into being. From the Middle Ages also emerged the romance epic, which over time evolved into the romance, which is defined as a novel or other prose narrative depicting heroic or marvelous deeds, pageantry, exploits, etc., usually in a historical or imaginary setting. In a relatively short period of time, romance took a 180 degree shift in meaning. Where it originally referred to a person's localized area of origin, romance transformed into a fantastical word that spoke of knights, dragons, and imaginary kingdoms.

Returning to the present day once more, the most concrete way romance is put into active use?

Courting (noun): A way of getting to know a person through gradual stages of increased intimacy by incorporating romance with social activities.

I'm sure you scale kids are already well aware how painfully unromantic the world is these days. Mention the word "courting" in the present time and most people will think you're referring to the latest basketball stats or your plans to actively sue someone. This has led many a Libran to become almost fully convinced that chivalry is dead and romance went out of style long ago. But that was all before you two met, of course.

When a Venus-ruled person is paired with another, the initial phases of dating are required to transpire through the romantic framework of courting (see definition listed above should you have shamefully forgotten it already).

Because two Libras know how to properly court each other, the initial phase of acquaintanceship, otherwise known as the honeymoon period, can be intoxicatingly romantic for both Venus-ruled parties. You'd think either scale person was living in a fairy tale world, given its romantic sensibilities were being so fully utilized and stimulated.

A suitor just as pretty as my beautiful self who obeys the proper guidelines of Venusian courting? What could possibly go wrong? Plenty.

After long being denied anything remotely romantic, when two Librans initially date, they could easily go into ROMANCE OVERLOAD, which could lead to ROMANCE OVERDOSE, which if not treated by large doses of reality could be followed more dangerously by HALLUCINOGENIC ROMANTIC IDEALISM!

Are you scale kids able to see the full scaled picture regarding the fantastical origin of romance having the potential of clouding everything over into one big idealistic untruthful L-word?

Since the sign of Libra is based in the mentally driven element of air, those born beneath the Scales are prone to becoming addicted to the romance-filled, fantasy land o' love that unfolds in their minds. If a Libran gets hooked on romantic idealism, its willpower to come back to the crass and coarse world of unromantic reality decreases at an alarming rate.

Should this occur, the partner of the romance OD'ing victim will be put on a pedestal and idealistically worshipped as if a deity. The more this happens, the less the OD'ing victim will want to know who its partner is in actual reality, desperately loving a fabricated idea of them and not the actual flesh and bones person.

If both Librans manage to fight their inherent need to fall in love with LOVE by maintaining a realistically grounded perspective of their partner, then life really will seem like a true romance. And that's no untruthful L-word.

Libra-Scorpio

You both must have heard the wise old adage that still applies in the modern day, right Libra and Scorpio? It goes something along the lines of a person can choose its friends, but not its neighbors.

This neighborly concept applies astrologically as well, yet also is completely irrelevant, especially when it comes to playing the zodiacal dating game. Take you two for example.

Nothing can change the astrological fact the signs of Libra and Scorpio are next door neighbors with each other on that big wheel of life, otherwise known as the zodiac. Yet that inalterable information is neither karmic apples nor cosmic oranges during those not so common times when the scales and the scorpion decide to join romantic forces.

Moving from old astrological adages to cosmic rules of thumb, it's generally understood the signs that border each other are categorized beneath a most unexciting descriptor of astrological compatibility: neutral.

(A solitary cough can be heard in the far off, remote distance.)

Every sign has the potential to work together. Some combinations take a lot more work than others just to achieve a state of equilibrium. With the joining of the signs considered to be neutral of each other, the state of equilibrium is something very much like that solid borderline that naturally forms whenever oil and vinegar are put into the same container. In other words, mixing the two isn't a bad thing, but a whole lot of shaking is needed for there to be any kind of blend.

At their core, the signs of Libra and Scorpio function from very different perspectives, making it seem many times as if they lived on the opposite ends of town versus being astrological next door neighbors. Having an elemental foundation of air, the Libra is a lighthearted sign that doesn't like getting bogged down by anything too intense. Having an elemental foundation fixed in the watery deep, the Scorpio's emotions probe its world with such depth of feeling that an all-encompassing, ever intense approach is its sign's standard for living.

The communication-based Libran loves small talk and can chit chat for hours, especially on the phone. The emotionally intense Scorpion secretly desires small talk and chit chat be made illegal offenses and fantasizes about communication would be reserved for emergencies only, ESPECIALLY anything phone related.

Although the Libra functions best when in a committed relationship, it enjoys the playful side of love and the harmless interplay of flirting. The only playful aspect with a Scorpio's approach towards love is its *War Games*-like strategy that hunts to kill. Flirting is pointless to the Scorpio looking for love since its depth of desire could never be considered harmless.

The Libra's motivation to be in a committed relationship with another can many times overpower its individual needs and overall sense of self. The Scorpio's sense of self would never allow any one person or relationship to overpower it ever. In fact, a good number of Scorpions would rather opt for complete control by having total domination over its partner versus any kind of submittal.

The Libra is a social butterfly that can approach any kind of person to engage in conversation. Unfamiliarity usually breeds distrust when a Scorpio must engage in conversation with those it doesn't know well, where any kind of person would perceive its overall demeanor as intimidating and unapproachable.

The Libra's sensitivity to its key relationships and overall environment leaves it with delicate digestions and weaker than average constitutions. The Scorpio's hardcore tenacity and will to survive is so strong that, according to your Love Author, following the nuclear holocaust the only things left standing afterward will be cockroaches, Cher, and Scorpios.

Despite the Libra and Scorpio being such diverse astrological creatures, two concepts exist that if mutually embraced could potentially serve as the unifying love glue that binds these two signs romantically together: affection and discretion. Both signs must view affection as love's middle ground.

Truth be told, the Libra can be a tad aloof regarding matters of the heart since its approach to love is mainly of a cerebral nature. Whereas the Scorpio feels love so intensely, the all-encompassing power the emotion has over it can often be totally overwhelming.

Affection (noun): A gentle feeling of fond attachment or devotion. Libra, take note the words feeling and devotion; Scorpio, mark the word "gentle."

Love can often bring out the most unevolved traits of the Scorpio personality, such as possessiveness and extreme jealousy, which in turn can make the Libra detach even further and eventually disappear. This is most especially the case when the two signs are first getting to know each other.

Libra and Scorpio are the middle representatives of each signs' respective elements. Libra is the middle representative of the element of air and Scorpio of water. The middle representatives focus on themselves predominantly from the perspective of one on one relationships.

Both signs derive a sense of well-being whenever focusing on its key relationships, especially while showing its partners the loving side of their personality that's gentle, yet devotedly heartfelt. In other words, the Libra's and the Scorpio's best qualities emerge whenever showing affection.

Discretion (noun): The quality of behaving or speaking in such a way as to avoid causing offense or revealing private information. It's a rather odd word when considering concepts that romantically bond two people together, but discretion applies to more than just being able to keep a secret when it comes to the interrelation between the Libra and the Scorpio.

Actually, your Love Author would first like to add another piece before extrapolating on the word that puzzles: less is more. Thoroughly confused? Discretion, in this astrological case, must be considered whenever looking at either sign's sense of aesthetics.

Libra's planetary ruler, Venus, not only reigns over the concept of love, but beauty and aesthetics as well. Venus' influence is what gives those born beneath the sign of the scales the best sense of taste and style of the zodiac. The scales' element of air adds to the Libra's overall sense of style both a rational elegance and a mentally cool richness that's never overdone.

On the surface, those born beneath the sign of the scorpion appear not to have any type of aesthetic whatsoever since many often live in bare bones environments that seem more like an ascetic monk's cell versus a home or apartment. However, with Pluto being its planetary ruler, the Scorpio prefers getting to the core essence of things without any distracting excess or periphery.

The desert deadly's taste is minimalist and never showy or ostentatious. Pluto's influence provides the Scorpio an inherent ability to know the core worth of things and gives it the desire to make its surroundings reductively basic or simple but always beautiful in the most powerful sense of the word.

When joining romantic forces, the Libra and the Scorpio should be able to thoroughly appreciate each other's inherent aesthetic of less is more. The Scorpio will admire the Libra's mentally cool sense of richness and the Libran will appreciate the Scorpio's sense of basic beauty. Both signs will most likely love how the other's sense of style and taste is never over done or too much. In other words, the Libra and Scorpio's aesthetic sense of discretion should be a mutual bonding point among the two signs.

The more the middle representatives of air and water try to take a middle of the road approach to its love union, the greater the likelihood the coupling of the Libra with the Scorpio will turn out to be anything BUT neutral, average, or middle of the road.

Libra-Sagittarius

Did you lovebirds know the most damaging forest fires occur in areas that don't necessarily have the most flammable material but are susceptible to high winds?

Flame, unto its solitary self, doesn't make a fire burn fast and furiously. Take said flame and infuse it with the oxygen from the windy air and the result is one serious scorcher, kind of like when the Libra and the Sagittarius begin dating each other.

In Astrology, the four elements of earth, air, fire, and water are naturally paired off. Each grouping consists of elements that are cohesive or naturally work well together, otherwise known as being complementary to each other. Hence, the elements of fire and air are complementary to each other.

Returning once more to our astrological forest fire analogy, with the element of fire's core energies being action oriented and the element of air's being mentally driven, the signs born beneath either element function best at a fast and furious pace that is much like a wildfire's wind-stoked flames.

However, when frenzied and fiery Sagittarius joins romantic forces with balmy breezed Libra, the erratic nature of the burning wildfire is made more constant and tempered down to that of a slow and steadily burning flame. Allow your Love Author to elementally explain.

The elemental foundation of fire is action, and the signs that make up the family of flame like being in as constant a state of action as often as possible. Hence, the fire signs function best when they are in motion or in the process of doing. Said another way, the members of the fiery family like to be busy.

The sign of Sagittarius is certainly no exception to this action-oriented rule. Being the last representative of the element of fire, those born beneath the sign of the centaur like its action to be as fast-paced and spontaneously varied as possible.

Sagittarius' embodies the burning dynamic the most amongst the fire signed family by virtue of its astrological quality. The centaur's astrological quality of mutable is what makes the last representative of this element truly flammable. Why? The mutable signs function best in environments containing variety and change and are the multitaskers of the zodiac.

Mix Sagittarius' mutable traits with the action-oriented element of fire and behold! The Tasmanian devil/Speedy Gonzalez/flaming Roadrunner of the zodiac! The element of air has the mental functions of communication and rational thought at its foundational core. Being a highly sociable creature by nature, the typical Libra can chat up anyone from every walk of life. The scales' inherent sense of decorum and manners gives those around it equal opportunity to converse.

Combining the Tasmanian devil of fire signs with the air-signed master of conversation may at first sound like a union of polar opposites due to the Sagittarius and the Libra working from such differing dynamics. However, joining Sagittarian fire with Libran air usually results in a steadily burning flame of romantic constancy versus a burning ball of passion that extinguishes itself as quickly as when it first started.

In fact, both sign's differences of dynamic tend to be seen as refreshingly fun by the other. The Libra's highly pleasant social skills should not only keep the ever busy Sag to stay still but amused and intrigued as well. The Sagittarian's infectious sense of optimism can easily captivate the attentions of each scale leaving the Libra agog with wonder.

Centaurs, if your easily distracted self retains anything from this chapter, it should be this: The best romantic way of tilting the scales of your Libran lover is by courting. And that doesn't mean suing it in a court of law or challenging it to a vigorous round of hoops on the court of basketball, Sag.)

Courting (noun): A way of getting to know a person through gradual stages of increased intimacy by incorporating romance with social activities. Another Libran commandment that's equally as important and should also be committed to memory is the following: Thou shalt not buy a Libra anything remotely cheap or gag-like.

Despite the sign of the centaur thoroughly enjoying any and all jokes of the dirty/cheap/potty persuasion, it does NOT in any way justify making romance purchases for its Libran love interest deemed to be cheap or of the gag gift variety.

Being ruled by Venus, the planet of both good manners and even better taste, the Libra does not consider potty humor in any way remotely funny, Sagittarius! For 'tis FAR better to present nothing or even some daisies you just picked off the highway over giving your scale-signed lover something it will consider cheap or gag gift-ish. Do so and risk having your air-signed trip of romance being permanently grounded due to it never even getting a chance to take off.

It's time to turn the romantic tables by teaching you love weighers a lesson. It may at first seem the scale kids have a much easier homework assignment by having to learn merely one aspect concerning how to date its centaur, but duly take note, Librans. Your Sagittarian rule of romance is just as challenging: Thou shalt keep the Sagittarian romantically interested by obeying the fire sign fun factor.

The fire sign fun factor states that in order for a fire sign to optimally function, fun needs to be present. The fire sign needs to feel as if it is having some semblance of fun at any given time. Libra, this does not mean having to ride the latest life threatening rollercoaster nor becoming a champion beer pong player (although doing either would rack up some extra pony points), but even an eyedropper's worth of fun goes a long way with the last of the fire signs.

As a member of the family of flame, Sagittarius likes to be busy as often as possible. And just for the romantic record scale kids, being busy for the typical pony boy or girl does NOT include the two of you staring open eyed and intensely professing your undying love for each other.

The un-fun side to the sign of the scales is the tendency to be prissy. You may want to look into buying some well-made but revealing active wear, along with new running shoes in order to partake in any of the following centaur activities: rock climbing, power sprinting (most likely after practical joking), dirt biking, gambling, along with any of the horsey oriented actions of steeple chasing and dressage.

The dreamy notions of romantic idealism that regularly occur in the mind of the Libra will need to stay exactly there since the Sagittarian will in all likelihood consider them invalid as activities to partake in, as well as seriously boring and totally un-fun. This leads us to the biggest pitfall of possible potential that lies beneath the surface of the Libra Sagittarius love union.

Libras, your Love Author won't yank your scale's chains. Where your sign's craving for romance and relationships makes you steadfast and faithfully loyal, the mutable quality of Sagittarius makes it crave variety and change. Said another way, Sags cheat.

Mind you, not all Centaurs cheat. But being unfaithful, along with nearly every other Sagittarian sin, is almost always caused by the same mutable signed source: boredom. Keep that factor of fun in the life of your Sag, Libra, and its wandering eye will stay faithful and focused strictly on you. If the Sag revvs up the romance while the Libra free falls into fun, the flame you both share as a complementary couple will torch steady and true well into the future.

Libra-Capricorn

Hold up, Libra and Capricorn. I need to find me a Red Bull and an energy bar 'cause you two are WORK.

Alrighty then! Now that I've done what's humanly best to crank my energies up to as maximum a non-illegal level as I can, allow me to start by being brutally blunt. The two of you are SURE you're dating each other, right?

I should preface things by stating that every sign has the potential to work together in a romantically involved way. It's just that some signs take a lot more work to achieve a state of equilibrium than others. And just to repeat what I stated earlier, you two are WORK!

Of the twelve signs, Libra and Capricorn are each other's biggest challenge to relate with naturally due to each sign's placement on the zodiac wheel. They are positioned from each other at the harshest astrological angle possible of 90 degrees, which is better known as the Square.

When two signs square each other, a consistently high probability exists for one to easily rub the other the wrong way, quite often because either or both signs are simply being their natural selves.

Not only do their inherent traits sound like polar opposites when compared to each other, the core foundations behind what makes a Libra and Capricorn tick appear to practically negate each other when observed together.

Capricorn is the work horse of the zodiac and will ceaselessly toil should it have a projected goal in mind. The few choice times a Libran will ceaselessly toil is when it finds itself either single or have a projected goal of a future marriage partner in mind.

The Libra's social skills and art of conversation gives it the ability to chat with anybody. The Capricorn's distant manner of business formal means it won't chat with just anybody, especially strangers. When excited, the Libra tends to communicate as fast and furious as a teenager. The Capricorn tends to communicate as detached and formal as an unamused librarian, and they don't get excited. Ever.

A main staple of the Libran diet is ROMANCE. Romance never even makes it on the Capricorn's menu, let alone its diet. More on the R-word in just a mismatched second.

Adjustments of astrological temperament are required of both signs if this romantic union wishes to have a pulse, let alone last. By far, the biggest problems potentially pose themselves during the earliest stages when the Libra and the Capricorn first begin dating.

Of the two, the Libra will need to do more of the initial adjusting than the Capricorn due to a quality that is abundantly inherent in their sign being abundantly absent in their partner: romance.

Libras, here are some things you need to tell yourselves from the get go. Your goat guy will not be the romantic knight in shining armor who will properly court you by chivalrously taking the lead with everything. Whenever in doubt, he'll most likely still be at work.

Your Capricorn lady will not be the damsel in distress nor the shrinking violet that'll swoon over each of your romantic gestures. To be blunt, the power suit was originally designed with the female corporate Cappie in mind. And whenever in doubt, she'll most likely still be at work too.

The Libra must accept the fact its romantic sensibility will more than likely not even be recognized with its Capricorn partner. Even with that said, the two traits that stand out with an earth-signed love interest, while although not dripping with passion, are quite admirable, none the romantic less: efficiency and earnestness.

This is not a sign you'll hear rattling off a list counting all the ways it loves thee. Rather, Capricorn is the sign that efficiently rattles off what needs to be done whenever a crisis or problem should emerge out of nowhere.

Know this up front, Libra. It is not in the Capricorn's astrological foundation to be overly or overtly complimentary. This is not the sign that will gush over the new outfit you just bought or openly admire your most recent haircut.

Breezily blowing along to the air-signed member of this love union. Cappies, we already know how important work is to your sign. This will in all likelihood NOT be the case with your Libran lover. In fact, when first exposed to the scales' love of luxury and attentiveness to its looks, a particular non-hard–working word might come to mind that the Capricorn must never utter aloud if it wishes to keep the affections of its Libran love interest: lazy. Accept the fact your Libra does not share the same self-identifying work ethic as you, Capricorn, and don't hold it against him or her by acting in an outwardly resentful way.

Libra and Capricorn actually do share two personality traits that could act as the love glue that holds this ill-fitting piece of romantic work together: appearance and discretion of taste. It shouldn't be surprising that appearance is of the utmost importance to both the Libra and the Capricorn. Here are two signs that would rather lose a limb versus being spotted in public donning sweatpants or showing an exposed body part that's either unmanicured or unshaved.

This rule of appearance for both the scales and the goat applies to any kind of public exposure, be it attending a gala charity event in the early evening or stopping at the local convenience store for milk in the early morning. Plus, of all the residents of the zodiac, Libra and Capricorn are the two signs tied for first place to have the most expensive taste.

Discretion (noun): The quality of behaving or speaking in such a way as to avoid causing offense or revealing private information. It's a rather odd word when considering factors that bind two people romantically, but discretion applies to more than just being able to keep a secret when it comes to the interrelation between the signs of Libra and Capricorn.

Actually, your Love Author would first like to add another piece before extrapolating on the phrase that puzzles: less is more. Thoroughly confused? Discretion, in this astrological case, must be considered whenever looking at either sign's sense of taste.

Libra's planetary ruler, Venus, not only reigns over love but beauty and aesthetics as well, giving it the best sense of taste and style amongst all the zodiac. The scales' element of air adds a sense of style in rational elegance and a mentally cool richness that's never overdone.

Similarly, those born with Saturn as its planetary ruler have an inherent aesthetic that's based on status (what a shocker!) but elegance as well. A Capricorn's tastes tend to always be refined and never ostentatious or flashy.

Saturn's influence provides the Capricorn an inherent ability to know the core worth of things and supplies it the desire to purchase things both status driven and tastefully beautiful in the most powerful sense of the word none the minimal less.

When joining romantic forces, the Libra and the Capricorn should be able to thoroughly appreciate each other's inherent sense of less is more. The Capricorn will admire the Libra's mentally cool sense of richness, and the Libran will appreciate the Capricorn's practical sense of basic beauty. Both signs will most likely love how the other's taste and style are never over done or too much. In other words, a factor that could romantically bind the Libra with the Capricorn is each sign's tasteful sense of discretion as long as the goat lover doesn't overdo the hunting scene portraits. Restrict their use for bathroom décor.

Libra–Aquarius

Welcome aboard, Libra and Aquarius!

Please be sure your seat belts of the first class extra-cushioned passenger seats are firmly adjusted because we'll be reaching some seriously high altitudes on this air-signed love trip!

Astrologically, the best love unions are those made of two people born beneath the same element. Since Libra and Aquarius are both air signs, it really doesn't get much better than when these two members of the house of easy breezes lift off into romantic flight.

Did either of you lovebirds know the element that both your signs foundationally share is unique amongst all the other elements of the zodiac? The signs of Gemini, Libra, and Aquarius aren't associated with any kind of animal imagery due to their unifying element of air being firmly based within the functions of the rational mind.

And in case either of your voraciously curious air-signed minds were wondering, the main processes of the rational mind are thought and communication.

The role communication plays for those born beneath the element of air is especially important since the breezy signs not only enjoy yakking away as often as possible, you Chatty Chads and Cathys of the Zodiac NEED to do so in order to optimally function.

Since Libra and Aquarius are both air signs, the mental stimulation factor goes through the proverbial roof when these two signs begin dating. Neither sign will be able to learn enough about the other upon first meeting, nor will either be lacking in questions to ask about the other's history, background, likes, dislikes.

Probably the best reason why the signs of the scales and the water bearer are so romantically compatible is due to this astrological combo having one of the highest probabilities against either airy person from experiencing its worst mental state of mind—being bored. Both signs' heightened mental curiosities along with their voracious hunger to learn should keep things romantically fresh and intellectually interesting.

While explaining the different communicative natures between your signs, do enjoy our newly converted cedar wood Finnish sauna flight cabin, Libra and Aquarius, and be sure to have a member of our love crew stimulate the blood flow to your open-pored skin with our newly purchased L.L. Bean birch branches. Air-signed romantic first class does have its privileges.

Although the scales and the water bearer are both air signs, the middle and last representatives of the airy elemental tend to communicate in markedly different ways, which both breezy signs will need to be aware about the other before their love flight even takes off from the romantic runway.

Both signs' planetary rulers are the key of communicative clarity as to how these two airy ones individually shoot its own breeze.

The scales' planetary ruler, Venus, is the heavenly body named after the deity of pretty. The goddess of gorgeous endows the Libran with a gift of gab to converse with any person from any walk of life. The planet of pretty's influence makes the scale person's chit chat attractively alluring by virtue of its Venusian voice being particularly pleasant on the ears.

The middle representative of air tends to be a master of conversation mainly due to its mannered sense of decorum to allotting itself as much time to listen as well as speak, along with knowing exactly when to start up the small talk and when not to say a word. Conversely, your Love Author must himself now communicate with the truth, which is the most honest of speech patterns associated with your sign, Libra.

Despite being a strict devotee to honesty, the sign of the scales isn't exactly known for being decisive, which is a particularly aggressive kind of communicative expression. To be painfully truthful once more, watching the Libra in the midst of making a defined decision can be likened to watching the seasons change, or listening to one's hair grow for the other residents of the zodiac. The weighing back and forth and hemming and hawing can be THAT time consuming.

Your Love Author cannot strongly enough suggest that the Libra allow its Aquarian love interest to decide the following BEFORE every date: which movie to be seen and what kind of food to be eaten or which restaurant to dine at for the evening. All romantic parties will be glad you did.

Invention (noun): A thing that did not exist previously and is recognized as the product of some unique intuition or genius. Water bearers, did you know that most inventors are born beneath your sign? Were you also savvy to the fact the sign of Aquarius rules over the Internet, as well as all things technological? It's easy to see why considering Uranus, the planet that rules over the sign of the water bearer, is the heavenly body that oversees the qualities necessary for invention to take place, such as intellectual brilliance and the future, itself.

Being the last of the air representatives, the role of duality is the most markedly pronounced for the sign of the water bearer. The communicative style of the Aquarius can be very much likened to the dualistic role an invention plays for society. Everything stems from the same planetary source.

Uranus oversees not just the concepts of genius and invention but also rebellion and anything that disrupts generally accepted norms. For just as an invention propels society into the future, its innovative nature breaks down society's status quo in the here and now in a most rebellious way as well.

Take one air-oriented concept of inventive genius, combine it with an air-blown sense of individualistic rebellion, and the end result is the communicative expression of the Aquarius—intellectually brash with the intent to clash with the general public.

Where the Libra speaks of sugar, spice, and everything Venusian nice, the Aquarian heatedly debates over topics of controversy. Where the Libra's civilized social skills deal with light hearted small talk, the Aquarian intensely speaks of heavily weighted subjects of high intellect. Where the Libra shoots the breeze with a voice most pleasant, the Aquarian's wind usually bellows with a voice most odd sounding.

Ironically, the inherently high intellect of the water bearer is the very thing that isolates it from freely conversing with the general public. The

Aquarian's daunting mental aptitude makes it loathe to discuss anything trivial, gossipy, or chit-chatty.

Dualistically, conversational warmth from an Aquarian is something that must be earned over time from this most complex of air signs since the communicative tone typically taken by the water bearer around those it doesn't know well is distant and frostily cool at best. The air truly becomes sweet for these breezy ones when they meet each other at the middle of the communicative road instead of opposite ends of the speaking spectrum.

The communicative capabilities of the Libra provide the Aquarian with some much needed warmth and infused social skills, and the innovative intellect of the water bearer supplies dimensional depth to the conversational musings of the person born beneath the sign of the scales. The more the scales and the water bearer borrow from each other's best abilities at shooting the breeze, the greater the likelihood of both air signs flying each other's friendly skies to romantic heights never before seen or experienced.

Libra-Pisces

Seriously, Libra and Pisces, I need to throw this one out there. Are you two SURE you're dating each other?

Maybe you each have different partners that got lost while foraging their way to this particular chapter of the book? Close, but no Cupid doll, huh?

Sorry for all the obnoxious obviousness just then, Libra and Pisces, but the two of you romantically joining forces is definitely NOT a common occurrence one hears about every day.

When looking at the prototypical wheel of the zodiac, the sign of Pisces lies at a 150 degree angle from the sign of Libra. The proper astrological term for this very particular angle is the quincunx. Everyone repeat along with me. Ready? "Ku-win-kwunx." Very good!

The quincunx is also known by the much easier pronounced, astrological reference word inconjunct. When two signs are placed at an inconjunct angle of each other, nothing remotely matches and every inherent aspect of one sign is square pegged against the natural energies of the other.

Some keywords associated with the inconjunct are: redirection, challenge, diversion, and requires adjustment.

I won't kid either of you, Libra and Pisces. Most of the outside world has a hard time picturing the two of you together due to your union's high factor of unobviousness. For the most part, the core differences within this astrological duo all boils down to their brains.

Libra is an air sign. Pisces is a water sign. The air signs initially react to the outside world via the functions of its brain's left hemisphere. The water signs initially react to the outside world via its right hemisphere.

The left hemisphere of the brain is known as the rational mind. The right hemisphere of the brain is known as the emotional/intuitive mind. A left hemisphered person is motivated most to exercise the processes of the rational mind, which are any of the following: thought, speech, and communication

A right hemisphered person is motivated most by its emotions and/or intuition. Sounds easy enough, right? Ah, but one last rule of mental play regarding all this brain matter must be mentioned. We humans have total control over the functions of our left hemispheres and no control whatsoever over the functions of our right hemispheres.

The mental muscles of those born beneath the element of air are so inherently strong the left hemisphere will often wrestle its feelings into submission by rationalizing them far from the surface of its conscious mind as often as possible. Conversely, being right hemisphere oriented, the water signs will sense how something feels at first before engaging in any kind of action or subsequent reaction.

Emotions for the last representatives of water hold a bit more influence besides merely being a first reaction to stimuli from the outside world. Picture the Piscean as if it was a radar station that picks up all energies intuitive and/or emotional from the general atmosphere that surrounds them. The typical Piscean naturally tunes into whichever emotional energies are present within its environment at any given time, be those energies from the past, present, or future. The tricky part is the emotional radar is always on for the Pisces.

Due to its emotional radar working 24/7, the world for the average Piscean will often be perceived as a very overwhelming place, rendering a good portion of the fish community speechless or very quiet at a watery minimum for better portions of its day. The reactive state of being for the typical Pisces is an environment where words simply don't cut it most of the intuitive time.

Piscean reality is an environment where verbal communication usually doesn't suffice in relaying all the feeling and sensitive energies taken in on a daily basis whether the fish person is operating from the conscious or subconscious mind, functioning with awake alertness, or from the deepest of dream states.

Returning once more to the inherent challenges with romantically pairing the scales with the fish, one part of this astrological duo identifies itself through the act of verbal communication (Libra), and the other half finds that same act to be a distractive nuisance that often falls short of adequately expressing its natural state of emotional being (Pisces). Fun, huh?

Even when these two signs first meet, misinterpreted misunderstandings usually run rampant from the get go. The Libra will often initially misinterpret the Piscean's silent nature as either being stuck up, standoffish, or disapproving. The Pisces will often misinterpret the Libra to be a wind tunnel of vanity that can't talk about anything besides its pretty self. Good times.

All romantic ironies aside, the scales and the cosmic fish actually do share a common trait that when ignited, motivates either sign far more than any hemisphered brain matter could ever possibly hope to achieve. In fact, this shared trait is such a powerful force of influence over both signs, it could very well be the glue that enables the Libra and the Pisces to stick together as a functioning love team: romantic inspiration

With the scales' planetary ruler named after the goddess of love and with the cosmic fish's ruling heavenly body of Neptune overseeing romantic poetry and the romance movement at large, Libra and Pisces aren't just signs that are romantic. These two signs take romance and make it seriously hardcore! Unfortunately, the world is a mighty unromantic place these days.

Mention the word courting in these present times and most people will think you're either talking about the latest basketball stats or your plans to actively sue someone. Even with that being the unromantic case, the signs of the scales and the fish still respond to and interact best through the process of courting.

Courting (noun): A way of getting to know a person through gradual stages of increased intimacy by incorporating romance with social activities.

Upon first meeting, the Libran and the Piscean should be quite adept at making each other's better romantic acquaintance by engaging in the proper rules of courtship. But both starry eyed lovers of LOVE must know the R-word isn't all sugar, spice, and everything idealistically nice. Romance has its downside too.

When committed to another, both the Libra and the Pisces have a naturally strong tendency to repress or suppress any problems, gripes, or differences experienced in the partnership.

Venus doesn't just oversee love. The planet of pretty rules over the concepts of peace and harmony as well. Should a Libran have a serious fish bone to pick with its partner, many times nothing will be said due to the scale person not wanting to rock the (fishing) boat nor disturb the peace.

Similarly, Pisces' planetary ruler not only deals with unconditional love and fantasy, Neptune also oversees the unevolved trait of self-imposed martyrdom. Too many fish people suffer through the most unhealthy of relationships without so much as uttering a Piscean peep of complaint due to always playing the role of Saint Selfless of the Uncomplaining Doormat.

Communication of every variation is necessary for a relationship to not just thrive but survive, Libra and Pisces. And just to inform you non-confrontational types, every relationship on this green earth needs to have an argument, debate, and a good old fashioned fight now and then in order to remain healthy and stable.

If this relationship is to romantically survive, both the scales and the cosmic fish will need to consistently work on vocally expressing its gripes and fears just as much as its romantic declarations of impassioned love for each other. The more both signs avoid their naturally non-confrontational tendencies, the better the chances this unobvious union has at becoming quite the romantic keeper.

Scorpio–Scorpio

Carmen is the name of the fantastically fatalistic opera written in 1875 by fellow desert deadly, Georges Bizet.

The opera is considered one of the best examples of a Verismo piece, a musical style that presented the underbelly of life in brutally realistic terms, often with degenerate or violent overtones. In your Love Author's astrological opinion, EVERYTHING about Bizet's musical masterpiece is Scorpionic, right down to the opera's male and female lead roles.

No, wait. Tail zing that last statement, scorpions. It's more like *Carmen* is in every way an UNEVOLVED scorpionic piece of Verismo art.

Each sign has characteristics that are good and bad or evolved and unevolved. No one sign is all good nor all bad. While we're at it, there isn't a particular sign that's either best or worst. The sign of the scorpion has undergone the oddest twist of astrological perception in these modern times. The inherent intensity and natural understanding of power associated with the sign of the desert deadly are more often than not completely misinterpreted. That and only its most unevolved personality traits are acknowledged, let alone known these days, with a most cartoon-like exaggeration: Vindictiveness with a vengeance, jealousy that borders on the psychopathic, possessiveness with a sadistic edge, and an insatiable sex drive that only Caligula could rival.

Admit it, you two. Your Love Author can almost guarantee upon first learning your love interest was born beneath the sign of the Scorpion, both of you initially experienced a jolt of inner trepidation based on what you've heard about Scorpios, despite the fact you are one.

Before romantically taking a step further, some housework needs to be done. The heavy, cobwebbed curtains within the scorpionic house of horrors need to be drawn back and aired out if a holistically proper perspective is to be given regarding the romantic merging of this most misunderstood of signs. We'll start by dragging some of the biggest scorpionic untruths into the rational light of day.

Scorpio Lie 1: Scorpios are unemotional. Before dispelling that first bit of scorpionic delusion, how about a desert deadly fun fact,? Did either of you know the scorpion is the only member of the animal kingdom that can consciously kill itself? Swear to Scorpio!

Only during the most dire of circumstances where the poisonous creature senses it is cornered with no chance of escape will the scorpion deliver its best tail zinger right through its own abdomen! This unique trait of scorpionic seppuku, or self-righteous suicide, will be referenced more than once throughout this rather intense chapter. Returning once more to scorpionic lie 1, contrary to popular belief, those born beneath the sign of the scorpion tend to be the deepest feelers of human emotion throughout all the zodiac. Even with that being the case, the typical Scorpio would rather undergo a daily colonoscopy than openly display its feelings in public or in front of strangers. Expressing emotions is THAT intensely private a process for the Scorpio.

Scorpio Lie 2: Scorpios are pig-headed stubborn and living definitions of the term "control freak." Oops, my bad. That last statement couldn't be any closer to the truth. I'll be honest with you two. There are a few exceptions (actually just one, and you two sure ain't it), but overall it's not highly recommended for a person born beneath one sign to date another of its own astrological kind.

Each sign encounters specific challenges whenever romantically doubling up with itself and Scorpio has some of the toughest challenges of pitfall potential when this sign dates its own.

Scorpio is a fixed sign by astrological quality, and joining two fixed signs together is one of the most challenging combinations to maintain due to the following fixed traits: a natural tendency to resist change; a mental proclivity to see things in a one dimensional, black or white way; an inherent inclination to not want to compromise; and a consistent knack for being pig-headed stubborn.

If anything, all romantic parties will save themselves a few decade's worth of wasted waiting time by always keeping this rule of scorpionic stubbornness in mind: You will NEVER get a Scorpio to do something they don't want to do.

It simply won't happen. To reference the opera *Carmen* once more, when the beautiful gypsy is confronted with death, her reaction is interpreted by most as strong and fearless. Carmen's stubbornness is what actually does her in. Our leading lady would rather commit scorpionic seppuku by walking into Don Jose's serrated hunting knife than compromise with him.

Things couldn't go any smoother when two Scorpios initially begin dating, however. It's when their first difference of opinion takes place where both water signs are shown just how fixed the other can be.

When a disagreement first occurs, both scorps will dig its tails into the ground determined never to move a millimeter for the duration of their scorpionic lives. Upon seeing its fixed sign partner doing the aforementioned tail digging, the other fixed sign will become even MORE inflexibly unrelenting and stupefied at how obviously wrong its fixed sign partner is about everything.

May your Love Author suggest to your double fixed bond a critically important relationship saver? COMPROMISE.

Not just one but BOTH fixed signs need to regularly compromise if this relationship is to have a pulse. Scorpio is one of the most stubborn signs you'll find and so unrelenting that millennia shall pass over this state of coupled checkmate if mutual compromise isn't put into effect.

Scorpio Lie 3: Not a single good trait has been assigned to this most maligned of signs. I beg to differ. The Scorpio has fierce loyalty, tenacity that never gives up, and a will to survive so strong the rest of the Zodiac crumples like flies just thinking about it.

Scorpio Lie 4: Pluto is not a planet. Scorpio's planetary ruler, Pluto, is the heavenly body last to be discovered and first to be demoted. In the first decade of the twenty-first century, Pluto was demoted by the scientific community by being decategorized to a dwarf planet.

Before obliterating such planetary perjury, the astrological influence Pluto holds over we earth folk must first be analyzed. Pluto oversees the following areas of human life: power, control, survival instinct, sexuality, domination, death, and what is beneath the surface.

The three planets furthest from the sun were each discovered over the last three centuries, and the events that occurred on earth at the time of their discoveries directly reflect their influence over us.

Uranus is the planet of individuality and revolution was discovered in 1781. The heavenly body that bears a Greek name versus the Roman named remainder was discovered in the midst of western history's two biggest revolutions: the American in 1776 and the French in 1789.

Neptune, the planet of the non-tangible and charity, was discovered without a telescope through the non-tangible means of mathematics in 1846. Immediately following Neptune's discovery, society's first charitable institutions such as hospitals, prisons, and orphanages emerged.

Pluto, the planet that oversees what is power driven yet hidden, was discovered in 1930. During that year, Prohibition was the law in the United States with bootlegging and the underground distribution of alcohol controlled by organized crime.

The year 1930 also saw the rise of Fascist regimes that would each overthrow their governing bodies, eventually exerting total dominance over the citizens they controlled. It all sounds pretty Plutonian, wouldn't you agree? Want to avoid your double signed love union from having to commit scorpionic seppuku? Neither Scorpio can behave like one.

Tail zing that last statement yet again. More like neither Scorpio can behave like one that's thoroughly unevolved.

Scorpio–Sagittarius

You both must have heard that wise old adage that's still applicable in the modern day right, Scorpio and Sagittarius? It goes something along the lines of a person can choose its friends, but not its neighbors.

This neighborly concept applies astrologically, yet is also completely irrelevant when it comes to playing the zodiacal dating game. Take you two, for example.

Nothing can change the astrological fact that the signs of Scorpio and Sagittarius are next door neighbors on that big wheel of life, otherwise known as the zodiac. Yet that inalterable information is neither karmic apples nor cosmic oranges during those not so common times when the scorpion and the centaur decide to join romantic forces.

Moving from old adages to more contemporary rules of cosmic thumb, it's generally understood the signs that border each other are categorized beneath a most unexciting descriptor of astrological compatibility: neutral.

(A solitary cough can be heard in the far off, remote distance.)

Every sign has the potential to work together. Some combinations take a lot more work than others just to achieve a state of equilibrium. Whenever joining the signs considered to be neutral of each other, the state of equilibrium is comparable to the solid borderline that naturally forms whenever oil and vinegar are put into the same container. In other words, mixing the two isn't a bad thing, but a whole lot of shaking is needed for there to be any kind of blend.

At their core, Scorpio and Sagittarius function from extremely different perspectives. It seems as if these two signs lived on the opposite sides of the planet versus being astrological next door neighbors.

With Jupiter, the planet of luck and abundance as its planetary ruler, the Sagittarius tends to have a hyper-positive (often to a fault) approach to things and doesn't like getting bogged down by anything too intense. Having an elemental foundation firmly fixed in the watery deep, the Scorpio tends to probe its world with such depth of feeling that an ever intense approach is its sign's standard for living life at large.

The Sagittarius is an open book. What you usually see is what you get with this typically straightforward sign. The Scorpio feels most secure having an aura of mystery. Its book is closed shut, and perish the thought what'll befall the poor soul that tries to uncover anything the Scorpio is unwilling to show.

The Scorpio's fixed nature gives it a methodical tenacity and focus, which although slow paced, makes sure goals and projects are followed through to completion. The Sagittarius' mutable nature is so naturally fast-paced, they're whirling dervishes of multitasking. But with the high number of mutual activities is an equally high potential for everything to be dropped due to the centaur succumbing to either distraction or boredom.

The Sagittarian is a highly social creature that can approach any kind of person to engage in conversation. Unfamiliarity usually breeds distrust when a Scorpio must engage in conversation with those it doesn't know well, where any kind of person would perceive its overall demeanor as intimidating and unapproachable. The Sagittarius loves practical jokes! The Scorpio loves the idea of disposing of those that love practical jokes.

The fixed quality of the Scorpio gives it a proclivity to plan in advance and approach its scheduled activities ON TIME! The mutable quality of the Sagittarius gives it a proclivity to procrastinate any kind of planning to the last possible minute, making it practically an unspoken guarantee that most of the time he or she is never on time.

Its fixed quality causes many a Scorpio to be commitment oriented, which in turn makes it loyally faithful to its partners. Its mutable quality causes many a Sagittarius to crave variety, which in turn can make it unfaithful to its partners.

The Scorpio has the patience of a saint. The Sagittarius is a saint's worse nightmare if it has to wait more than five nanoseconds longer than necessary. With the above said, one of the biggest challenges this particular combo will need to face, especially upon first meeting, will determine how long the Scorpio Sag union lasts: ADJUSTMENT.

Because their energies function at such differing levels and speeds, adjustments will be required for both signs. Namely, the Scorpio needs to pick up the pace with dispelling its aura of mystery while initially getting to know its Centaur partner, and the Sagittarian needs to hold back on its usual galloped pace by not jumping into things where the spark of romantic interest fizzles not too long after it began.

Conversely, the Scorpio will need to put the brakes on its naturally intense approach to things, which the Sag may find a bit too unnerving in a creepy, serial killer kind of way if left unmonitored. Likewise, the centaur will need to put the pedal to the metal on its tendency to drag its heels with such love union factors as commitment and displaying affection.

Should romantic commitment be imminent, the Sagittarius must also be well aware of the following: When dating or committed to a Scorpio, nothing is casual! When a Scorpio commits itself romantically to another, it does so for the long haul. The Sagittarian needs to be aware that scorpionic romance has nothing to do with seeing each other now and then or simultaneously playing the field. There shall be no impulsive changes of heart nor displays of fickleness, Sagittarius! Do so and proceed at your own romantic risk!

For those centaurs chomping at the bit to test drive its racing skills in the bedroom based on what it has heard about Scorpios and their sexual prowess, guess what? Every dirty detail you've been told about Scorpios and their sexual powers are all true but with a big ol' but.

Unlike your sign, which has a rep for being the player of the Zodiac (a nice way of saying many a centaur tends to cheat as often as it changes horseshoes), when a Scorpio is committed to another, it tends to be loyal to a fault. And Jupiter save your Sagittarian soul should you romantically commit to a Scorpio and it comes upon your centaur self to play horsey with anyone else.

How's this for extra romantic reinforcement, pony people? Scorpio is the LAST sign you'd ever want as an ex, especially should it have just cause for wanting to send your horsey self to the glue factory.

When the Scorpio cuts all ties off for good, there's no turning back. Worse, if the desert deadly has ended things because you've deeply wounded its heart then Godspeed is all your Love Author can utter in a hushed, fearful whisper while desperately searching for the nearest exit.

In the period directly following the romantic breakup, the Sagittarian who has gravely sinned against the Scorpio may be justified in having pony panic attacks of worry, sprinkled with healthy horsey helpings of paranoia.

But that's not where the fear factor lies, o hedonistic horse folk. Time must pass and the Sag must once again become fully relaxed for the tail of the wounded scorpionic ex-lover to deliver its most effective sting.

For it's when the Sagittarius is back to feeling like its old self and in the mood to FINALLY hit the town and partay is exactly when the centaur prances over to its closet looking for its dancing shoes and doesn't notice that the pair in the furthest dark corner isn't empty.

The pony person must refrain from becoming the object of the Scorpio's very intense affections unless ready to fully commit. Don't say your Love Author didn't warn you.

Scorpio-Capricorn

If your love union had to be reduced to merely one word or solitary phrase, it would be Kodomo-no-Asobi, Scorpio and Capricorn. Allow your Love Author to explain.

Kodomo-no-Asobi is a Japanese parlor game played by upper class teenage girls in the early nineteenth century. The game is for the most part Blind Man's Bluff but with extra rules of play added for maturing measure. Just as in Bluff, one person is designated "it" and blindfolded in the midst of a large, open space. Like Marco Polo, the rest of the players must call out to the person designated "it," while avoiding being touched by whoever is "it."

Unlike Blind Man's Bluff or Marco Polo, Kodomo-no-Asobi stands apart from the typical parlor game involving blindfolds. It was played amongst young adults, namely Japanese teens on the verge of becoming young ladies of status. With that in mind, this particular game of the blindfolded variety went beyond the chaotic motions typically displayed amongst little children.

Kodomo-no-Asobi incorporated the maturing concepts of trust and relaxation through its two additional rules of play: all participants were dressed in their best kimono while playing; and the traditional device of the blindfold was still used, but the "it" person not only had to seek and find the rest of the players blindfolded, it did so while holding a full cup of tea.

Holding a full cup of tea while blindfolded forced the "it" person to strategize with a relaxed sense of decorum versus impulsively groping about at the open air. The person designated "it" had to acutely listen in order to ascertain the location of the other players' voices for the purpose of seeking them out with a relaxed motion of intent. That or they stood the risk of staining her best Kimono, or worse, scalding herself (depending on whether the tea used during the game was heated or at room temperature).

On one level, Kodomo-no-Asobi seems like quite the easy game by virtue of its straightforward rules of play. On another level, the added rules to this coming of age Blind Man's Bluff made it deceptively challenging and socially complex, which is much like when the Scorpio and the Capricorn join romantic forces.

On one level, the scorpion and the goat possess the ease and advantage of astrological cohesion by virtue of being elementally complementary to each other. On another level, this particular pairing has the potential of never experiencing the ease and flow of complementary cohesion due to both signs' inherently intense natures, but more on the intense stuff in just a bit.

In astrology, the four elements of earth, air, fire, and water are naturally paired off. Each grouping consists of two elements that are cohesive, or naturally work well together, otherwise known as being complementary to each other. The elements of earth and water astrologically complement each other. By virtue of their elemental foundations, the earth and the water signs share a core motivational trait: security.

The earth signs derive the most security from the tangible. The term tangible can be translated to the possessions an Earth sign owns, the money in their bank, and the work output they do. With their sign naturally ruling over the House of the Public and Career, the Capricorn is driven by primarily two things, work and status.

Representing the middle embodiment of water and ruling over the house of death and transformative change, Scorpio is known as the survivor sign. This is the sign that can make do with the barest minimum of resources. The Scorpio derives security from its most basic of necessities. Anything additional is considered to be either icing on the cake or totally superfluous.

Both the scorpion and the goat tend to approach things with an intensity that's rather intense. The Capricorn's intensity is evident through its work ethic that's unlike any other sign. The Scorpio's intensity is so all-encompassing it will only bother with things it feels will have complete and total follow through. The cause behind either signs' inherent sense of serious intensity can be reduced to one astrological source: their planetary ruler. And just to enlighten everyone, intensity does have its upsides.

With its planetary ruler of Saturn overseeing the concepts of both karma and time, the childhood of the Capricorn is non-existent by virtue of being given the mantle of adult responsibility not too long after exiting the womb, such as having to take on the job of being parent to one of its parents or having to work at an appallingly early age.

With Pluto, the planet of power and death its planetary ruler, the Scorpio is never stunned with shock or naivete whenever dealing with any of life's darker difficulties, given its ability to picture the worst possible scenario.

The Capricorn's intensity provides it the analytical approach needed to come up with workable solutions to any of life's crises. The Scorpio's intensity gives it the objectification to withstand being swept away by its deeply felt emotions whenever facing life's darker side.

The cohesion of the complementary elements of earth with water can also be likened to something more modern and concrete: a river dam. A constructed obstruction placed directly in the path of a flowing body of water can produce any number of effective results, from a re-routed water supply to a hydro-electric energy source.

The key to a dam's effectiveness is its foundation. The proper positioning of a dam's foundation requires consideration of the earthy component of the dam itself, along with equal evaluation being given to the pressure and speed of its watery counterpart. Should either side be overlooked or not taken into full consideration, the dam may initially stand, only to disintegrate a short time after its construction.

The union of the Scorpio and the Capricorn often will begin quite soundly, only to fall apart a short time later due to either half overlooking or not taking into full consideration the needs of the other. This is usually due to the intense nature of either sign focusing on a particular purpose or goal and assumptions will be made without the reinforcement of communication.

With the image of the river dam in mind, let us imagine communication to be the binding cement that holds the dam's foundation securely into place. Open communication is critical for any relationship to not just thrive but survive by virtue of it dispelling any erroneous assumptions.

Your Love Author would like to reinforce things by reintroducing our Blind Man's Bluff game for late nineteenth-century status climbing Japanese teens, Kodomo-no-Asobi. This version of Bluff sets itself apart from a bunch of hyperactive tots screamingly flailing about by two factors the Scorpio Capricorn Love union must possess if they wish to achieve any semblance of romantic success: trust and relaxation.

By wearing her best kimono and holding a full cup of tea in her hand, the Japanese teen who is "it" must find within herself the poise to move fluidly in as a relaxed manner as possible, as well as trust in herself that she will eventually no longer be "it."

If our "it" girl became too intense while playing, she risked more than just staining her good clothes. Kodomo-no-Asobi taught by example that one's placement in society was best maintained with a consistently relaxed composure. For where there is trust and relaxation, intensity can never be found.

So Scorpio and Capricorn, the romantic merger between two complementary signs at first sounds like the biggest piece of astrological cake to swallow. But after reading this chapter, both of you now know better.

Scorpio–Aquarius

This chapter has barely begun and already you both have put me in quite a pickle, Scorpio and Aquarius! Your Love Author planned on generalizing the positive and negative dynamics when the scorpion and the water bearer join romantic forces under the format of "I have good news and bad news," but even THERE we have issues. When asked to choose, I can already see both signs instantly responding with opposing answers at the exact same time.

Scorpio is intense and no nonsense. If there's any pain to be addressed it would rather tear that ace bandage of bad news off first in one swift, painful motion regardless if any hair follicles or patches of skin be ripped up right along with it.

Aquarius likes things, well, different. Why should it conform to such limitation as good or bad when an entire universe's worth of news choices lay in between? It's as bourgeois as asking the politically savvy if one is merely a Republican or Democrat.

(Smiling hard while slowly backing away.)

How about we start over from satirical scratch.

Oh hey, Scorpio and Aquarius! So, a question for you guys. Are either of you familiar with the concept of non-beginner chili sauce?

I should ask, are both of you knowledgeable about the range of specialized chili sauces that cater to a very specific portion of the consumer population, namely advanced chili sauce lovers to the extreme?

Only one factor determines this particular range of extreme chili sauces not made for beginners: heat, be it oral or gastro-intestinal. The variation of heat for the advanced chili sauce lover comes down to three selections: super hot, deadly hot, and HF, which stands for human flamethrower.

Since we're dealing with a portion of the consumer population already well versed with gustatory discomfort, heat is the unifying factor within every variety of extreme chili sauce. It all really boils down to how much heat the consumer is willing to internally handle.

The same can be likened to when the scorpion and the water bearer join romantic forces, but instead of heat, a different concept—challenge— is used for variation, which will be present anytime the Scorpio and the Aquarius interact together.

It all boils down to how much challenge the two love consumers are willing to internally handle. And what nails the concept of challenge so firmly into the foundation of the Scorpio Aquarius love union?

Both signs are of the same astrological quality: fixed. The fixed signs experience the most challenge in achieving a state of relationship equilibrium far more than any of the other astrological qualities.

As a whole, the fixed signs do not have the easiest time seeing other people's perspectives. Other fixed characteristics that are anything but easy are as follows: a mental proclivity to see things in a one dimensional, black or white way; an inherent inclination to not want to compromise; or a consistent knack for being obstinate, which is a polite way of saying "pig-headed stubborn."

Your Love Author likens the Scorpio Aquarius dating process to that Japanese genre of a cult classic, early sci-fi horror film—the *Godzilla* movie.

Much like the unfolding plot that is the formulaic standard for any of the *Godzilla* movies, the atmosphere needs to be picture postcard perfect when the Scorpio and the Aquarius first begin dating. Everything has to be super great in order to juxtapose the truly horrific nature of what lies above or below, which soon shall volcanicly descend upon the fright flick's idyllic surroundings and peaceful townsfolk.

When the Scorpio and the Aquarius begin dating, all parties put every effort into looking their best, and just as importantly, being on their best behavior. Things may seem so intoxicatingly good at first that assumptions are often made that the atmosphere surrounding their fixed love union will always be one of harmonious ease.

But it's exactly that same type of sentiment in the *Godzilla* film when the lovers are walking hand in hand down the promenade, right past the school as the closing bell rings. The teacher stands in the doorway, waving in slow motion, saying "Goodbye, children!" to her happily exiting students. The camera pans up and away to allow the viewing audience to see the churning volcano, darkening sky, or bubbling ocean's surface in the distance. Terror is about to descend upon Romanceville!

In other words (dramatic orchestral chords while a woman hysterically screams), the Scorpio and the Aquarius are about to have their first difference of opinion!

Picture the water bearer and the scorpion walking hand and stinger together, strutting amidst the puffy clouds of honeymoon phase bliss, and then a disagreement or difference of opinion occurs. Instantaneously both fixed signs will dig their heels into the ground, determined never to budge a millimeter for the duration of their Aquarian and Scorpionic lives!

Upon seeing its fixed sign partner doing the aforementioned heel digging, the other fixed sign will become even more inflexibly unrelenting, stupefied at how obviously wrong its fixed sign love interest is about everything.

Godzilla has officially crossed paths with Mothra/Ghidora/Rhodan or Hidorah the Smog Monster, ladies and gentlemen!

Like the townspeople who reside in the celluloid Japanese seaside hamlet of placid perfection, everyone is taken completely off guard. No one sees it coming when the raging bubbles begin to surface and a screaming Godzilla emerges from deep within the ocean's depths, while Ghidora, the threeheaded dragon king, flies down from the sky to pick a monster showdown of unbending will with the prehistoric lizard.

But just like the dapper male lead whose mouth moves well before the audience hears his dubbed in English voice, your Love Author would like to inform the feuding fixed couple, "There may just be a way."

Hold on to your love interest and plug your ears because this one's gonna be a real screamer: COMPROMISE.

It's Romanceville's only hope, Scorpion-o-sama and Aquarius-san!

Not just one but both fixed signs need to regularly compromise if this relationship is to NOT have a horror flick ending of romantic armageddon. Both Scorpio AND Aquarius are two of the most stubborn signs within the known universe, and many seasons shall change before either fixed sign realizes its pig-headed partner is just as stubborn as itself.

And if no form of compromise is put into effect, the relentless stubbornness indicative within the personalities of the Scorpio and the Aquarius will propel their stalemate of will through the unfolding future with neither fixed sign showing the slightest inclination of ever caving in.

The two *Godzilla* film lovers may have been separated while Ghidorah was deflecting that flying school bus hand-flung by Godzilla, but they always manage to tearfully find each other towards the film's end just as the camera pans up and away, displaying the smoking carnage as peace once again returns to the town of Romanceville. Or does it?

I won't kid either of you, Scorpio and Aquarius. The love union between your signs is never a simple romantic matter. Much like how the concept of heat is a constant component with the various renditions of extreme chili sauce, the dynamic of challenge will always be present within the Scorpio Aquarius love union.

However, that's not to say all is gloom and doom for the Scorpio and the Aquarius romantically joining forces! Should both fixed parties actively participate in the art of compromise, as well as accept the notion that challenge will regularly feature into their relationship, this powerhouse partnership should be well equipped to romantically handle the heat, no matter how extreme.

Scorpio–Pisces

Imagine if you will, Scorpio and Pisces, the futuristic fantasylands weaved within the plots of some of the best examples of twentieth-century science fiction.

Case in point, *Logan's Run*, the 1967 sci-fi novel turned 1976 cult classic film by the same name (LR for short), and *Brave New World*, the 1931 futuristic work elevated to literary classic, (BNW for short), by the British satirist, Aldous Huxley.

In both stories not of this time or place, hedonistic pursuits of pleasure are the main focal points for all literary parties involved. Whether one loses itself in mental ecstasy after taking soma, BNW's hallucinogenic pill like no other; or excitedly enters LR's government sponsored Orgy Center with wild abandon, the stratospheric self- satisfaction in either sci-fi story creates an almost zen like state where words can't adequately describe the barrage of pleasure causing endorphins experienced. It's kind of like when the Scorpio and the Pisces first begin dating each other.

Astrologically, the best love unions are those made of two people born beneath the same element. Since Scorpio and Pisces are both water signs, it really doesn't get much better than when these two members of the element of wet meet and romantically mingle!

The flow of human emotion is at the core of every water sign, and what many humans, including many a water-based one, tend to forget is that emotions are non-rational things. The rational mind resides strictly within the left hemisphere of the human brain. Anything emotional or intuitive is housed within the brain's right hemisphere.

If you want to speak to your partner, your brain oversees that task by having its left hemisphere send impulses to your mouth, which makes it move in order to say what needs to be said. Speech is a function of the rational mind and is under the domain of the left hemisphere.

Now, let's theoretically say you still need to speak to your partner, and rather desperately this time around. The only difference is your partner is nowhere physically near you. Just then your phone rings. You pick it up to hear your water-signed partner on the other end say, "Hi, honey. I just felt a strong sensation you needed to speak to me." The right hemisphere of your partner's brain had just been engaged and put to full use.

When dealing with any and all stimuli from the outside world, those born beneath the element of water will utilize their emotions before anything else. The water sign will literally see how something makes it "FEEL" before going into any kind of action or subsequent reaction.

Non-water signs like to think its feelings fit in custom-made gift-boxes where each emotion resides in a nice little compartment while waiting for its name to be called out at some point in the distant future.

The water signs know better. They know all too well that human emotion is a force much like Mother Nature herself. We cannot MAKE the weather happen. We live with it and adjust accordingly whenever it chooses to change.

Those born beneath the element of wet naturally understand they have no control over true emotion when it hits their radar. When in touch with their emotions, the water sign flows with them.

Returning once more to our current love scenario, the duo in question isn't comprised of merely one astrologically wet one, the romantic pairing of the Scorpio with the Piscean is truly harmonious since it involves the union of two water signs.

An interesting phenomenon tends to occur after two water signs have initially joined romantic forces and an emotional bond has been formed between them. Overall things get quieter.

Because both parties share a watery astrological foundation, the Scorpio and the Pisces are more than likely to develop an innately intuitive sense of the other's presence without either sign needing to analytically discuss how or why it has come about. Nor will one water sign necessarily have to explain to the other what is being mutually felt.

This non-verbal, intuitive bond that forms whenever two water signs become emotionally close is, for the most part, a glorious thing much along the romantic lines of the pleasure experienced by the characters from LR and BNW whenever venturing on their pursuits of self-satisfaction.

But this emotional bond of the water-signed kind does have its down sides too. Inherently Pisceans tend to be naturally sensitive and Scorpios tend to be naturally intense. What both water signs need to be mindful of once their emotional bond has begun to form is for neither sign to become so super sensitive about things that every slightest hurt is retained and stored away in an emotional arsenal to be used as future weaponry (keep that in mind, Pisces). That, along with both wet ones must never allow things to get so emotionally intense where one lover ends up becoming scarily jealous or hyper-possessive of the other (mark and remember, Scorpio).

Should either the Scorpio or the Pisces start to see any of these negative trends beginning to form, it's highly recommended that one or both of the following options be implemented: lightening things up or openly communicating.

Nothing dispels an atmosphere of heavy emotion faster than a little laughter, and a change of scenery never hurts either. In spite of the aforementioned world of wordless wonder created whenever two water signs emotionally bond, in order for every human relationship on this planet to not only thrive but survive, communication must be regularly exercised by all romantic parties involved.

Once an emotional bond has been firmly established, all water signs will need to avoid two forms of behavior that specialize in breaking down the flow of open communication: passive aggression and assuming.

Passive aggression is a non-confrontational tactic where one states its case / displays its willfulness / attempts to get one's way through behavior that is both non-active and non-communicative that's never direct but always undermining. Your Love Author likes to believe that open communication is the solution for any kind of deep seeded problem in a relationship, but not so in the case of passive aggression.

Should one water sign experience a constantly relentless show of passive aggressiveness over time from its water signed lover, the best thing it can do is, in a word, run. At least the energy exerted will be put to good use versus the vast amounts that'll be wasted in trying to directly confront the most non-direct of confrontational tactics.

This next form of communication avoiding behavior is often utilized by a goodly portion of the unevolved water signed family, but most especially is a favorite choice of emotional bond breaker utilized by many a non-evolved Piscean.

Because of its non-verbal tendencies, a Piscean pitfall expressed by many an unevolved fish person or water sign is a tendency to assume. The unevolved communicator will assume those around it will automatically know what it is thinking or needing without having to verbally express itself.

Assuming is a tactic where one wishes to avoid having to deal or speak with others. It provides an unevolved person with a false license to avoid all forms of clear communication such as asking questions outright or specifying details so that all parties are on the same page.

Swimming back into a much warmer love current, regularly implementing open communication without the presence of either passive aggression or assuming will only make the waters of your emotional bond even more crystal clear, Scorpio and Pisces. Doing so creates the best chances for both watery ones to be swept away to romantic shores more blissful than any pleasure seeking sci-fi novel could ever hope to present.

Sagittarius–Sagittarius

Just so we're on the same page, Sagittarius, you DO know you're romantically interested in one of your own, right? I'll be honest with you pony people. There are a few exceptions (actually just one, and you two sure ain't it), but overall it's not highly recommended for a person born beneath one sign to date another of its own astrological kind. When two centaurs decide to join romantic forces, the potential pitfalls that emerge make themselves more than abundantly obvious from the Sagittarian start.

But before galloping forward to discuss the overt pitfalls of problematic potential two Sags might face when romantically teaming up together, a quick overview of the traits and qualities associated with the sign of the centaur is required.

Sagittarius is a mutable fire sign ruled by the planet Jupiter. The fire signs are action oriented, and enjoy being in as constant a state of action as often as possible. The fire signs function best when they are in motion or in the process of doing. Said another way, the members of the fiery family like being busy and are at their worst when inactive. Sagittarius is certainly no exception to this action oriented rule.

The mutable signs occur as each of the four seasons draws to a close, right before another begins. They function best in environments containing some level of variety and change and are the multitaskers of the zodiac. The mutables are known for doing as many simultaneous actions as physically possible, but they are equally known for dropping said actions at choice times due to their susceptibility of being easily distracted. And here is where Sagittarius' planetary ruler, Jupiter, comes in.

Jupiter is by far the most gargantuan of heavenly bodies orbiting our Sun and because of its voluminously vast proportions, the King of Planets astrologically oversees the human concept of expansion. When person-alized, Jupiterian expansion is about an openness of choice within one's daily life to do whatever one wants to do, whenever one wants to do it. It's a long-winded way of describing Sagittarian personal freedom.

From a big picture perspective, what's the most direct way a person can expand its world? By venturing to other parts of the globe it has never been before. In other Sagittarian words, foreign travel.

Your Love Author recommends every child of Jupiter should sched-ule a trip to the most exotic of unexplored locales every three to five years in order for it to optimally function and stay Sagittarian sane.

Travelling the globe is nice and all, but it must be emphasized the most important thing to every child of Jupiter is its freedom. Even with that said, are you ready for a Sagittarian shocker? Dating another person curtails the Sag's personal sense of freedom, regardless if that person is of the pony persuasion or not.

Look at it this way, centaurs. Having one's personal freedom reduced isn't so horrible if it's for the purpose of investing one's time to make better acquaintance with a dating partner who, like your horsey self, is always fun and never boring.

Dates for two Sagittarians tend to be as physically active as romanti-cally possible. The typical Sag takes its action-oriented core by doing things against a big picture-sized backdrop, such as attending a (insert any/all sport) game in an arena setting, gambling the night away at a casino, or travelling to the most exotic locales on the globe.

The super positive side with two Sagittarians dating each other is neither centaur will have an issue with doing the other's physical activ-ity. And if one horsey half's suggested activity is spontaneously switched at the last minute request of the other, it stokes up the fun even more.

Speaking of the F–word, your Love Author must seriously stress the importance of having the presence of the F–word, which is FUN, as often as possible whenever two fire signs come together. The fire signs function best when they sense there is some level of fun taking place at any given point in their action-oriented lives. As little as an eyedropper's amount of fun goes a long way for those born beneath the element of flame.

But even with the F-word being tossed around like a (insert any/all sport) ball, two Sagittarians dating risks its own set of potential pitfalls. We'll start with an issue the sign of the centaur is most susceptible to amongst all the zodiac.

Double Sag Potential Pitfall 1: Physical Exhaustion. Your Love Author has come up with a saying, "When a fire sign actually says it's tired, it's usually too late." As already mentioned, Sagittarius is the multitasker of the zodiac and its energy is best burned up doing as many things as possible all at once.

Doing a bunch of things while throwing them all up in the air and needing the arms of Shiva to juggle everything all at once is fine and good, Sagittarius, but what about when you're tired, rundown, or on absolute empty?

Since the fire signs enjoy being busy as often as possible, they tend not to hear their bodies' SOS call of alarm whenever approaching the brink of physical exhaustion. Hence, even though its body may have been warning him or her at a much earlier time, the overly active fire sign will still burn itself out with not an ounce of energy left even in its fingers to attempt hailing a cab or a stretcher.

When two Sags begin dating, their excitement is usually quite hard to contain. So much that they'll run each other ragged while attempting to do things together as often as their physical bodies will allow.

Both romantic parties must also remember each was born beneath the same sign that's naturally competitive and can be quite the risk-taking daredevil at times. Besides not being able to lift a limb whenever physically spent, both Sagittarians must refrain from raising the probability of also having their limbs lifted in traction.

Double Sag Potential Pitfall # 2: Anger Issues. The human emotion all fire signs have at their immediate disposal is anger. Despite their natural luckiness and good timing, the children of Jupiter tend to have bad tempers and anger issues. One punchy Sag with anger issues is bad enough. Throw another into the mix and the backdrop becomes the Ultimate Fighter Octagon in the blink of a black eye if not monitored.

Those dating a female Sag should be warned. This is NOT your shrinking violet or acquiescing doormat of a girlfriend or wife! The fire-signed female does what she wants to do, and heaven pity the fool who stands in her way! These feminine flames think like dudes. They're strong willed, go after what they want, and can deliver a powerful right hook if they're told to be in any way submissive or subservient. You can't say your Love Author didn't warn you.

Double Sag Potential Pitfall 3: Cheating. The centaur's astrological quality of mutable makes many a Sagittarian naturally crave variety. When applied to two Sagittarians dating each other, variety can often translate to philandering, being unfaithful, and adultery. You get my bed-creaking drift.

Sagittarius is a sign naturally endowed with a stronger than average sex drive. Should the burning need for adulterous activity arise, both horned horses are more than capable of amping and switching up the sexual fun exclusively with each other. Most Sags cheat because they're bored. Want your pony lover to jump through sexually exclusive hoops for you only? Keep boredom out of the bedroom.

Enjoy your double Sag romance, centaurs. By all means, make the very most of each action-filled minute with your pony partner. But do try to love moderately.

Sagittarius–Capricorn

You both must have heard that wise old adage that still applies to the present day, right Sagittarius and Capricorn? It goes something along the lines of a person can choose its friends, but not its neighbors.

This neighborly concept also applies astrologically yet is completely irrelevant, especially when it comes to playing the zodiacal dating game. Take you two, for example.

Nothing can change the astrological fact the signs of Sagittarius and Capricorn are next door neighbors on that big wheel of life, otherwise known as the zodiac. Yet that inalterable information is neither karmic apples nor cosmic oranges during those not so common times when the centaur and the mystic mountain goat join romantic forces.

Moving from old astrological adages to more contemporary rules of cosmic thumb, it's generally understood the signs that border each other are categorized beneath a most unexciting descriptor of astrological compatibility: neutral.

(A solitary cough can be heard in the remote distance.)

Every sign has the potential to work together, but some combinations take a lot more work than others to achieve a state of equilibrium. When signs considered to be neutral of each other join, the state of equilibrium is something very much like the solid borderline that naturally forms whenever oil and vinegar are put into the same container. In other words, mixing the two isn't a bad thing but a whole lot of shaking is needed for there to be any kind of blend.

Of all the combinations of neutral signs, Sagittarius and Capricorn are by FAR the most drastically different from one another. They are so different it often seems as if these two signs lived on the opposite ends of the planet versus being astrological next door neighbors.

Nowhere is this more evident than in two areas of human existence that truly separate the horses from the goats: WORK and FUN.

Capricorn rules over the tenth house of career, and is the workhorse of the zodiac. A Cappie's labors are its most productive whenever associated with an established goal. Elevated status and assured success are practically inevitable for this most hardworking of signs whenever a firm goal is set.

There are times when those born beneath the sign of the centaur establish long term goals for themselves as well. Kind of. With the king of planets overseeing the concept of expansion, many a Sag will come up with goals befitting an Olympian god or Superman rather than within the reach of mere mortals.

Jupiter's children will be motivated to broadcast their chosen objective for the future in front of as large of an audience as possible. They'll picture themselves already at the pinnacle of their achievements, relaying the details like the most animated of storytellers. Unfortunately, the Sag's goal usually serves more as a distraction to keep the last of the fire signs from focusing on its tasks at hand by avoiding work altogether.

Both the neutral signs of Sagittarius and Capricorn have two distinctly different work ethics that play a huge factor in the dating process between these two signs.

The work ethic of the typical Capricorn can be likened to a 1970s slogan for Smith Barney Investment Firms: "They get money the old fashioned way. They earn it."

A Capricorn enters this plane of existence with an inherent awareness that anything of value has a price, and if something is wanted, one must work for it. (Work, for the Capricorn, is valid only when it's comprised of good, old-fashioned elbow grease.)

When the concept of luck is personified, which is another way of saying when an inanimate force is supplied with human traits or qualities, it will often be depicted as being mentally compromised along with an acute case of nearsightedness. Why? Luck is both blind and dumb.

The force of fortune so many of us worship in the modern day is haphazard and random. We don't earn luck. It simply lands in our laps for no definable reason. Of the twelve signs, Sagittarius is by far the luckiest. Being ruled by Jupiter, the planet of luck, centaurs have a propensity to be consistently lucky and possess an uncanny knack for being in the right place at the right time.

Unfortunately, many a child of Jupiter will become so accustomed to its atypically good luck or to things going his or her way, it will often overlook developing a defined work ethic simply because it has not had to work too hard for anything.

This reliance on an abundance of luck can lead to an equal abundance of such non-lucky things as irresponsibility, carelessness, recklessness, and empty promising, just to name a few.

Where luck is relied upon by many a Sagittarian, nearly every Capricorn negates it by never relying or even believing in this unearned force of fortune. Let's now look at the opposite end of the labor spectrum by examining how these two neutral signs deal with the concept of fun.

Your Love Author has come up with a theory regarding fun and the typical fire sign called "The Fire Sign Fun Factor." The fire signs function best when they sense there is some level of fun taking place at any given point in their action-oriented lives. Even an eyedropper's amount of fun goes a long way for the average fire sign. The last representatives of the family of flame are no exception to the fire sign fun factor.

Oxymoron (noun): A rhetorical figure of speech when incongruous or contradictory terms are combined, as in the phrases "a deafening silence" or "a mournful optimist." Or how about one of your Love Author's favorites: fun and the Capricorn. For the vast majority of Saturn's children, the word "fun" doesn't even exist within their vocabularies. While we're at it, neither do the words "vacation," "relaxation," or "snort laughing."

With its business formal demeanor emanating the warmth and congeniality of an unamused librarian or distant bank teller, it's not too hard to see why fun and the Capricorn usually never cross paths.

Where the Sagittarius needs fun at some level of bare minimum in order to optimally function, the Capricorn can go through an entire life cycle and never even encounter the F-word.

For many a Cappie, the concept of fun is a cousin a few times removed from chaos. From its Saturnine perspective, fun and chaos are both housed together beneath a domain that truly terrifies every goat guy and girl to its core.

The Capricorn's high-goaled sense of status drives it to always appear perfectly put together, which over time can be rather un-fun. If the Capricorn can work at maintaining the bare minimum of the fire sign fun factor for its Sagittarian love interest while the Sag consistently keeps gainful employment during the duration of their love union, you two neutrals might just stand a romantic chance after all.

And Sag, should you find yourselves in the Capricorn hot house, here are three valuable words of advice: skin care products. The Capricorn may not necessarily forgive your Sagittarian sins, but it will ALWAYS be a sucker for high quality SCPs, even if repetitively given each year as the all-in-one Christmas and birthday gift.

Sagittarius–Aquarius

Did you lovebirds know the most damaging forest fires occur in areas that don't necessarily have the most flammable material but are susceptible to high winds?

Flame, unto its solitary self, doesn't make a fire burn fast and furiously. Take said flame and infuse it with the oxygen from the windy air and you have one serious scorcher. Kind of like when the Sagittarius and the Aquarius date each other.

In astrology, the four elements of earth, air, fire, and water are naturally paired off. Each grouping consists of two elements that are cohesive or naturally work well together, otherwise known as being complementary to each other. Hence, the elements of earth and water, but more importantly for this particular pairing, the elements of fire and air are complementary to each other.

Returning once more to our romantic forest fire analogy, with the element of fire's core energies being action oriented and the element of air's being mentally driven, the signs born beneath either element function best at a pace that is much like a wildfire's wind-stoked flames: fast and furious.

However, when fiery Sagittarius joins romantic forces with the fixed air sign of Aquarius, the erratic nature of the furiously fast burning wildfire is made more constant and tempered down to that of a slow and steadily burning flame. Allow your Love Author to elementally explain.

The elemental foundation of fire is action, and the signs that make up the family of flame (Aries, Leo, and your Sagittarian self) enjoy being in as constant a state of action as often as possible. Hence, the fire signs function best when they are in motion or in the process of "doing." Said another way, the members of the fiery family like being busy. The last representative of fire (aka Sagittarius) is certainly no exception to this action-oriented rule.

The mutable signs occur as each of the four seasons draws to a close, right before another begins. The mutable sign of Sagittarius takes places at the end of autumn, right before the winter solstice. The mutables function best in environments containing some level of variety and change, and are the multitaskers of the zodiac. The mutables are known for doing as many simultaneous actions as physically possible, but they are equally known for dropping said actions at choice times due to their susceptibility of being easily distracted.

Blowing right along to the airy half of our complementary couple, human intellect is the foundational core of the element of air and functions best through the mental processes of thought and communication. The range of intellectual complexity and the communicative output of the signs that comprise this element (Gemini, Libra, and Aquarius) can be likened to something along the lines of a *Goldilocks and the Three Bears* astrological scenario.

Much like the three different variations of bear sizes in the children's fairy tale, the first representative of the air signs, Gemini, can be likened to the Baby Bear of the air-signed bunch due to that sign's constant state of mental curiosity. The middle representative of the airy ones, Libra, is comparable to the Mama Bear due to the scales' mental capabilities being so graciously well-mannered. Last but certainly not intellectually least, the Aquarius can be no one else but the Papa Bear of the air-signed family by virtue of the water bearer's innovative intellect towering way above every other resident of the breezy bunch and the rest of the zodiac as well.

What evens out the fire of the Sagittarius-Aquarius union into a steadily burning flame of high romantic potential is the astrological quality of the stoking wind supplied by the last of the air signs. In other words, the fixed quality of the water bearer.

The fixed signs are each positioned at the mid-point of each of the four seasons, and the sign of Aquarius occurs during the dead of or very middle of the winter season. Unlike Sagittarius' mutable quality, the fixed signs usually have a hard time beginning things and/or find it difficult summoning the necessary motivation to get things started.

But where the mutable sign can be easily distracted, the fixed person, once started, keeps its energy concentrated and focused on whatever task it has slowly begun until it's reached its full completion. Among the fixed, nothing is ever rushed or approached with a fast and furious pace. Slow and steady wins the race with these heavy hitting signs.

Now, combining the Tasmanian devil of fire signs with the fixed sign of airy genius may at first sound like a union of polar opposites due to the Sagittarius and the Aquarius working from such differing dynamics.

However, returning once more to our original "wind + fire = serious scorcher" formula of complementary elements, joining the romantic energies of the centaur with the water bearer more often than not results in a serious romance of long-lasting potential versus a burning ball of passion that extinguishes itself as quickly as when it first combusted.

In fact, both sign's core differences of dynamic tend to be seen as refreshingly fun by the other versus any kind of romantic obstacle that could get in the way of the Sagittarius and Aquarius' budding intimacy upon first dating each other.

The Sagittarius' highly energetic and equally high positive approach to things has a knack for keeping the brilliant mind of the Aquarian thoroughly preoccupied. While the water bearer's unique thoughts of inventive genius can easily captivate even the most fidgety of centaurs, leaving it sitting silently still with wonder.

With all the super great aspects behind the complementary nature of fire and air, potential problems arise should either element become too isolated.

In each of its very own strong ways, both Sagittarius and Aquarius are signs of solitary independence. No matter how good the lovin' is for either sign, both the centaur and the water bearer will always need some alone time. This is a natural component for the Sagittarian, whose biggest form of motivation is its sense of individualized freedom.

For the Aquarian, this is an imposed state of mind despite the water bearer being otherwise known as the sign of groups. Upon entrance onto this plane of existence, the Aquarius longs to be part of a social group.

However, this almost always never materializes to the water bearer's liking, especially during its teen years and twenties due to its inherently fierce sense of individuality.

Without even trying, the Aquarian's natural quirkiness and ahead of its time flair makes it stick out like a sore thumb within any group, be it friends, classmates, co-workers, or social clubs. Over time, the water bearer becomes accustomed to being a lone wolf due to years of longing to belong, but admiring those together from the outside.

Those born beneath the influence of Jupiter, the largest heavenly body of all the solar system (aka Sagittarius) like having the freedom to do its own thing whenever it wants to do it. Ruled by the planet of expansion, the last representative of fire is not used to considering the perspective of others within the framework of its spontaneously impulsive life.

But that's exactly what needs to happen when Cupid's arrow slams the centaur with amorous intentions for an Aquarian love interest!

If the Sagittarius can step outside of its own self-concerned perspective to coax the Aquarian out of its own self-imposed solitary confinement by reassuring the water bearer its sense of being different isn't incomprehensible but so uniquely lovable, then let the good times roll and burst into air-stoked flame!

Sagittarius–Pisces

Hold up, Sagittarius and Pisces. I need to step out for a bit and find me a Red Bull and an energy bar 'cause you two are WORK.

Alrighty then! Now that I've done what's humanly best to crank my energies up to as maximum a non-illegal level as I can, allow me to start by being brutally blunt: The two of you are SURE you're dating each other, right?

I should preface things by stating that every sign has the potential to work together in a romantically involved way. It's just that some signs take a lot more work to achieve a state of equilibrium than others. And just to repeat what was stated earlier, you two are WORK!

The inherent energies and overall personalities of the Sagittarius and the Pisces operate from such different foundational points that combining the centaur and the fish in any kind of one on one partnership requires a consistent level of hard work from both parties.

Of the twelve signs, Sagittarius and Pisces are each other's biggest challenge to relate with naturally due to each sign's placement on the zodiac wheel. They are positioned from each other at the harshest astrological angle possible of 90 degrees, which is better known as the square.

When two signs square each other, a consistently high probability exists for either sign to rub the other the wrong way quite often because either or both signs are simply being their natural selves.

Along with squaring each other, the core foundations of the centaur and the fish drastically differ from each other fundamentaly, and on multiple levels.

The action-oriented fire signs enjoy being in as constant a state of action as often as possible. Hence, the fire signs function best when they are in motion or in the process of doing. Said another way, the members of the fiery family like being busy and are at their worst when inactive.

The element of water is based in human emotion and the water signs initially react to the outside world with their feelings. In other wet words, those born into the watery family will gauge how something makes them feel at first, prior to taking any kind of action and/or subsequent reaction.

Even with that said, for the last representatives of the watery element, emotions hold a bit more influence besides merely being a first reaction to stimuli from the outside world. Imagine the Pisces as if it was a radar station that picks up all intuitive and/or emotional energy from the general surrounding atmosphere. The typical Piscean will, by default, naturally tune into whatever emotional energies are present within its environment at any given time, be those energies from the past, present, or future. The tricky part for the Pisces is its emotional radar is always on.

Due to its emotional radar working 24/7, the outside world will often be perceived as a very overwhelming place for the typical Piscean, rendering a goodly portion of the fish community speechless or very quiet for the better part of its day.

The signs of Sagittarius and Pisces do share the common ground of having the same astrological quality. Both the centaur and the cosmic fish are mutable signs. The mutable signs function best in environments containing some level of variety and change and are the multitaskers of the zodiac. The mutables are known for doing as many simultaneous actions as physically possible, but are also equally known for dropping said actions at choice times due to their susceptibility of being easily distracted.

For many a Sag and Piscean, the biggest challenges occur upon their first meeting where misinterpreted misunderstandings tend to run rampant.

The Sagittarian will often initially misinterpret the Piscean's silent nature as either being stuckup, standoffish, or disapproving. The Pisces will often misinterpret the newly introduced Sagittarius as an obnoxiously pushy loudmouth that is utterly self-possessed. Good times.

If the centaur wants to make amends for something it wrongfully did or didn't do within its relationship, it will naturally go into action by attempting to actively do something with its water-signed love interest.

The Pisces will then block the centaur's chess move by proceeding to thwart every bit of fire-signed action through the tactic of non-reactive non-action, which is better known as passive aggression.

Passive aggression is a non-confrontational tactic where one states its case, displays its willfulness, or attempts to get one's way through behavior that is both non-active and non-communicative and never direct but always undermining.

Your Love Author likes to believe that open communication is the solution for any kind of deep seeded problem in a relationship but not so in the case of passive aggression. Should one romantic party experience a consistently relentless show of passive aggressiveness over time from the other, the best thing it can do is, in a word, run. At least the energy exerted will be put to good use, versus the vast amounts that'll be wasted in trying to directly confront the most non-direct of confrontational tactics.

One last piece of the puzzle of problematic potential for the Sagittarius Pisces union still needs to be addressed. Because of their mutable astrological natures, the signs of the centaur and the cosmic fish both have a rep of partaking in the number one relationship killing pastime: CHEATING.

Most mutables cheat simply because they're bored. Want your mutable-signed lover to jump through sexually exclusive hoops for you only, Sagittarius and Pisces? Keep boredom out of the bedroom.

Sag, you have the energy to come up with a bunch of new positions, locales, and accoutrements to keep things spicy and fresh in the bedroom. Pisces, you have the imagination to make all of the above an erotic reality.

Now Sag and Pisces, after all that did you think this chapter wouldn't have even the tiniest of good romantic tidings to deliver about your partnership? Guess again! Besides sharing the common ground of both being mutable signs, a less obvious and more unique tie bind the sign of the centaur to the sign of the cosmic fish. It's a tie of ancient proportions.

Before there were cars, computers, or ice cubes, there was the ancient universe. In other pre-electric words, the ancient universe was the solar system that existed from the perspective of man's naked eye without the assistance of a telescope.

The planetary ruler of Pisces is not included within the ancient universe due to Neptune being discovered in 1846. At this point, some of you might be asking yourselves, didn't Pisces people exist prior to 1846? Most definitely, although your Love Author didn't know any of them personally. Despite that fact, Pisceans who existed prior to the discovery of their planetary ruler, Neptune, were still ruled by a heavenly body. It's the very same gargantuan space ball that happens to also rule over the sign of the centaur.

The signs of Sagittarius and Pisces share a not so well known common tie of having the same ancient planetary ruler of Jupiter, the heavenly body that oversees the fortuitous concepts of luck, blessings, and expansion.

If the Sagittarius and Pisces consistently make an effort at instilling their love union with the Jupiterian qualities of optimism, good humor, and an overall positive attitude, the king of planets will expand its blessings upon a partnership otherwise rife with potential problems into a romantic keeper of a relationship that's able to laugh off whatever obstacles they face together as a loving team.

Capricorn–Capricorn

It's no secret, goat guys and girls. Earth signs like their stuff.

The element of earth, which is the foundation beneath the sign of the mystic mountain goat (aka Capricorn), reacts to the outside world with and derives the most security from what is tangible: possessions, homes, cars, diamonds that are at least five carats (never lower) in variations of white, pink, brown, with the occasional yellow thrown in. Ya know. Stuff.

Even with that said, since Capricorn is the last representative of the element of earth, those born beneath the sign of the mystic mountain goat take the concept of the tangible to a whole new extreme! But honestly you two, does the Bentley REALLY require the installation of a juice bar? And I think you goat kids will survive if the vacation villa doesn't have its own coat of arms AND flag.

Don't misunderstand me, status seekers. There's nothing wrong with owning nice things and having wads of cash. It's when the tangible becomes master over those based in the tangible that things can become a smidge problematic.

Speaking of the tangible, your Love Author picked up a little something to celebrate your horn-headed union. A couple of dual-purposed souvenirs picked up for quite a pretty penny (you each can pay me back later) that serve as both gifts as well as realistic reminders for the earth-signed couple to keep their love of the tangible in check for the duration of their romantic time spent together. But your Love Author jumps far too ahead of himself.

I'll be honest with you two. There are a few exceptions (actually just one, and you two sure ain't it), but overall it's not highly recommended for a person born beneath one sign to date another of its own astrological kind. Each sign encounters its own unique set of challenges whenever dating itself, and Capricorn has some of the most overt challenges of pitfall potential when romantically doubling up.

For some couples of the double Capricorn persuasion, their biggest challenge is quite often age related. Many a Cappie will pair up with another who is significantly older or younger. The greater the age difference often correlates to the greater the likelihood of rift-causing potential to actually take place. Capricorn case in point is the short lived double Cappie marriage between goat guy Cary Grant and his thirty-three years younger goat girl Dyan Cannon.

For other double Capricorn couplings, their biggest challenge is never being able to see each other. The last representative of earth possesses a work ethic that is truly like no other. Unfortunately this same work ethic can prove to be a Capricorn's worst enemy due to both romantic parties being married to its job.

Every goat guy and girl should know upfront their labors are their most productively effective when a particular concept, THE GOAL, is present. No matter how high up or far off, the work ethic of the Capricorn functions best when it has an aspired goal in mind.

Besides being the career driven sign that functions best with the presence of a pre-established goal, the most important trait central within the life of the typical Capricorn is the achievement of STATUS. The natural propensity for hard work instills an inherent need within those born beneath the sign of the mystic mountain goat to drive the latest model of Mercedes or wear the most frightfully expensive eye gear as an expression of its Saturnine work ethic.

In other words, the Capricorn has a natural need to outwardly display its high priced items of status as if openly declaring to the world: "I EARNED THESE FRIGHTFULLY EXPENSIVE THINGS BY WORKING MY GOAT HOOVES TO THE BONE!"

Can anyone make its best goat's guess as to what happens when a person born beneath this status seeking sign with a work ethic like no other joins romantic forces with another cut from the same Capricorn cloth?

Behold our final pitfall of double Capricorn romantic potential. The Cappie couple competes against each other. This sense of Capricorn competition usually comes in two varieties. The first and not so common form is of a working goat team that relentlessly labors together in order to accomplish a mutually chosen goal of the highest order.

A case in Capricorn point is, when double Cappie couple Matthew and Tina Knowles ended their Saturnine marriage of twenty-nine years after their combined efforts achieved their goal of their daughter Beyonce becoming an international superstar.

More often than not, Capricorn coupled competition will emerge in the form of opposing work camps with each Saturnine side toiling in direct competition against the other.

Picture a goat couple officially announcing their engagement to soon be married. Both members of the Cappie couple each have forged its own well-established career path and both are about to reach new and improved levels of status and success within its respective lines of work.

Picture not too long after announcing their official engagement, improved status and success comes a knockin' for both halves of this hard working team, but with a big 'ol goat butt. Both earth signs have been offered job promotions with considerably more pay but with one Capricorn needing to relocate to its job's corporate headquarters in the southeast, and the other's company requests a move to the newly built offices in the Pacific Northwest. Status driven success has now caused a stalemate for our soon-to-no-longer-be-betrothed Cappie couple due to neither goat capitulating to the other's career aspirations.

Let's take that same Cappy couple except this time their promotions don't require any cross-country uprooting or home relocating. Their wedding goes full steam ahead, resulting in both goats' conjoined finances and assets abundantly expanding like never before.

Goatishly great, right? Not so fast, kids. The universe wanted to remind all earth-signed parties that too much abundance isn't always an automatically good thing. Should either Capricorn tap into the unevolved side of their Thing amassing behavior, chances are quite sound its same signed partner will also fall prey to that most dangerous kind of Thing needing, otherwise known as blatant materialism.

Oops! I almost forgot your love tokens! Ready goat guys and girls? POP THE CAGES OPEN AND LET 'EM OUT, BOYS! My gift for the happy Cappy couple? Giant peacocks on the verge of molting!

The male form of this species of bird is the version we associate with the peacock. Its massively grand tail is the tool of attraction the peacock employs to impress the aviary opposite sex of its kind, otherwise known as the peahen.

But there's a price to pay with being the mate of choice amongst the choicest chicks of peahen persuasion. If the peacock's tail becomes too expansively large without actively molting or having any excess feathers removed, it will restrict the cocky bird to the material plane by making him too weighted down to fly or even strut in a brisk manner. If not quickly addressed, the plight of the portly peacock becomes a most welcome dilemma for the lions or tigers located anywhere within the near vicinity of these overtly oblivious birds.

Let the peacock's paired down tail of floating emerald green and ultra-marine serve as an earthy reminder for both Capricorns to keep their mutual need to amass Things on as grounded a level as possible. The more this is mutually done by both same signed parties, the greater the chances you lovers of the tangible have at being catapulted far from the material plane into an altogether heavenly realm of romantic bliss.

Capricorn–Aquarius

You both must have heard that wise old adage that applies in the modern day, right Capricorn and Aquarius? It goes something along the lines of a person can choose its friends, but not its neighbors. This neighborly concept also applies astrologically yet is completely irrelevant, especially when it comes to playing the zodiacal dating game. Take you two for example.

Nothing can change the astrological fact the signs of Capricorn and Aquarius are next door neighbors with each other on that big wheel of life, otherwise known as the zodiac. Yet that inalterable information is neither karmic apples nor cosmic oranges during those not so common times when the mystic mountain goat joins romantic forces with the water bearer.

Moving from old astrological adages to contemporary rules of cosmic thumb, it's generally understood the signs that border each other are categorized beneath a most unexciting descriptor of astrological compatibility: neutral.

(A solitary cough can be heard in the very far off, remote distance.)

Every sign has the potential to work together. Some combinations take a lot more work than others to achieve a state of equilibrium. With the joining of the signs considered to be neutral of each other, the state of equilibrium is something very much like the solid borderline that naturally forms whenever oil and vinegar are put into the same container. In other words, mixing the two isn't a bad thing, but a whole lot of shaking is needed for there to be any kind of blend.

Normally these astrological next door neighbor rules of play would apply to any two signs that border each other. If only one half of the playing field wasn't comprised of the sign that considers normal to be the dirtiest of swear words and refuses to be enslaved by any kind of standardization, astrological or whatsoever. Guess who, Aquarius.

Your Love Author has good news and bad news, Capricorn and Aquarius. Since Capricorn is ruled by the heavenly body whose nickname is "The Great Malefic," how about we rip the bad news bandage off first in one swift and extremely painful motion? The bad News is the next door neighbor rules that apply to the rest of the zodiac are null and void should the neighbors in question be the mystic mountain goat and the water bearer.

That may not necessarily be bad news for the sign that dares to always be different. You again, Aquarius. But the astrological news flash may be quite unsettling for the most status oriented of signs that's beyond hypersensitive to public opinion. Front and center, Capricorn.

Before dropping the good news bomb, let's focus first on the inherent differences between these two very different signs. Capricorn, your planetary ruler of Saturn oversees all that is seasoned with age and time honored. Aquarius, your planetary ruler of Uranus gives the middle finger to anything aged or time honored by overseeing all that is futuristic and completely unconventional.

The Capricorn most enjoys working within a pre-established defined structure. The Aquarius least enjoys working outside of any given structure that isn't of its own making. The Capricorn is most concerned with what is tangible, namely the things it owns, along with the sense of status derived from them. Affairs of the mind are of the utmost importance to the Aquarius, who frowns upon any overt attachment to the material plane and any kind of status derived from it.

The Capricorn functions best when it is assigned tasks from the authorities above them that it can tangibly complete. The Aquarius functions best rebelling against the authorities or any assignment or task it is told it must tangibly complete. The Capricorn's sense of style is costly yet conservative. Style or otherwise, the Aquarius couldn't be conservative even if it had to at all costs.

Still starved for that yet to be delivered good news regarding what sets your next door neighbor partnership apart from everyone else, goats and water bearers? Even with its blatant differences, what makes the romantic pairing of the Capricorn with the Aquarius so unique can be summed up in three words: ancient planetary rulership.

Prior to the existence of cars, computers, or ice cubes, there was the ancient universe. In other pre-electric words, the ancient universe was the solar system that existed from the perspective of man's naked eye without the assistance of a telescope. Aquarius' planetary ruler wasn't a part of the ancient universe due to Uranus being discovered in 1781.

Some of you now may be wondering, didn't Aquarians exist prior to 1781? Most definitely, although your Love Author didn't know any of them personally. Despite that fact, Aquarians who existed prior to the discovery of Uranus still had a planetary ruler. Before 1781, the heavenly body that ruled over the sign of Aquarius was Saturn, the very same ringed planet that rules over its astrological next door neighbor,.

The signs of Capricorn and Aquarius are bound together by the not so common tie of sharing the same ancient planetary ruler of Saturn, which is the planet that oversees hard work and time itself. To be blunt, a partnership bound by the lord of karma will in no way resemble an easy breezy romantic joy ride. Nor will it be a bond of high passion either.

Saturnine relationships tend to be serious unions bound by the more sobering aspects of life, namely obligation, duty, and time rather than passion-filled high romances. Even so, along with overseeing such heavy duty concepts as karmic retribution, restriction, and loss, Saturn also rules over such relationship affirming things as commitment, structure, tangible security, and grounded stability.

Whereas the spark of a passion-filled romance can be extinguished just as quickly as it began, a Saturnine union moves forward at a more tempered, gradual pace and its bond grows ever stronger with the passage of time. It must be emphasized that Saturn is an earthy or tangibly driven planet. The ringed planet bestows tangible reward to its Saturnine team members that contribute their fair share of work.

It's good to know upfront the hard stuff that takes place during the initial stages of your newly formed union, Capricorn and Aquarius. Whereas most love birds experience the heavenly bliss associated with the initial phases of dating, which is better known as the honeymoon period, the Saturnine couple must face the nuts and non-romantic bolts reality of adjusting to its partner's idiosyncrasies, habits, and overall lifestyle while becoming better acquainted with each other.

The lord of karma doesn't look favorably upon those who cut corners or take the easiest path of least resistance, Capricorn and Aquarius. The ringed planet's rewards are earned by one's labors consistently being done over a reasonable length of time.

The more the goat and the water bearer actively work at not making any set expectations, the more your ancient planetary ruler will reward your union, Capricorn and Aquarius. If both signs manage to make it through the initial phases of their newly forming union, the ancient planetary ruler of both the goat and the water bearer will reward this atypically neutral union with the satisfaction of knowing its bond like no other is a real keeper of a relationship that will outlast even the most lovey dovey of passion-filled romances.

Capricorn–Pisces

Behold, Capricorn and Pisces! Your Love Author places before your coupled selves a concrete example impressively representing the union of each of your elemental foundations of earth and water: the Hoover dam.

This early twentieth-century feat of man-made ingenuity symbolizes the cohesion of the tangible harmoniously working within a fluid environment. It's much like when the Capricorn and the Pisces join romantic forces.

In astrology, the four elements of earth, air, fire, and water are naturally paired off. Each grouping consists of two elements that are cohesive or naturally work well together, otherwise known as being "complementary" to each other. Hence, the elements of fire and air, but more importantly for this particular pairing, the elements of earth and water are complementary to each other.

Both the earth and water signs share a core motivational trait: security. The earth signs derive their best sense of security through the tangible. The term tangible can be translated to the possessions an earth sign owns, the money in its bank account, as well as its work output. The Capricorn gains the most security from two particular areas of life: work and status. The water signs react to anything first and foremost through their emotions. The Pisces derives security from what or whoever gives it a sense of psychic calm and emotional contentment.

The material stability of the last of the earth signs matched with the other-worldly intuition of the last of the water signs at first sounds like a relationship dynamic of polar opposites. In actuality, romantically combining the goat with the fish more often than not results in a partnership of balanced contentment by virtue of their mutual energies merging the weighted with the weightless and the material with the immaterial.

Despite the Capricorn Pisces union working so naturally well, this astrological combination has its own unique set of challenges and pitfalls. The challenges can be housed beneath an overriding marker of problematic potential: REALITY

When focusing strictly on the concept of reality, Capricorn's earthy lot could be called the sign of reality. In turn, the Pisces crew could be described as the sign of UN-reality.

Capricorn is ruled by Saturn, the planetary task master that dishes out nothing but hardcore reality. Whereas Pisces is ruled by Neptune, that giant gas ball that oversees anything intangible that floats in the fluid world of non-reality. Both planets significantly contribute in a major way to the core personalities of the signs they rule.

Saturnine (adjective): (1) One who is reserved in speech. (2) One whose manner is stern, dour, or silent. The word saturnine has altered over the centuries, but it's believed to have originated in the 1500s and refers to, you guessed it, Saturn, Capricorn's planetary ruler.

When first used in the Middle Ages, the original connotations for Saturn's descriptor were far more extreme. Along with the other dour definitions already listed, in the sixteenth century the word saturnine also included those who displayed outward tendencies of being intensely gloomy and depressingly morose. And all because of the ringed planet's overseeing such saturnine things as fear, restriction, hardship, and loss.

The childhood of the typical goat kid is non-existent by virtue of it being given the mantle of adult responsibility not too long after exiting the womb, such as having to be parent to one of its parents or working at an appallingly early age. Facing such daunting responsibilities while still so young contributes to many a Cappie being naturally serious in a most intense way.

Said another way, the Capricorn's existence is based strictly in hard, cold reality. This is a sign who never allows a single "time is money" moment to be associated with such non-realistic stuff as luck, daydreaming, or fantasizing. The sign of the goat bears the distinction of having the best problem solving skills of the zodiac due to its approach to reality being so hardcore in a saturnine way.

Neptune: From the Latin *Neptunus*, which is of unknown meaning, possibly related to the Indo-European root "nebh" referring to wet, damp clouds. Whereas the name of Capricorn's planet can clearly be seen within words that describe it, not only does Pisces' planetary ruler lack any descriptors, the origin of its name has no defined meaning.

Neptune was the first planet discovered by intangible means when a Piscean named Urbain Le Verrier determined its existence through mathematical deduction in 1846. With its presence being first noted by such non-tangible means, it's no wonder the bluish green gas giant astrologically oversees anything deemed to be unclear and situated far from the harsh realities of reality itself.

Despite Pisces' planetary ruler hazing things over and distorting such reality based things as accuracy and defined boundaries, it does so for a purpose: Neptune refines.

In order to escape the real world, another place must unrealistically exist that's far more refined than reality itself. Places that can be internally explored via one's imagination, fantasies, or dreams, be they of the day or night varieties.

Not surprisingly, those who invest the most time in these non-realistic worlds consistently are born beneath Neptune's ruling sign of the cosmic fish. The real world of the here and now is a harsh place for the typical Piscean. The last sign of the zodiac is by far the most sensitive of the twelve. Neptune's influence of blurring reality over for the purpose of refining perception instills within those born beneath its ruling sign with the need to escape the glaring brashness of reality as often as they feasibly can. This Piscean need can be pursued through either evolved or unevolved means.

Evolved examples of Neptunian escapism from reality include producing creative or imaginative work, writing poetry, doing volunteer or charity work, partaking in yoga or meditation classes, and making or enjoying music or visual arts of all kinds.

Unevolved examples of Neptunian escapism from reality include alcohol, drugs (most especially of the hallucinogenic kind), pornography, constantly being on the internet, and watching too many movies or always being glued to the TV.

The Piscean need to escape reality is a valid one and must never be ignored or denied, especially by its dating partners. This is most important to those born beneath the hyper-realistic sign of Capricorn. Fortunately, the complementary nature of the goat fish relationship provides both signs an astrological check and balance system of addressing each other's very different approaches to reality.

The Capricorn can effectively monitor the Pisces to make sure its escapist tendencies aren't too prolonged or get in the way of its real world responsibilities (provided the monitoring is gentle and never too harsh or abrupt). Conversely, the Pisces can expand the palette of the Capricorn's hyper-realistic world with a more expansive array of creatively imaginative colors.

Returning once more to the Hoover dam representing the well-functioning union between the elements of earth and water, let us imagine communication to be the binding cement that holds the mighty structure securely into place.

Open communication is a critical component for any given relationship between two humans by virtue of it dispelling any erroneous assumptions being made between all parties. Should reality become hazy or confusing, both the Capricorn and the Pisces must allow for communication to be the factor that keeps the romantic power generated by its complementary relationship to continue flowing smoothly. And should that regularly occur, the Capricorn Pisces love union will be catapulted far from reality to a more heavenly place of romantic bliss.

Aquarius–Aquarius

Brrrrrr! Is it just me, or did it get seriously chilly in here? Hold that thought, you two, while your Love Author throws on an extra heavy cardigan sweater. How things got so nippy is beyond me. Oh wait! The downhill drop in temperature couldn't be more astrologically apparent! We're dealing with the joining of romantic forces between two Aquarians.

Before delving into any Aquarian explanation, how about a little trivia? The element of air, namely the signs of Gemini, Libra, and your highly cerebral selves, are the only residents of the zodiac represented by non-animal symbols. Why? The elemental foundation of air is based in human intellect versus any kind of animal instinct and functions predominantly from the workings of the rational mind.

Aquarius is the last of the air, not water, signs (your Love Author's drying toothbrush contains more water than the entire astrological lot of you combined). The last representatives of each of the four elements function best from a mass level dealing with the general public, specific groups, or the entire globe at large.

Being elementally based in human intellect, those born beneath the sign of the water bearer tend to possess a level of intelligence high above the collective of the common man. The air signs are mentally stimulated most by the concept of duality, or the joining of polar opposites. With Aquarius gravitating towards the highest of intellectual capacities that function best from a group level, it stands to dualistically reason whenever dealing with this sign from a personalized perspective, things get mighty chilly.

That's NOT to say those born beneath the sign of the water bearer lack the capacity to be warm and interpersonally congenial. Warmth and congeniality, like every other trait of the human personality, exists within the personae of every Aquarian, but the average water bearer doesn't readily expose itself without the presence of familiarity over time. The high chill factor behind the Aquarian personality is based upon two core sources: the water bearer's astrological quality and its ruling planet.

The fixed signs occur at the midpoint of each of the four seasons, with Aquarius taking place during the middle or dead of winter. The fixed do not have the easiest time seeing other people's perspectives that aren't their own. Other non-challenging fixed characteristics are: a mental proclivity to see things in a one dimensional, black or white way; an inherent inclination to not want to compromise; or a consistent knack for pig-headed stubborn.

Because of their tendency to be set in their ways, change is a force openly resisted by those who are fixed. When newly meeting a fixed sign, it's highly advised to never take an overtly overfriendly approach. For example, walking up to a fixed person you've never met while announcing, "Let's totally be BFFs!" or "I'm head over heels in love. Please marry me!" is tantamount to having the police summoned or being maced in the face due to the fixed person involuntarily reacting to such overfamiliar overtones.

Things like friendship or romantic intimacy must be gradually earned over time by those pursuing the fixed personality. The more unfamiliar a fixed person is, the more detached and chilly it will behave.

Speaking of friendship, keeping in mind that Aquarius is the sign of groups and identifies its sense of self with whatever group it belongs to, it must be emphasized that friendship is THE most important thing to the typical water bearer. So much that if an Aquarian considers you its friend, it is your friend for life.

It would behoove those with amorous intentions for the last of the air signs to always remember the following statement. An Aquarian's friends will always come first on its priority list with everyone else taking a backseat whenever this occurs.

By now both Aquarians must have realized this love interest is in no way normal, average, typical, and not comparable to any non-Aquarians you've dated in the past. The water bearer is the sign that dares to be different and marches to the beat of its own drummer and every other trite phrase used to describe anything but trite. This is all because of the water bearer's ruling planet, Uranus.

Just as its ruling sign sets itself apart from the rest of the zodiac, Uranus does the same amongst the other planets of our solar system. For starters, the seventh furthest planet from the sun has a planetary axis that's tilted sideways, resulting in THE most erratic of orbital paths. Picture an egg flying through outer space on its side.

Because of its orbital motion propelling itself practically on its side, Uranus' magnetic field doesn't emanate from its center. Its north and south poles lie where all the other lemming space balls have their equators. Like Saturn, Uranus has encircling rings. But these aren't just your average, run of the mill, around-your-planetary-waist, hula-hoop rings. OH NO! Uranus' rings circle up and around its oddly arranged orb as if the planet was playing cosmic jump rope.

If that wasn't astronomically non-conformist enough, where the other planets have poser Roman names, Uranus is the only heavenly body within our solar system that bears a name originating from the ancient Greek.

With all of that uniqueness fresh in mind, the planetary ruler of the last of the air signs astrologically oversees the following life concepts: uniqueness, non-conformity, inventiveness, high intellect, futurism, modernism, egalitarianism, computers, technology, outer space, science and the scientific method.

It's no coincidence the planet that rules over the disruptive forces of rebellion and revolution was officially discovered in 1781. A year that was smack dab in the middle of two of western history's most noteworthy rebellions, namely the American Revolution of 1776 and the French Revolution of 1789.

Completing the crash course of Uranus 101, we now return to the potential dilemmas two fixed signs face when first dating each other. Far more than any of the other astrological qualities, the fixed signs experience the most challenge in getting along with one another and achieving a state of relationship equilibrium.

When two Aquarius begin dating, things couldn't go any romantically smoother! Both fixed signs put every effort into looking their best, and just as importantly, being on their best behavior. Things may flow so smoothly at first that all water bearing parties may be lulled into a false sense of romantic security. "A love interest who's a fellow MENSA and is as non-conformist and intellectually brilliant as my genius self? What could possibly go wrong?"

The honeymoon period quickly comes to an abrupt halt when our Aquarian couple has their first difference of opinion. When this occurs, both air signs will instantaneously dig their heels into the ground, determined never to budge a millimeter for the duration of either of their water bearing lives! Upon seeing its fixed sign partner doing the aforementioned heel digging, the other fixed sign will become even MORE inflexibly unrelenting, stupefied at how obviously wrong its partner is about everything.

Only one thing in the known universe can release such a stale mate of stubbornness. COMPROMISE.

Not just one but both Aquarians need to regularly compromise if they wish their double fixed relationship to survive. Should compromise not be utilized, millennia shall pass with neither water bearer showing the slightest inclination of ever caving in.

However, should both Aquarians work at keeping their brilliant minds wide and open by learning the art of mutual compromise, UV protective eye gear will be regularly required for all water bearing parties due to the romantic future beaming so brightly before them.

Aquarius–Pisces

You both must have heard that wise old adage that still applies in the modern day, right Aquarius and Pisces? It goes something along the lines of a person can choose its friends, but not its neighbors. This neighborly concept also applies astrologically, yet is completely irrelevant as well, especially when it comes to playing the zodiacal dating game. Take you two for example.

Nothing can change the astrological fact the signs of the water bearer and the cosmic fish are next door neighbors with each other on the big wheel of the cosmos, otherwise known as the zodiac. Yet that inalterable information is neither karmic apples nor cosmic oranges during those not so common times when the Aquarius and the Pisces decide to join romantic forces.

Moving from old astrological adages to contemporary rules of cosmic thumb, it's generally understood the signs that border each other are categorized beneath a most unexciting descriptor of astrological compatibility: neutral.

(A solitary cough can be heard in the far off, remote distance.)

Every sign has the potential to work together. Some combinations take a lot more work than others just to achieve a state of equilibrium. With the joining of the signs considered to be neutral of each other, the state of equilibrium is something very much like the solid borderline that naturally forms whenever oil and vinegar are put into the same container. In other words, mixing the two isn't a bad thing, but a whole lot of shaking is needed for there to be any kind of blend.

At their core, the signs of Aquarius and Pisces function from very different perspectives, making it seem as if these two signs lived on the opposite ends of the globe versus being astrological next door neighbors.

The inherent differences between the Aquarian and the Piscean personalities are best observed beneath the header of human emotion. It all boils down to their brains. Allow your Love Author to explain both literally and physically.

Aquarius is an air sign. Pisces is a water sign. The air signs initially react to the outside world via the functions of the left hemisphere of their brain. The water signs initially react with their right hemisphere. A left-hemisphered person is motivated most to exercise the processes of the rational mind, which are any of the following mentally driven functions: thought, speech, and communication.

A right-hemisphered person is motivated most by things that reside under the domain of the non-rational mind, namely its emotions and/or intuition. Sounds easy enough, right? Ah, but one last rule of mental play regarding all this geographical brain matter must be mentioned. We humans have total control over the functions of our left hemispheres and no control whatsoever over the functions of our right hemispheres.

Aquarius is an air, not a water sign, as many erroneously believe. The foundational core behind the element of air is human intellect. Being the last representative of air, Aquarians tend to possess high levels of intelligence that tower far above the collective mental capacities of the common man.

However, along with its big fat brain, the chilliest of descriptors such as cold, icy, or frostily cool are also associated with the Aquarian personality. Why? The outward persona displayed by the Aquarius is one of near total emotional detachment.

The mental muscles of the typical water bearer are so strong, anything even hinting of emotion is immediately rationalized away versus its cerebral energies being subjected to the influences of the non-rational mind.

Ready for an astrological knee slapper? Aquarius, along with the other signs that are fixed in astrological quality, actually believe it can control every aspect of life. The fixed signs share a common personality trait of being obstinate (aka pig-headed stubborn), along with a delusional sense of having total control over every dimension of their waking lives. It's only when such uncontrollable things as fate, illness, the aging process, and death make their presence known that the fixed personality is forced to see otherwise.

The emotional realm's inability to be controlled greatly contributes to the emotional detachment of the Aquarian personality. For the sign of the cosmic fish, emotions are an entirely different matter of challenge altogether.

The element of water is foundationally based in human emotion, and the water signs initially react to the outside world through their emotional state. Those born beneath the element of wet will initially determine how something makes them feel before taking any kind of action or subsequent reaction.

For the last representatives of water, emotions hold a bit more influence besides merely being a first reaction to stimuli from the outside world. Fish folk will naturally tune into whichever emotional energies are present within its environment at any given time, be they from the past, present, or future.

The tricky part is the Piscean emotional radar is always on. Due to its emotional radar working 24/7, the world for the average Piscean will often be perceived as a very overwhelming place, rendering a goodly portion of the fish community to be speechless or very quiet for better portions of its day.

One half of this dynamic astrological duo (Aquarius) functions best through the rational act of verbal communication with a near to total detachment from its emotions and innermost feelings. Meanwhile, the other half (Pisces) finds verbal communication to mainly be a distractive nuisance due to its limitation in adequately expressing its emotions and innermost feelings.

When romantically combined, the emotional detachment of the water bearer merged with the heightened emotional sensitivities of the cosmic fish skyrocket the problematic chances of one sign's actions to be completely taken the wrong way by the other.

The Piscean could oversensitively translate the Aquarian's absence of emotion to mean the water bearer clearly does not care or even like him or her, resulting in overwhelming hurt feelings of overreaction. Hurt feelings that can result in the Piscean fish darting off in a different direction, never to be heard from again.

Should that occur, the Aquarius will subsequently interpret the Pisces' absence of explanation for its disappearance to be offensively cruel and insensitively rude, since the worst thing one can do to an air sign is purposely not communicate to them.

For this fiendishly tricky astrological combo to even have a pulse, both romantic parties will need to adjust, as well as accept each other's inherently different approaches to life. That and both sides must never take things immediately to heart whenever reacting to the actions of the other.

A common trait that both signs actually share is the water bearer and the cosmic fish are the last representatives of each of their respective elements. The last representative of an element functions best from a mass level dealing with the general population, groups, or the entire globe at large.

The last representatives of air put its naturally high intellect to best use whenever viewing the world with a humanitarian scope. Since this is the sign that truly believes in the possibility of Utopia, a society where each person from every walk of life is treated exactly the same.

The last representatives of water put its naturally intuitive power to best use whenever serving others, most especially those who need assistance the most. This is the sign that empathically defends and protects the underdogs of the world.

Should the last representatives of air and water invest the time in adjusting to their differences and discover that not only are they still together but also have come upon causes that both can fight for as a romantic team, the only thing left to both feel and say is, "Look out, world!"

Pisces–Pisces

Peace, Pisces dudes! It's seriously awesome you two are, ummm, what is it you two were doing again? Dating! That's right! Dating each other! No seriously, man. My soul's essence is joyous just knowing you fish folk were ummmm, you're happy because of what now?

Sorry to hit both of you over the fish head with such exaggerated silliness, Pisceans, but the brain dead hippie portrayal was meant to symbolize the hazy aura of confusion your planetary ruler wields over we humans. The heavenly body that rules over the sign of Pisces is, in your Love Author's opinion, the most challenging of the planetary bunch.

In the positive spectrum, Neptune astrologically oversees such transcendent things as unconditional love, spirituality, intuition, charity, and the highest aesthetics of artistic expression.

In the negative spectrum, the giant sea-green gas ball rules over such destructive things as deception (of the self and others), passivity along with its behavioral counterparts, passive aggression and denial, and last but certainly most damaging, addiction.

But that's not all, fish folks. Neptune's most challenging influence is the need for the self to become completely lost in the other. I'll have more on that "losing of the self in the other" business in just a bit.

In order to navigate Neptune's waters, we'll need to better understand the astrological foundation of its ruling sign, the cosmic fish of Pisces.

Pisces is a water sign. The flow of human emotion is at the core of every water sign, and what many humans tend to forget is that emotions are non-rational things. When dealing with outside stimuli, the water signs will utilize their emotions first and foremost by determining how something makes them feel before going into any kind of action or subsequent reaction.

Non-water signs like to think their feelings reside in custom-made gift-boxes where each emotion sits while waiting for its name to be called out at some point in the very distant future. The water signs know better.

They know all too well human emotion is a force much like Mother Nature herself. We cannot MAKE the weather happen. We live with it by adjusting accordingly whenever it chooses to change.

An interesting phenomenon occurs whenever two water signs first emotionally bond. Overall, things get quieter. Each water sign develops an intuitive sense of the other's presence without either needing to analytically discuss how or why it has come about. Nor will one water sign necessarily have to explain to the other what is being mutually felt. This non-verbal, intuitive bond that forms whenever two water signs become emotionally close is, for the most part, a glorious thing!

Inherently, Pisceans are acutely sensitive. What both fish folk need to be mindful of once their emotional bond has formed is for neither to allow its already heightened sensitivities to become over-amplified where every slightest hurt is absorbed and retained.

In spite of the aforementioned world of wordless wonder created when two water signs emotionally bond, in order for every human relationship on this planet to not only thrive, but survive, communication must be regularly exercised by all wet parties.

That and both Pisceans must refrain from actively partaking in two forms of behavior that are the most effective at blocking the flow of clear communication: passive aggression and assuming.

Passive Aggression is a non-confrontational tactic where one states its case, displays its willfulness, attempts to get one's way through behavior that is both non-active and non-communicative, and is never direct but always undermining.

Your Love Author likes to believe that open communication is the solution for any kind of deep-seated problem in a relationship, but not so in the case of passive aggression. Should one water sign experience a constant and relentless show of passive aggression over time from its water signed lover, the best thing it can do is, in a word, run. At least the energy exerted will be put to good use versus the vast amount wasted in trying to directly confront the most non-direct of confrontational tactics.

This next form of non-communicative destruction is the relationship killing weapon of choice employed by many an unevolved Piscean: assuming. This occurs whenever one assumes those around him or her will automatically know what it is thinking or needing without having to verbally express itself.

At its unevolved core, assuming is a behavior tactic where a person wishes to avoid having to deal or speak with others. It provides the unevolved person with a false license to avoid all forms of clear communication such as asking questions outright or specifying details where everyone is on the same page.

Even with that said, asking a child of Neptune to openly communicate is much easier said than done due to its heightened sensitivity regularly inhibiting the Piscean's ability to communicate in clear and concise ways. Due to its emotional radar working 24/7, the world for the average Piscean will often be perceived as a very overwhelming place, rendering the majority of the fish community speechless or very quiet for better portions of its day.

I won't kid you, fish folk. There are very few exceptions (actually there's only one and it so ain't you), but the astrological rule of thumb regarding dating one's own sign is that while it's not necessarily impossible, it sure can't be called easy.

Each sign generates problematic potential specifically oriented for that particular sign whenever a person dates another of its own astrological kind. The problematic potential specified for the sign of Pisces when dating itself is confusion. For two Pisceans joining romantic forces, things become more confusing than ever before.

Take all of Neptune's non-communicative traits and apply them to both sides of this particular love duo and the result usually is both Pisceans being thoroughly confused about how its partner feels about nearly every given thing but too sensitive to speak up and ask for clarification.

The confusion becomes even more pronounced when considering the Piscean need to escape reality. As previously mentioned, reality is harsh for the typical Pisces, resulting in its need to occasionally escape it. This can be pursued by either evolved or unevolved means.

Evolved examples of Piscean escapism from reality include producing creative or imaginative work, writing poetry, doing charity work, partaking in yoga classes, and making or enjoying music or visual arts of all kinds.

Unevolved examples of Piscean escapism from reality include alcohol, drugs (most especially of the hallucinogenic kind), pornography, constantly being on the internet, and always being glued to the TV.

The Piscean need to escape reality is a valid one and cannot be ignored, overlooked, or denied. When a child of Neptune dates another, the need to escape reality becomes stronger than ever and with a higher occurrence than usual.

As mentioned earlier, the most challenging of Neptune's influences is the need for the self to be completely lost in the other. This need often has permanent consequences with those fully losing themselves and never being seen again due to them choosing any of the following unevolved routes: drug overdose, alcohol poisoning, drunk driving, and suicide just to name a deadly few.

Conversely, when romantically joined together, not only can one Pisces influence the other's outlet of escape, both can partake in escaping together should that outlet be both evolved and life affirming, such as volunteering as a couple at a homeless shelter, attending an opera or ballet together as a romantic team, or partaking in transcendental meditation classes as a united love union.

Should the Piscean couple implement clear communication as well as regularly escape reality together via evolved means, both fish folk stand to be whisked away to unchartered waters of romantic bliss that truly transcend this world.

To Write to the Author

If you wish to contact the author or would like more information about this book, please write to the author in care of Llewellyn Worldwide Ltd. and we will forward your request. Both the author and publisher appreciate hearing from you and learning of your enjoyment of this book and how it has helped you. Llewellyn Worldwide Ltd. cannot guarantee that every letter written to the author can be answered, but all will be forwarded. Please write to:

Brad Kronen
℅ Llewellyn Worldwide
2143 Wooddale Drive
Woodbury, MN 55125-2989

Please enclose a self-addressed stamped envelope for reply,
or $1.00 to cover costs. If outside the U.S.A., enclose
an international postal reply coupon.

Many of Llewellyn's authors have websites with additional information and resources. For more information, please visit our website at http://www.llewellyn.com

GET MORE AT LLEWELLYN.COM

Visit us online to browse hundreds of our books and decks, plus sign up to receive our e-newsletters and exclusive online offers.

- Free tarot readings • Spell-a-Day • Moon phases
- Recipes, spells, and tips • Blogs • Encyclopedia
- Author interviews, articles, and upcoming events

GET SOCIAL WITH LLEWELLYN

 Find us on Facebook
www.Facebook.com/LlewellynBooks

Follow us on
www.Twitter.com/Llewellynbooks

GET BOOKS AT LLEWELLYN

LLEWELLYN ORDERING INFORMATION

 Order online: Visit our website at www.llewellyn.com to select your books and place an order on our secure server.

Order by phone:
- Call toll free within the U.S. at 1-877-NEW-WRLD (1-877-639-9753)
- Call toll free within Canada at 1-866-NEW-WRLD (1-866-639-9753)
- We accept VISA, MasterCard, and American Express

Order by mail:
Send the full price of your order (MN residents add 6.875% sales tax) in U.S. funds, plus postage and handling to: Llewellyn Worldwide, 2143 Wooddale Drive Woodbury, MN 55125-2989

POSTAGE AND HANDLING:

STANDARD: (U.S. & Canada)
(Please allow 12 business days)
$25.00 and under, add $4.00.
$25.01 and over, FREE SHIPPING.

INTERNATIONAL ORDERS (airmail only):
$16.00 for one book, plus $3.00 for each additional book.

Visit us online for more shipping options. Prices subject to change.

FREE CATALOG!

To order, call
1-877-
NEW-WRLD
ext. 8236
or visit our
website

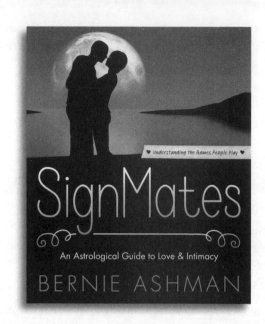

SignMates

An Astrological Guide to Love & Intimacy

BERNIE ASHMAN

In this book you'll learn what your inner motivations in a relationship are, and how they can conflict with the desires—both conscious and un-conscious – of your partner. You will also learn about the hidden motivations of your partner that may push your buttons. The book also explains methods for overcoming these problems and why your relationship can be strong and vibrant.

This book will save hours of time for astrologers who can quickly find potential problems in a relationship (it's based on Sun Signs) and how to deal with them. It can also aid counselors of any type. With this book you can have a secret tool that can put you ahead of others in your field.

But I think this book is also important for all of you who are neither counselors nor astrologers and simply want to make your relationships better. This book will show you possible pitfalls and points of disagreement, as well as giving you strategies for overcoming them. In short, it could save your relationship.

So give your relationship a chance! Use this book.

978-1-56718-046-6, 504 pp., 7½ x 9⅛   **$21.99**

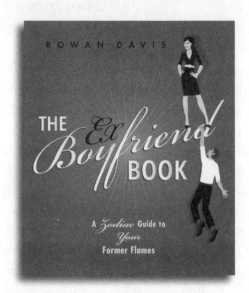

The Ex-Boyfriend Book
A Zodiac Guide to Your Former Flames
Rowan Davis

Bye bye love, hello moving on. Is your ex-boyfriend really out of your life? Sometimes the leftovers of a relationship linger like a bad cold. Astrological compatibility can have a lot to do with how your relationships end. Pining for that charmer Gemini? Can't seem to kick that Taurus couch potato off your good pillow? Check the astrological rapsheet of your ex and get all the answers. His Sun sign will remind you of his sweet—and sour—sides. His sign will also show you how to send him packing or (if it's what you really want) how to get him back.

Even if you're happily settled with a new mate, reading up on a former flame with this star guide will remind you why you're now better off!

978-0-7387-1143-0, 216 pp., 5 x 6   **$12.95**

JESSICA SHEPHERD

Venus Signs

· Discover Your
Erotic Gifts and *Secret Desires*
Through Astrology

Venus Signs

Discover Your Erotic Gifts
and Secret Desires Through Astrology
Jessica Shepherd

Take an intimate tour of the inner world of all twelve Venus signs. For millennia, Venus swaggered through the history books with unrivaled self-possession and sexual self-confidence, as notorious for seducing others as making her own pleasure and enjoyment central. Yet many women today have lost touch with the very aspects of our self she represents: joy, self-worth, sexual vitality, and eroticism.

In *Venus Signs*, Jessica breathes life back into the Goddess. As she leads you through a personal journey into the Venus sign of your self and your loved ones, prepare to become reacquainted with your innermost secret desires and your erotic strengths. Discover the must-have qualities of your soul mates, how to keep a long-term relationship happily humming, how to align with your own feminine energy, and how to draw your deepest heart's desires toward you. These are Venus powers that you can use to create, laugh, and love exceptionally well!

978-0-7387-4194-9, 240 pp., 6 x 9   **$16.99**

sun signs
& soul mates

An Astrological Guide to Relationships

LINDA GEORGE

Sun Signs & Soul Mates
An Astrological Guide to Relationships
Linda George

Today's overly materialistic and ego-centered world makes it difficult to recognize our inner selves, let alone connect on a spiritual level with another person. Thankfully, astrology reveals the true patterns in ourselves and in others.

Evolutionary astrologer Linda George looks at the nature of the soul and relationships through the lens of astrology, exploring the lighter and darker sides of the twelve Sun signs of the zodiac. She reveals the compatibility potential for each pairing and offers entertaining and insightful relationship clues to help you better relate to your partner. Learn about each Sun sign's strengths, challenges, and behavioral quirks. From deciding whether to date that flirtatious Gemini to identifying your soul's fundamental needs, *Sun Signs & Soul Mates* will help you understand yourself—and your partner—more completely.

978-0-7387-1558-2, 240 pp., 6 x 9   **$17.95**
